Dust

Special Issue guest edited by Deborah Valoma

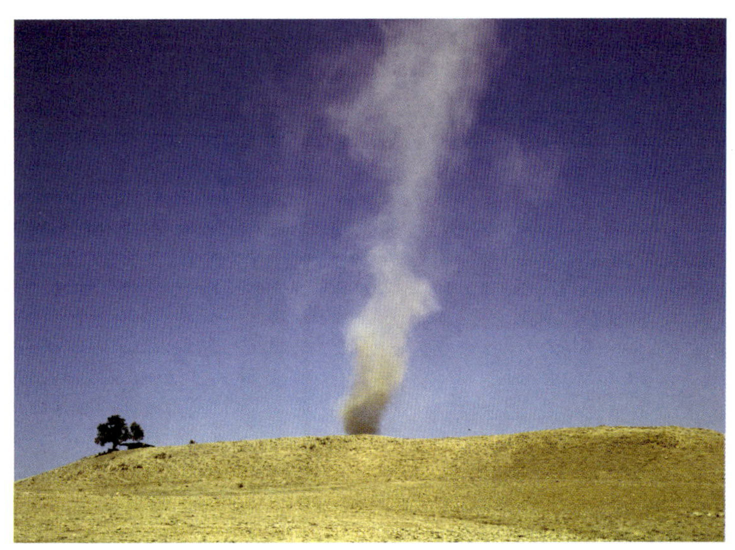

Textile

EDITED BY
CATHERINE HARPER
AND DORAN ROSS

THE JOURNAL OF
CLOTH AND CULTURE

VOLUME 8
ISSUE 3
NOVEMBER 2010

ORDERING INFORMATION

Three Issues per volume. One volume per annum.
2010: Volume 8
ONLINE
www.bergpublishers.com
BY MAIL
Berg Publishers
C/O Turpin Distribution Services
Pegasus Drive
Stratton Business Park
Biggleswade
Bedfordshire SG18 8TQ
UK
BY FAX
+ 44 (0)1767 601640
BY TELEPHONE
+ 44 (0)1767 604951
For Subscription Enquiries
email custserv@turpin-distribution.com
ENQUIRIES
Editorial: Julia Hall
email jhall@bergpublishers.com
Production: Ken Bruce
email kbruce@bergpbublishers.com
Advertising: Ellie Graves
email egraves@bergpublishers.com
SUBSCRIPTION RATES
Institutional
Print and online: 1 year: £162/US$316; 2 year: £260/US$506
Online only: 1 year: £138/US$269; 2 year: £221/US$430
Individual
Print: 1 year: £47/US$81; 2 year: £76/US$130
Full color images available online
Access your electronic subscription through
www.ingentaconnect.com
Berg Publishers is the imprint of
Oxford International Publishers Ltd.

EDITORS

Catherine Harper
University of Brighton, UK
Doran Ross
Fowler Museum at UCLA
Founding Editor and Associate Editor:
Pennina Barnett, Goldsmiths, University of London, UK
p.barnett@gold.ac.uk
Founding Editor and Associate Editor:
Janis Jefferies, Goldsmiths, University of London, UK
j.jefferies@gold.ac.uk
Associate Editor:
Mary Littrell, Colorado State University
mlittrel@cah.colostate.edu
Editorial Assistant:
Lucy Gundry
lucygundry@gmail.com
Book Reviews Editor:
Victoria Mitchell, Norwich School of Art & Design,
St George Street, Norwich NR3 1BB, UK
v.mitchell@nsad.ac.uk
Exhibition Reviews Editors:
UK and Rest of World
Deborah Southerland, Faculty of Creative Arts, University of the
West of England, Bower Ashton Campus, Kennel Lodge Road,
Bristol BS3 2JT, UK
Deborah.Southerland@uwe.ac.uk
USA
Geraldine Ondrizek, Art Department Chair, Reed College,
Portland, OR 97202, USA
ondrizeg@reed.edu
Rebecca Stevens, Contemporary Textiles, The Textile Museum,
23250 S Street NW, Washington, DC 20008-4088, USA
stevensgrj@aol.com

AIMS AND SCOPE

Cloth accesses an astonishingly broad range of human experiences. The raw material from which things are made, it has various associations: sensual, somatic, decorative, functional and ritual. Yet although textiles are part of our everyday lives, their very familiarity and accessibility belie a complex set of histories, and invite a range of speculations about their personal, social and cultural meanings. This ability to move within and reference multiple sites gives textiles their potency.

This journal brings together research in textiles in an innovative and distinctive academic forum for all those who share a multifaceted view of textiles within an expanded feld. Representing a dynamic and wide-ranging set of critical practices, it provides a platform for points of departure between art and craft; gender and identity; cloth, body and architecture; labor and technology; techno-design and practice—all situated within the broader contexts of material and visual culture.

Textile invites submissions informed by technology and visual media, history and cultural theory; anthropology; philosophy; political economy and psychoanalysis. It draws on a range of artistic practices, studio and digital work, manufacture and object production.

Berg Publishers is a member of CrossRef

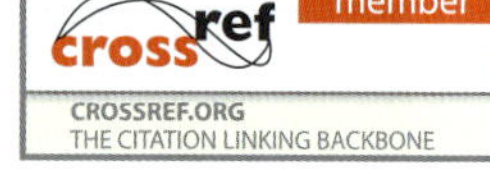

SUBMISSIONS

Should you have a topic you would like us to consider, please send an abstract of 300–500 words to one of the editors. Notes for Contributors can be found at the back of the journal and style guidelines are available by emailing kbruce@bergpublishers.com or from the Berg website (www.bergpublishers.com).

ISSN: 1475-9756
www.bergpublishers.com

Textile is indexed by Abstracts in Anthropology; AIO (Anthropological Index Online); ART Bibliographies Modern; British Humanities Index; Current Contents/Arts and Humanities; DAAI (Design and Applied Arts Index); IBR (International Bibliography of Book Reviews of Scholarly Literature in the Humanities and Social Sciences); IBSS (International Bibliography of the Social Sciences); IBZ (International Bibliography of Periodical Literature on the Humanities and Social Sciences); ISI Arts and Humanities Citation Index; Scopus; World Textiles.

Contents

EDITORS

Catherine Harper
School of Architecture and Design
University of Brighton
Grand Parade
Brighton BN2 4AY
UK
Catherine.Harper@brighton.ac.uk

Doran Ross
Fowler Museum at UCLA
308 Charles Young Drive
Los Angeles, CA 90095-1549
USA
dross@arts.ucla.edu

Dust Chronicles

Dust Chronicles

But oh *how the wind seems to own it,*
making it rise and move through us
though we'd swear we'd seen nothing.

Roberta Spear. "Dust." *A Sweetness Rising.*

Not long after I was invited by Catherine Harper to guest edit this special issue of *Textile: Journal of Cloth & Culture* on the topic of dust, a respected colleague—an artist working in metal—remarked that textile artists "give everything away." She was referring to the ongoing conceptual tug-of-war in the craft world between the forces holding fast to tradition and those who have seemingly abandoned the past. As a textile artist with a foot in both camps, I immediately understood her good-natured, yet pointed, comment.

In recent decades, makers in the field of textiles have been crossing the increasingly porous boundaries between craft, art, design, and activism. Along those pathways, some have given up hard-and-fast codes of conduct and adopted unconventional tactics. At moments, skill has relaxed into sloppiness, tactile processes have been superseded by digital technologies, material has evaporated into concept, object has been supplanted by performance, and making has given way to unmaking. To some, we have given away too much.

DEBORAH VALOMA

Deborah Valoma is the Director of Fine Arts and Associate Professor of Textiles at California College of the Arts, where specializes in research on the cultural history of textiles as a global aesthetic practice. She also teaches a series of courses on textile history and theory, and has written several articles, including "Cloth and African Identity in Bahía, Brazil," published in *Berg Encyclopedia of World Dress and Fashion.* She is currently working on a book entitled *The Past in Present Tense: Four Decades of Baskets by Julia Parker,* forthcoming from HeyDay Books. Also a studio artist, Valoma explores the material, conceptual, and poetic nuances of the medium through a hybrid practice incorporating both digital weaving technologies and hand processes.

Textile, Volume 8, Issue 3, pp. 260–269
DOI: 10.2752/175183510x12868938341321
Reprints available directly from the Publishers.
Photocopying permitted by licence only.

Yes, I said, we textile artists assume loss as a fundamental principle of our art form. Unable to rest on the sturdy material convictions of ceramics, glass, metal, or wood, we practice in a zone of unpredictability and pliability. Our materials have an uncertain presence and require an ultimate letting go: they are, by their very nature, transient. And so, acutely sensitive to the properties of our materials, we have become masters of gathering, integrating, and liberating particulate matter.

Spun of the fluff of nothingness, textiles yield to nothingness. They surrender to pressures of time and trauma—subject to staining, decomposition, and inevitable ruin. Textile artists contend daily with the dread of unraveling. Like Penelope, we weave and we unweave. We loop and we unloop. We stitch and we unstitch. We tangle and we untangle. We cast on and we cast off. The indigenous language of textiles is a vernacular of loss, and by necessity, we have become fluent in a poetics of the ephemeral. Like true believers, we follow the dictates of Genesis 3:19 (King James Version), "for dust thou art, and unto dust shalt thou return."

Swayed by gravitational pull from opposite polar zones, textiles waver between the seemingly contradictory principles of integration and disintegration. At the positively charged pole, metaphors of interconnectivity abound: we speak of the worldwide web, the fabric of society, and spinning a tale. Unlike reductive methods of shaping matter, spinning, weaving, knitting, and crocheting are additive and integrative. The formation of a cohesive whole from minute, disparate, yet equally valued elements is achieved though multiple points of contact. As an organizing principle, textiles offer a blueprint for thinking about interconnecting structures in linguistic, political, and scientific discourses.

On the negatively charged pole swirl chaotic clouds of dust that settle on the horizon line in sheets and blankets. Cloth, as Lois Martin points out in "The Direction of Cloth: The Horizontal Dimension," offers a "nonviolent resistance" to verticality (2002: 9), and the same could be said of dust. The disobedient limpness of cloth and the gravitational sink of dust lend an abject horizontality to both. Bedclothes and shrouds wrap prone bodies and disintegrate into loss and longing—the residual materiality of the uncontrollable and the undone. And so, because the bodies of textiles ultimately fail as our own fragile bodies do, we must arm ourselves with the *thought* of textiles—the delicate conceptual nuances of this humble yet poetically charged medium. It is these that provide conceptual solidity to our aesthetic practices.

My love affair with dust began when I was seven years old. Stomping through foot-high puffs of pure grey powder on Tell Nagila in the Negev Desert, I delighted in the soft, dry physicality on my bare feet and legs. And occasionally—when the perfect atmospheric conditions converged—millions of particles would spin excitedly on the winds, gather momentum, and soar high above me in a whirlwind. Most days, I played in the crumbling stone buildings built in the Bronze Age while archaeologists cautiously brushed debris, layer by layer, from the site. In buckets of muddy water, workers washed the extraneous dust from each potsherd, glass fragment, and metal scrap, and scratched each with a number in pen and ink. But the coiled baskets, plaited mats, and woven fabric that had once dominated the cultural landscape were never recovered, tattered and soiled, up out of the sediments—even in the minds of the archaeologists. I did not realize it then, but I was bathing in the dust of fibrous material long ago disintegrated and forgotten— breathing into my lungs the almost imperceptible particles of an unremembered existence.

Dusty lessons of loss continued throughout my life. In a neighborhood of Jerusalem, an entire community tumbled out of their stone-wall apartments to the call of a wailing woman. There she sat cross-legged, tearing her dress, clawing at the dry earth, and flinging fistfuls of dust into her unbound hair. This was a Biblical enactment of symbolic ruin—a defiant response to the tenuousness of life practiced for thousands of years. Cited numerous times in the Old Testament, the rending of cloth and the flinging of dust are parallel acts of ritualized mourning—exposing the frayed edges of grief and the tattered space of loss.

A few years ago, the union of dust and loss descended on me again in a kaleidoscope of particles. Over a period of days, I watched the creation of a five-foot sand *mandala* by Buddhist nuns from Kathmandu. First of its kind to be made by nuns in North America, the polychrome diagram represented compassion and the enlightened mind. At the end of eight days of painstaking, breath-stopping work, onlookers pushed forward to witness its purposeful destruction. I struggled to keep my composure in the rising anxiety of the crowd, and only caught a glimpse of the sudden, almost violent gesture as the nuns carved into the pristine carpet of dust. Shaken, I relaxed into the bodies of strangers, looked up into the sun-soaked air, and watched as a billowing cloud of vividly colored sand dusted the crowd with a euphoric experience of surrender.

In the Western drive to concretize human experience, time is conceived of as linear, fixed, and progressive. We erect the monumental to forestall the erosion of time, and strive toward containment and management of the unruly. And yet, the nature of dust disrupts the comfort of predictability and solidity and "belies the grandeur, strength and lucidity of masculine materials" (Kennedy 2005: 2). Dust floats, shifts, travels erratically on unseen currents of air, and coats our throats with the sweet, burnt taste of moments never to be relived. Dust does not forge ahead: it dances in spirals, circles backward—and when wind dies or breath fades—dust descends. It falls, like pliable cloth, into and around itself.

The settling of dust brings us to an ethereal standstill in a hushed, folded dustscape—aptly described by Charles Dickens in *Great Expectations* as "dust of desuetude" (1880: 533). In the first essay in this issue, "Dust the Ghostly Twin: A Study of Latency in the Writing of Celeste Olalquiaga," Melissa Laird states that dust, "more than any other element, signifies the passing of time." Using Olalquiaga's writing on dust in *The Artificial Kingdom* as a starting point, Laird asserts that layered dust is the quintessential metaphor for time-induced dormancy and articulates how the poignant aesthetics of dust act as a "softening presence" in the transition of an artifact from bright to dull, from distinct to subtle, and from perfect to imperfect.

In the *Oxford English Dictionary*, the third definition states that dust is anything reduced by disintegration. And though we recoil from the messiness of the decaying process, we also long wistfully for the past. We are seduced by surfaces draped with patinas of dust: the age-old and the well-worn are lovingly handled with "the oddly eroticized appreciation of decay" (Dillon 2009: 4). The dusty odor of handcrafted lace, bought for a heart-sinking two dollars in a flea market, intoxicates us with the nostalgia of unremembered lives, the touch of an unknown hand, and the haunting recollection of something just beyond the edge of our memories. Dust conjures the past. Dust *is* the past—particles of temporal chaos—floating just under our noses.

When my father's body was cremated, it was separated according to specific instructions in his will into twin piles of dust: one delivered to me, and the other to his wife. I promised my father I would carry my allotment of his body dust to Petra, Jordan—a place we had once traveled on the backs of Bedouin horses. In preparation for my mission, I wove a densely coiled, black basket, *Father Ossuary*, which would hold his dusty remains. In a gesture of unrequited love, I gingerly folded a handful of grey ash and bits of white bone into a vat of melted beeswax—a material reference to the Hebrew meaning of my name— and coated the surface of the basket thick with dusty sorrow.

But what is dust? According to Hannah Holmes, author of *The Secret Life of Dust*, dust is a bit of everything reduced to "particles so small that gravity has to fight to get control of them" (2001: 7). Full of inorganic and organic matter, dust particles ride the winds by the unavoidable billions: desert sands, salt rising from the oceans, decayed matter, sulfur compounds, soot of burned forests, volcanic ash, pollen, and flakes of skin shed from extinct dinosaurs and the billions of people that have inhabited the earth. Millennia ago, human technologies supplemented the dusty haze with soot from fires, microscopic particles of smelted metal, and of course the dust of plant and animal fiber that floated up from prehistoric encampments.

By the late nineteenth century, the rapid-fire intensification of the industrial revolution blanketed manufacturing centers with the residue of modernity. Coal fires burned over Britain, western Europe, and the northeastern part of the United States, spewing tons of soot into the air, darkening skies, and coating the overcrowded cities with a film of blackness that seemed to be a visual manifestation of a growing communal anxiety.

Peasants, who had for centuries been considered by the upper classes to be dirty and coarse—the "closest companions of dust" (Amato 2000: 36)—flooded the urban areas, where they preserved their dusty reputations by working in trades such as chimney sweeping and dust collecting. Social critics and reformers fought a battle against unchecked urban grime— what John Ruskin condemned as the "perpetual plague of sulphurous darkness" (1859: 61).

Relentless invention in the textile industry fueled the swift intensification of cloth production and generated its own unique form of toxic dust. "Cities of spindles" such as Manchester, England proliferated rapidly—their voracious growth fed by the millions of bales of raw cotton fiber streaming in from the colonies. As the machinery of mass production churned, clouds of white fluff billowed out of factory doors and clung to every surface of the mill towns. Brown lung settled into the bodies of thousands of workers—often women and children—who were exposed to long-term inhalation of cotton dust in inadequately ventilated factory environments.

In this issue, Elodie Neuville depicts the dusty enactment of class and gender in her article "Women, Cloth, Fluff and Dust in Elizabeth Gaskell's *North and South*." Set in an industrial center of cotton production in northern England, cotton dust floats through Elizabeth Gaskell's 1855 novel as a motif that "makes pregnant the alienating character of modern production processes and their devastating effect on both feminine interiors and feminine bodies."

Neuville's analysis traces cloth backward to its origins as fluff, and argues persuasively that cotton is used throughout the narrative to "explore and represent femininity in its negotiation of dawning modernity."

Like brown lung, fear of dust settled into the social consciousness of the Victorian middle classes. As Brian Dillon describes in "A Dry Black Veil," the bourgeoisie "feared the insinuation of dust into the domestic interior, where it was transmuted from a threat of civil health into the marker of household disarray" (2009: 3). Because moral uprightness and mental clarity were equated with a state of domestic dustlessness, Victorian interiors were feather-dusted daily, linens boiled, and bodies scrubbed. Richard Henry Horne's panoramic vision of a squalid encampment in "Canvass Town," published in Charles Dickens's *Household Words*, vividly exposes the Victorian revulsion for the barely controlled, dust-filled domestic landscape and the disorderly female body with its potential for stain making. He describes "a confusion of odiously dirty and torn blankets and coverlets; some of a dull yellow, hammy color; some mottled, and some of a shade approaching to pale black, while over all of them lay a fine bloom of dust" (1853: 365).

Though in the nineteenth century dust was an "explicitly domestic feminine trope" (Kennedy 2005: 2), class and race were the dustiest of all fields of engagement. The job of controlling middle-class domestic dust was placed into the hands of working-class women, and

in the United States in particular into the hands of women of color. Native American girls housed in Bureau of Indian boarding schools were exclusively trained to clean and launder; domestic service was the most common employment for African American women up until the Second World War; and today Latinas constitute the largest category of domestic workers in the United States. Writing in *Dirt and Domesticity*, Cara Mertes points out that women of color not only attended to the physical dust and dirt, "but also contained the psychological dirt as well" (1992: 70).

Some contemporary artists are kicking up the psychological dust. Angela Hennessy's *Blacklets* (2007), depicted on the cover of this issue, is the reduction of "black velvet"—a nineteenth-century eroticized slang word for a black-skinned woman—to an insignificant and unruly pile of fuzz. Through countless quiet hours spent in the destructive act of unraveling, Hennessy charted the physical deterioration and mental collapse of her schizophrenic father. The title cites Andrew Wynter in *Our Social Bees* (1861: 25), who bemoans the "dim canopy of soot hovering over London" and the "blacklets that invisibly permeate the air." Referencing her father's sooty death in a fire years earlier, Hennessy folds the dusty horizon inward and maps the internal terrain of blackness. Black fuzz covered her studio, clung to her body, and traveled with her. She inhaled it, consumed it, and over time absorbed her father's absence (personal communication).

Seizing the metaphor of dusty otherness, Columbian artist María Adelaida López's *Dust Houses* (2004–2007) are encased in household dust and dirt she emptied from vacuum cleaner bags while supporting herself through graduate school as a house cleaner in Philadelphia. American photographer David Maisel similarly proposes dust as a signifier of the marginalized in his haunting series *Library of Dust* (2005–2006). Maisel photographed over one hundred copper canisters containing the unclaimed cremated remains of Oregon State Insane Asylum patients who died over a period of nearly a century. Each stark image represents a single, isolated canister erupting with a colorful blossom of corrosion caused by the chemical reaction of human ash, copper, and moisture—dusty portraits of the forlorn and the forgotten.

And in this issue, collaborative artists Sean Miller and Kelly Cobb discuss the aesthetics of dust in "Art Museum Dust Collection: Wearing Away Museum Grounds—Dust Bunnies, White Lies, and New Measures." Miller is the organizer of the ongoing project *Art Museum Dust Collection*, and has been harvesting dust in museums for over a decade. His interventions shift perceptions from the substantial to the minute, invert definitions of high and low, and point convincingly toward the unlikely claim that "dust is the most beautiful material present in many museums." As a collaborator on the ongoing project, Cobb designed dust cloth: woven at The Jacquard Center in North Carolina, the surfaces incorporate microscopic snapshots of Miller's museum dust. Defining dust as "a spontaneous, tumbled non-woven" textile, Cobb weaves dust into dust and creates work that foretells its own certain demise.

These aesthetic statements transgress the hierarchies of value upheld within the white walls of gallery and museum. Dust obscures our myopic focus on the pristine, the singular, and the solid. Dust crumbles the certainty of one-point perspective, refracts light democratically, and dilates our peripheral vision to reveal the overlooked dustscapes collecting along the distant edges and in the deeply set corners. This is the territory of the dusty have-nots: women of color with skins dusted brown, dusty Global South populations, the urban homeless sleeping under blankets of dust, the infirm dressed in linty, threadbare gowns, and the mentally ill rocked by internal dust storms. Dust is the insidious interloper—the specks that belie the falsity of white neutrality.

Dust is the color of the unseen and the inconsequential, the ever-shifting color of the other. In "Dust to Dust: A Particular History of Khaki," Catherine Moriarty cleverly shifts our attention in this volume to the color of invisibility. The author tracks the British Army's abandonment of the arresting bright-red uniforms worn in traditional battlefield formations in Europe, and its adoption of dust-colored fatigues in the mid-nineteenth-century military campaigns in Africa and Asia where "the nature of warfare on the margins of colonial incursion was much more unpredictable." Derived from the Farsi word _kāk_—translated as dust-colored—service uniforms sewn from khaki cloth rendered soldiers virtually invisible in the dusty geography of the colonized.

Scientific researchers too have been training their eyes on the unseen and overlooked. Because organic material is preserved intact only in extreme cold, dryness, or wetness, most archaeological sites yield only significantly degraded fiber specimens, if anything at all. Far from spectacular, most are decomposed and fragmentary. Issues of preservation have made the study of ancient textile technologies challenging, but commonly held interpretive biases in the male-dominated field of archaeology have also played a significant role in the assignment of scientific value. The "unsexy field of perishable artifacts" (Adovasio et al. 2007: xii) has been neglected by generations of scholars, and as a result the importance of textiles—and the contributions of women who generally made them—have been obscured in the reconstruction of prehistoric culture.

Two articles in this collection redress these oversights. Recognizing the scientific value of even the most insignificant textile dust, two teams of researchers applied current methodology to the analysis of material collected in excavations of prehistoric North America. In "Revealing Clues from Textile Particulate through Microscopy, Infrared Spectroscopy, and X-ray Microanalysis," Kathryn Jakes, Amanda Thompson, and Christel Baldia investigate dust particles shed from degraded, charred, and mineralized textile fragments discovered decades ago at Seip Mound, Ohio (*c.*100 BCE–400 CE). Instead of brushing away the seemingly irrelevant dust, these researchers collected fibrous debris from storage boxes and glass cases at the Ohio Historical Society and were able to tease a wealth of data from "material that would otherwise be thrown away."

In "Moundville: Forgotten Textile Fragments Reveal the Past," Virginia Wimberley and Amanda Thompson focus on textile specimens discovered at Moundville, Alabama (*c.*1250–1550 CE) during excavations conducted in the 1970s. These minute fragments—originally considered insignificant compared to the lithic, ceramic, and metal artifacts found at the site—remained unexamined until the recent study. Based on careful chemical and structural analysis, their findings rectify past oversights, reveal significant information about the prehistoric culture of Moundville, and confirm the relevance of further research on the inconsequential and unvalued.

As the dust settles on this volume, the words, sentences, and paragraphs settle one by one like lightly compressed strata in an archaeological site. Heeding Olalquiaga's assertion that "dust is the transformation of reality from unitary to fragmentary, from continuous to chaotic" (2002: 94), I wanted to stir up a bit of editorial dust. At first I considered scattering this collection of articles like particles across several issues, but decided it was critical to construct one volume where the

dust could drift and collect into a layered composition of meaning. And although poetry has never been included in prior issues of *Textile: Journal of Cloth & Culture*, it seemed a fitting topsoil to scatter on the dusty topography of this special issue.

Poetry is dusty, or perhaps more accurately, fuzzy: an unraveling of Roland Barthes's often cited "weave of signifiers" (1977: 159). In the poem "home," Joseph Lease addresses—in both form and content—the poetic caress between dust and loss. Swarms of words drift lightly above the clean pages, coming to rest only briefly in seemingly random, yet meaningful patterns like "little arcs of dust on a couch." Language particles—both spoken and unspoken—rise again off the poem's white landscape and land gritty in our eyes, blurring the journal's crisp edges. If we can avoid the impulse to wipe clean, we can perceive in the quiet haze the unformed, the unseen, and the unheard.

Silence, writes Marie-Luisa Achino-Loeb, is a "repository of the unselected, unfocused, unprivileged: a domain of silent sounds, silent meanings, silent structures" (2006: 42). Like poets, jazz musicians know about dustiness, though they do not call it that. Lesser musicians play into the silence, but the masters *play the silence*—the pause in music, the lyrical, dust-filled void between counts, chords, and melodic phrases where the meaning can settle on its own. Like skillful jazz musicians, textile artists have learned that emptiness heightens the poignancy of mutable presence. We work our strings, plucking

and pausing, purposefully giving the moment away—bringing presence to absence and voice to voicelessness.

So, yes, we textile artists give away. We surrender to dusty loss—we *use* loss as a fundamental principle of our art form. We employ the aesthetics of order and disorder, composition and decomposition, form and formlessness. We drift purposefully in the liminal territory between the fluff before and the dust after, poised between becoming and disappearing and becoming. We revel in the strength of working on the fringe—no, *being* the fringe, the tear in the whole, and the frayed edge. In the battle against the hierarchy of order and permanence, we squirm under fences, squeeze through gates left ajar, and scale walls. And like Alfred Tennyson's "maniac scattering dust" (1849: 192)—we too scatter dust as we go.

Pablo Picasso's statement "Art washes away from the soul the dust of everyday life" demands revision here. Dust *is* the art of everyday life.

References

Achino-Loeb, Maria-Luisa. 2006. "Silence and the Imperatives of Identity." In *Silence: The Currency of Power*, 35–51. Edited by Maria-Luisa Achino-Loeb. New York: Berghahn Books.

Adovasio, J.M., Soffer, Olga and Page, Jake. 2007. *The Invisible Sex: Uncovering the True Roles of Women in Prehistory*. New York: Smithsonian Books.

Amato, Joseph A. 2000. *Dust: A History of the Small & the Invisible*.

Berkeley and Los Angeles: University of California Press.

Barthes, Roland. 1977. *Image, Music, Text*. Translated by Stephens Heath. New York: Hill and Wang.

Dickens, Charles. 1880. *Great Expectations*. Illustrated by F.A. Fraser. Boston: Estes and Lauriat.

Dillon, Brian. 2009. "A Dry Black Veil." *Cabinet: A Quarterly of Art and Culture* 35 (fall): 59–65.

Holmes, Hannah. 2001. *The Secret Life of Dust: From the Cosmos to the Kitchen Counter, The Big Consequences of Little Things*. New York: John Wiley & Sons.

Horne, Richard Henry. 1853. "Canvass Town." In *Household Words: A Weekly Journal*. Ed. Charles Dickens. Volume VII. New York: McElrath and Barker.

Kennedy, Jake. 2005. "Dust and the Avant-Garde." *CLC Web: Comparative Literature and Culture* 7 (2). http://docs.lib.purdue.edu/clcweb/vol7/iss2/4/

Martin, Lois. 2002. "The Direction of Cloth: The Horizontal Dimension." *Surface Design Journal* 26 (winter): 6–13.

Mertes, Cara. 1992. "There's No Place Like Home: Women and Domestic Labor." In *Dirt and Domesticity: Constructions of the Feminine*, 58–73. Organized by Jesús Fuenmayor, Kate Haug, and Frazer Ward. New York: Whitney Museum of American Art at Equitable Center. Exhibition catalogue.

Olalquiaga, Celeste. 2002. *The Artificial Kingdom: On the Kitsch Experience*. Minneapolis: University of Minnesota Press.

Ruskin, John. 1859. "Modern Manufacture and Design." In *The Two Paths: Being Lectures on Art and Its Application to Decoration and Manufacture, Delivered in 1858–1859*, 47–67. Edited by Christine Roth. West Lafayette, IN: Parlor Press, 2004.

Spear, Roberta. 2007. *A Sweetness Rising: New and Selected Poems*. Ed. with Intro. by Philip Levin. Berkeley, CA: Great Valley Books/HeyDay Books.

Tennyson, Alfred. 1849. "In Memoriam A.H.H." In *The Poetical Works of Alfred Tennyson; Poet Laureate*, 179–218. New York: John B. Alden, Publisher, 1883.

Wynter, Andrew. 1861. *Our Social Bees; or, Pictures of Town and Country Life, and Other Papers*. London: Robert Hardwicke.

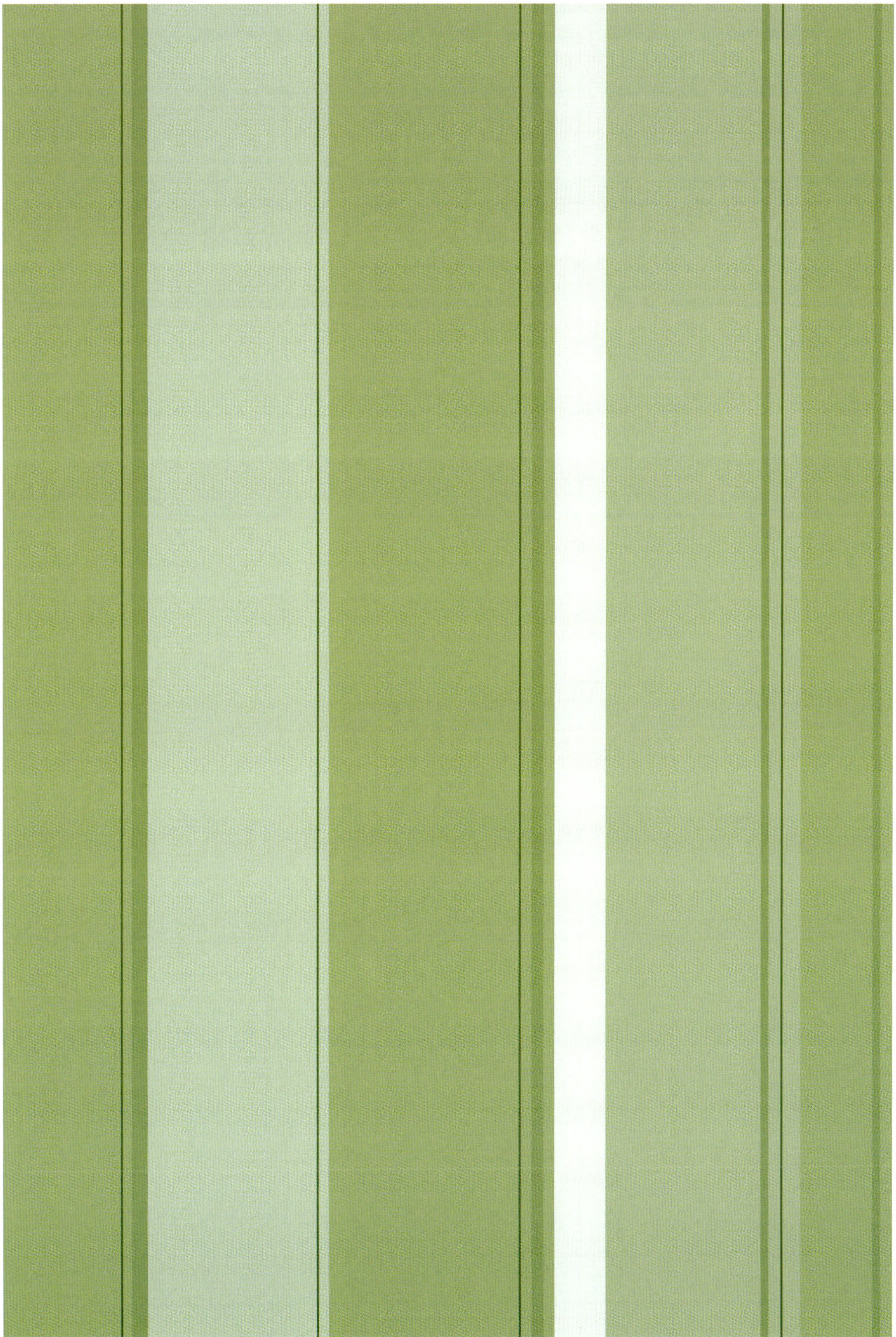

Dust the Ghostly Twin: A Study of Latency in the Writing of Celeste Olalquiaga

Abstract

This article examines the aesthetics of time wrought through the cultivation of neglect, where dormancy, latency, and the mechanical failure of artifacts act to facilitate accumulations of dust on their fragile surface. Notions associated with the provenance of artifacts, their protection or subjection to dust, the creation of subtle patinas from once vital hues, and dust's function as a conduit from time past to the modern day are discussed through the writing of cultural theorist Celeste Olalquiaga.

Keywords: fragmentary remains, latency, dormancy, aesthetics of damage, aureatic authenticity, Celeste Olalquiaga

MELISSA LAIRD

Melissa Laird is Academic Coordinator at the Whitehouse Institute of Design, Australia. Trained as a practitioner in the fields of fashion and graphic design, she has research interests including material culture scholarship and visual intelligence. She is currently working on a book documenting women's historical memory in the Australian Colonial period, 1788–1901, and will soon present her Doctoral research at the University of Oslo. Laird is part of the UTS Challenge Grant—Blueprints for Sydney research undertaking, and is actively engaged in research/ art practice with the Hyde Park Barracks Museum, Sydney.

Textile, Volume 8, Issue 3, pp. 270–273
DOI: 10.2752/175183510X12868938341367
Reprints available directly from the Publishers.
Photocopying permitted by licence only.
© 2010 Berg. Printed in the United Kingdom.

Dust the Ghostly Twin: A Study of Latency in the Writing of Celeste Olalquiaga

Dust, more than any other element, signifies of the passing of time. It suggests latency, immobility, the tangible reality of dormancy, sleep, and the static; an artifact devoid of activity. Dormancy can be witnessed through accumulations on the surface of artifacts; the accretion of dust and webs, the highly dynamic processes of decay, mould, decomposition, and rust, which can only be accomplished on immobile fragments, evidence of the passing of time, stillness, and death. Artifacts have many qualities which help define their aureatic visibility. These contribute to the significance of the artifact as historical marker, a signifier of time and place. While the surface itself may be highly active, the artifact itself must remain static for such residues to accumulate. Provenance then, may be suggested through cracks, imperfections, flaws, blemishes, and signs of failing function and weakness harnessed and revealed through dust's inevitable envelopment. Filtering the gaudy excesses of brilliant color once adorning shining artifacts, dust's softening surface mutes them to subtle patinas in their morbid stillness. Raging red diminishes to a gentle coral; ultramarine, to a smoky haze-like grey; gold's blazing lustre lessened to dappled caramel. The viewer gains aureatic insight from such detail; cobwebs become gossamer; rust the subtle patina of shadow. Dust the ghostly twin: a study in latency.

The passage of time and space, rather than lessening the value of artifacts, augments it. Rather than detracting, dust gives the aged artifact credibility, a sense of historical authenticity. Cultural theorist Celeste Olalquiaga (1999) describes well-worn artifacts suffering "the mortal trials of time and space" as revealing of "the wear and tear of age and use" (p. 88). She continues, "As if in suspension in limbo, instead of being empty or blank, [the artifact] carried the imprint of the duration, one that is measured, not in the productive accumulation of years or days, but rather in the subtle persistence of a stubborn anachronicity, the stoic refusal of things to depart once their usefulness is exhausted" (p. 5). Not only does dust connect the past with the present, it creates a gentle fusion of the interior object with an augmented exterior. Olalquiaga (1999) states, "Dust is what connects dreams of yesteryear with the touch of nowadays" (pp. 94–5). Dust equalizes the ragged surface textures of sculpted forms, filling cracks and crevices, in a form of negative relief work. Filigree and lace become ill-defined, openwork reduced to harmonious wholes, as dust pervades and balances positive and the negative space. Dust settles, fills, grows, bonds, and makes "new." Artifacts glean new identities through their dust-enhanced latency.

During this latency, function becomes less significant as fragments show signs of age, malfunction, failure, decay, and dust, "the signature of lost time" (Olalquiaga 1999, p. 95). But in these derelict artifacts, fragmentary remains of once whole objects, showing significant signs of mechanical and aesthetic failure, material-culture scholars find data: the rich aesthetics of damage. Through their transition from completeness to decay, artifacts can undergo a metamorphosis through their rediscovery and interpretation. Dust acts as a companion to such a transition from the perfect to the imperfect. In their dormancy, selected remnants and relics undergo a variety of processes: loss, entombment, protection, secrecy. Provenance, then, helps provide some evidence of the type of conditions fragments may have been exposed to.

Artifacts with inherent precious, personal, or sentimental value may have been cloistered in protective coverings, guarded, sealed and stored and less prone to dust's softening presence. This type of artifact, which Olalquiaga (1999) describes as "personalised in the privacy of someone's specific universe," tends to have attracted considered care, its passage through time and space lovingly guided by family or friends (p. 17). A sacred or iconic object may be kept in "camere auree" in a protected or private environment for viewing and communion (p. 211). Similarly, a secret artifact, intimate souvenir, or personal memento may be hidden or concealed from public view and inhibited from the incidence of dust. Artifacts awarded with little significance by an owner may be forgotten or lost and become increasing consumed by an unceasing layering of dust particles, blending with its environment, camouflaged. A broken item may be disregarded, discarded, and ultimately consumed: by dust.

Dust serves as one of the archives' allies, the traditional curator's *raison d'être*. Through the rigorous procedures to safeguard against it, many objects have been preserved by protections imposed on an artifact. Olalquiaga charges "albums, armoires, boxes, glass cases ... protecting [artifacts] from this era's archenemy—dust" (p. 89). Glass shrouds, cabinets of curiosity, protective drapery, and vigilant fluttering of cloth have served to mediate exposure to dust's delicate and translucent form. Glass boxes, concealed shelves, archival drawers, specimen bottles, and compartmentalized storage sections form part of the physical frameworks associated with the traditional library and the archive which house artifacts, and are used as devices for protective placement. Olalquiaga (1999) states, "Glass cases used to protect collectables from dust unwittingly raised them to the status of relics" (p. 52). The protective placement of artifacts create notions of privacy, scale, and intimacy, sound and ambience, the hushed, ephemeral, and intangible elements of these traditional spaces built into the environments into which dust cannot permeate. It is important to note, however, that an artifactual aura created through sacred ambience may be vastly more emotive for the viewer than the profane environment of the public, open, or untempered viewing space. Notions of age and use, decay and dust, find a new relevance within the contemporary practices of dynamic exhibit design. These ideas are wrought through the cultivation of neglect, harnessing the aesthetics of time and damage, of which dust is prominent in its contribution to historical and aureatic authenticity.

... the beauty of the marks of time. (Olalquiaga, 1999: 86)

Reference

Olalquiaga, C. 1999. *The Artificial Kingdom: A Treasury of Kitsch Experience*. London: Bloomsbury.

Women, Cloth, Fluff and Dust in Elizabeth Gaskell's *North and South*

Women, Cloth, Fluff and Dust in Elizabeth Gaskell's *North and South*

From Penelope's tapestry to Hester's Scarlet Letter, women and cloth have a long and intimate narrative history together. Elizabeth Gaskell's *North and South* (1854–55) holds a place of its own in that history. The novel is full of the things and stuff that have come to be regarded as typical of the genre that flourished in an era that inaugurated new ways to enjoy and celebrate materiality.

North and South focuses on Margaret Hale, daughter of a Lady and a country clergyman, who has spent an idyllic early childhood with her parents in Helstone, a village "like (…) in one of Tennyson's poems" (Gaskell 1998: 12)[1] in the South of England. At age nine, she "was brought, all untamed from the forest, to share the home, the play and the lessons of her cousin Edith" (NS, 8) in London. At the start of the novel, Margaret is eighteen and coming back to Helstone, but her return is, however, short-lived as her father's dissenting opinions compel him to resign his position as a vicar and move north. In Milton Northern, Mr. Hale will teach John Thornton, a rich cotton-mill owner who wishes to resume an education too early discontinued. The novel thus opposes a pastoral and bucolic South to an industrial and seemingly rough North. The geographical and cultural opposition is dramatized through the characters of Margaret Hale and John Thornton and the evolution of their relationship through desire and defiance to romance.

The novel's treatment of cloth follows and develops the seeming opposition between North and South, or men and women, for cloth is both industrially transformed product and merchandise and the basis of a homelike and private occupation. By organizing in her novel the collusion of the two worlds where cotton is used in different ways and to different purposes, Gaskell asks the question of the possible coexistence of the private, the traditional, the historical, and the feminine with what is public, modern, and new.

When the novel's heroine first enters Milton she is struck by its purposeful, businesslike, matter-of-fact air. Cotton is everywhere she looks, in "every van, every wagon and truck … either in the raw shape

ELODIE NEUVILLE
The author can be contacted
at ecjneuville@yahoo.com

Textile, Volume 8, Issue 3, pp. 274–285
DOI: 10.2752/175183510X12868938341402
Reprints available directly from the Publishers.
Photocopying permitted by licence only.

in bags, or in the woven shape in bales of calico" (NS, 59). Factory-made, ubiquitous, volatile, and versatile, this cotton is synonymous with the modernity that the Hales—and others besides them—must confront.

By studying the trajectory of this material in the lives of the women of the novel, I argue that cloth, because of its polymorphous quality, is being used to explore and represent femininity in its negotiation of dawning modernity. My argument follows the life of a piece of cloth backward, starting with the final product in the shape of shawls or pieces of upholstery and slowly unraveling it to reach back to raw cotton and to the cotton dust, or fluff, created during the carding process. I start by discussing the way socially prescribed feminine behavior is challenged by women's relationship to their clothes and to their own bodies as well as by the social fabric binding women to each other. I then explore the effects of the mechanization of the industrial process on that social fabric and on women's relation to their interior and their interiority.

In Chapter 1 Margaret is made to stand in the middle of her Aunt's drawing-room "as a sort of lay figure on which to display the [Indian shawls]" (NS, 9), her whole body devoted to setting off "the long beautiful folds" for the assembled ladies.

> *Occasionally, as she was turned round, she caught a glimpse of herself in the mirror over the chimney-piece, and smiled at her own appearance there ...*

> *She touched the shawls gently as they hung around her, and took a pleasure in their soft feel and their brilliant colours, and rather liked to be dressed in such splendour—enjoying it as a child would do, with a quiet pleased smile on her lips. ... Mr. Henry Lennox was suddenly announced ... Margaret stood perfectly still ... but looking at Mr. Lennox with a bright, amused face, as if sure of his sympathy in her sense of the ludicrousness at being thus surprised.* (NS, 9)

Although this scene might seem trivial, it in fact explores the multiple semantic layers embedded within the central figure of Margaret enjoying the feel of a beautiful piece of cloth she does not own in a private setting. The shawls are clearly bourgeois upper-class objects, telltale signs of a social status that is not quite that of Margaret. She is the family's poor relation, the daughter of a lady and a modest country clergyman, whose social status within the household is uncertain. Narratively, the expensive shawls emphasize Margaret's predicament as one whose place in society is ambiguous.

On a broader socio-historical level, the shawls' geographic origin is here as a reminder of the interdependence between imperialism and the necessary association of women with home and the private sphere. Here the imperial venture finds its usual justification in that it helps maintain and prettify the private sphere in the homeland, thereby reinforcing the distinction between abroad/public space and home/ private space. That distinction is, however, somewhat questioned by the look Margaret directs first to herself in the mirror and then to Henry Lennox. Instead of being the object of everyone's gaze, Margaret is shown to be the origin, or subject of that gaze. The shift from passive to active voice in the first sentence also marks a shift in point of view: the look in the mirror is a look inward which comes as a questioning of the established order of things. Margaret has been put on display at the centre of the room, and is still in that position when the only man comes in. By glancing at herself and then at Lennox, Margaret takes charge of her image, her representation. This is akin to someone being filmed suddenly taking hold of the camera. As Margaret catches "a glimpse of herself in the mirror over the chimney-piece," she becomes a source of pleasure to herself, not needing to please or be pleased by anyone.

We can gain some insight into how Margaret's representation partially eschews expected patriarchal codes by turning to Griselda Pollock in her exploration of the works of Mary Cassatt and Berthe Morisot in her article "Modernity and the Spaces of Femininity" (Pollock 2003). In this article Pollock engages with the traditional or mainstream definition of femininity as represented in early modernist works of art—specifically impressionist paintings—and consolidated through its critique in mainstream modern art history. Pollock's aim is not to deny the existence of sexual difference and

its inscription in the work of art but to "explore … the concrete ways in which women negotiate and refashion that position [femininity] to alter its meanings. We can ask of Elizabeth Gaskell's representation of femininity what Pollock asks of the work of the two painters: 'Is femininity confirmed as passivity and masochistic or is there a critical look resulting from a different position from which femininity is appraised, experienced and represented?'" (Pollock 2003: 124). Here Margaret's gaze is empowering because it brings about a heightened consciousness of herself through a sensual enjoyment of her image and the material she's wearing. She is bold enough to know her own worth and confront a man with her gaze rather than waiting for his own. If, as Pollock argues, "the sexual politics of looking function around a regime which divides into binary positions, activity/ passivity, looking/being seen, voyeur/exhibitionist, subject/ object" (ibid.), then we can say that in the shawls scene, Gaskell through Margaret rearticulates these positions. There the feminine occupies both ends of each binary position. (There are ladies looking and there is Margaret looking back or looking elsewhere.) Even with the arrival of Henry Lennox into this so far exclusively female meeting, he is not given the traditional male role of the voyeur, but instead his arrival starts an exchange of looks, a relationship, a "sympathy" with Margaret. The drawing-room, this space traditionally construed as feminine, "ceases to function as the space of sight for a mastering

gaze, but becomes the locus of relationships" (ibid.).

In chapter VII, Margaret's first encounter with Mr. Thornton goes even further toward reinventing the gendering of space and looks. Not yet settled in Milton, Margaret comes back to her hotel to learn that her father's friend and pupil, Mr. Thornton, is waiting in their sitting room. This time Margaret has lost all sign of passivity and is given most of the traditional male prerogatives: she commands space by opening the door to let herself in and asking Thornton to take a seat. But she is also defined in words arguably in this context calling up masculine qualities: "straight," "fearless," "frank," "unabashed," while being somewhat deficient in the feminine ones resulting in her feeling "no awkwardness," not being "surprised or discomfited," and most of all totally lacking the "flush" on her complexion which would at least have intimated some feminine internal turmoil. Her dress is an enigma in its blend of utter simplicity and grandeur, the latter residing in "a large Indian shawl, which hung about her in long heavy folds, and which she wore as an empress wears her drapery" (NS, 62). Margaret does not use her dress as an artifact for seduction, she wears it as an outside reflection of her personality. Mr. Thornton, through whose eyes we look at her, sees in those elements of dress a natural ability to rule. The comparison he makes with an empress links the person with an official function requiring the exercise of power, which was most unusual for a woman. Margaret is shown to disrupt the established decorum of feminine behavior by controlling her image.

When Margaret's image escapes her, she becomes the focus of representation and interpretation. Sketching with her friend Henry Lennox in the bucolic and picturesque landscape surrounding the parsonage in Helstone, Margaret takes off the bonnet which "makes [her] head so hot" (NS, 26). In such an informal setting, she is understandably heedless of the city's strict etiquette. However, as Henry is anxiously waiting for a sign in Margaret's behavior that could be interpreted as an encouragement to his courtship, her bare-headedness becomes an invitation. Without this little piece of cloth attesting to her modesty, Margaret is taken to silently signal her availability to be represented both literally in Lennox's drawing and figuratively in his imagination. The interpretative breach of representations opened up by the same careless gesture in Milton proves otherwise important. Coming to Mrs. Thornton's to ask for a water-bed for her ailing mother, Margaret finds herself trapped within the mill-owner's house at the moment when the striking workers, having broken down the mill gates, stand before the house steps. After she has convinced Mr. Thornton to go and face them "man to man," she takes up "her place by the farthest window" and wishes "Mr. Thornton would but say something to them—let them hear his voice only ... But perhaps he was speaking now ... She tore her bonnet off; and bent forwards to hear. She could only see ..." (NS, 178). Margaret's bonnet hinders her hearing; if it indeed stands for female modesty then the signs of female modesty are what prevents her from both understanding and playing a part in what is going on outside. It is significant that taking off her bonnet is necessary to connect with the world outside. Soon she will further break down barriers between herself and the outside world by actually unbarring the door of the house and joining Thornton on the steps, facing the crowd.

For Sally Shuttleworth, Margaret's "stepp[ing] out bare-headed" is "a sure sign in the Victorian novel of female abandonment." According to her, Margaret's "actions simultaneously embody the two dominant, but opposing, models for womanhood in Victorian Culture," on the one hand "the spiritual helpmeet" and on the other "the passionate female body" (Shuttleworth 1998: xxviii). Margaret is certainly "trapped between the polar opposites of her own desires and motivations" but she is mostly torn apart by the different interpretations assigned to her looks and actions by those watching. It is as though this moment existed almost purely for the sake of its exegesis, it is the focal point around which revolve questions about Margaret's identity. To Margaret, stepping out bare-headed is first and foremost a way to be able to take part unhindered in the world surrounding her. She is a prisoner of sorts since John Thornton orders her and the other women of the house to stay inside, just as he ordered the "Irish hands" come to work instead of his striking workers. To everyone else, Margaret, in throwing off her bonnet before standing in front of an all-male assembly, has revealed the bold and shameless nature of a temptress.

What Margaret is in fact reproached with is the turning inside out of her private self and its exposure to strangers, to publicity. The negative value associated with the insufficient covering and hiding of the female body is contrasted with the sometimes positive consequences of letting others reach out and abolish the usual private/public boundaries. Rather than being the focus of misinterpretations, cloth becomes the material that makes tangible a sense of female solidarity and community.

When Margaret goes on an errand to look for a servant in the course of her first weeks in Milton, she finds herself caught up in the throng of mill workers on their way between factory and home. On such occasions, her clothes help break down the distance between her and working-girls from the mills who,

with their rough, but not unfriendly freedom, would comment on her dress, even touch her shawl or gown to ascertain the exact material; nay, once or twice she was asked questions relative to some article which they particularly admired. There was such a simple reliance on her womanly sympathy with their love of dress, and on her kindliness, that she gladly replied to these inquiries, as soon as she understood them; and half smiled back at their remarks. (NS, 71)

No notion of class or rank guides the girls' behavior. This absence of decorum almost comes as a relief to Margaret from the affected London manners she had to submit to while at her Aunt Shaw's. The freedom she enjoys in the streets of Milton and the inescapable proximity with the factory-workers are two sides of the same coin. In touching "her shawl or gown," the girls break down a formal barrier that language more often than not builds up. Because of its intimate contact with our bodies, dress and articles of dress come to represent us or our meaning—they are the acceptable visible counterpart of our incarnate nature. Clothes and cloth in general also touch women in such context very closely in that a considerable part of their time is devoted to sewing, embroidering, knitting, or mending articles of dress or upholstery: the garments they work on and wear envelop them in one common universal experience born out of the intimacy created by long hours spent poring over the material.

The bond between women of different conditions is intimately portrayed through the friendship between Margaret and Bessy Higgins, which takes up elements of Margaret's encounter with the world of working people. Here again, the bond between the two girls is not based solely on words, but relies heavily on touch, mediated once again by cloth: "Bessy lay back silent, and content to look at Margaret's face, and touch her articles of dress, with a childish admiration of their fineness of texture" (NS, 100). As the friendship between the two girls develops, but also as Bessy's

lung infection progresses, the latter's reliance on her friend's articles of dress for comfort takes on a new dimension. As they discuss Margaret's choice of a white silk gown for the Thornton's dinner, Bessy is reminded of a dream she had of her friend before she even met her. Bessy's dream is very much imbued with a spiritual and religious significance: in it Margaret wears a "shining raiment" that she insists is identical to the white silk gown. "Let me come and see you in it. I want to see yo' and touch yo' as in very deed yo' were in my dream" (NS, 149). Bessy's need to make sure of Margaret's realness through touching her clothes is reminiscent of Christians contemplating relics in order to strengthen their faith.

On Bessy's death, Dixon—the Hales's maid—explains to Margaret that "the young woman who died had a fancy for being buried in something of yours, and so the sister's come to ask for it—and I was looking for a night-cap that wasn't too good to give away" (NS, 216). Bessy's wish to lie for eternity not *with* but "*in*" something of Margaret's emphasizes the indestructibility of their mutual attachment as well as the power that cloth and garments are invested with as repositories and vehicles for emotions.

The ability of cloth to absorb emotions and history in its fabric is precisely what Mrs. Thornton must confront. Although she insists on her pride at living right next to her son's mills, with the sound of workers reminding her of "a hive of bees," she is keen to protect herself and her furniture and objects as much as possible from "dust and destruction" (NS, 112). In the eyes of Margaret, visiting the Thornton drawing room for the first time, the chief impression is that of a fossilized world:

> It seemed as though no one had been in it since the day when the furniture was bagged up with as much care as if the house was to be overwhelmed with lava, and discovered a thousand years hence. The walls were pink and gold; the pattern on the carpet represented bunches of flowers on a light ground, but it was carefully covered up in the centre by a linen drugget, glazed and colourless. The window-curtains were lace; each chair and sofa had its own particular veil or netting, or knitting ... The whole room had a painfully spotted, spangled, speckled look about it, which impressed Margaret so unpleasantly that she was hardly conscious of the peculiar cleanliness required to keep everything so white and pure in such an atmosphere, or of the trouble that must be willingly expended to secure that effect of icy, snowy discomfort. Wherever she looked there was evidence of care and labour, but not care and labour to procure ease, to help on habits of tranquil home employment; solely to ornament, and then to preserve ornament from dust and destruction.
> (NS, 112)

Ironically, Mrs. Thornton protects her possessions from the dust of the mill by covering them up with cloth, which is exactly what the mill produces. Her drawing room looks like a stage set, the main purpose of which is to display the signs of an upper-middle-class interior. But it is precisely all these correct outward signs that send the "wrong" message about Mrs. Thornton's class origins. She gets the colors and materials right but she fails to get the inhabiting it right. In other words, things, with her, retain the character of commodities. The drawing room is an accumulation of goods that never become fetishes because they are prevented from deterioration through human contact. To Margaret's perception, the drawing room is somewhere between Pompeii and the Crystal Palace, a museum or a shop display. It contrasts with the Hales's interior, in which objects lose their commodity status to become extensions of their owners' personality. In that respect the owners are, if we follow Walter Benjamin's reflections in *Paris, capitale du XIXème siècle* (Benjamin 2000: 58), true bourgeois whose traces get "imprinted in [their] interior" and who value objects precisely because of their ability to reflect the passing of time. As Benjamin explains in his exegesis and commentary on Marx's *Capital*, from roughly the Great Exhibition of 1851 onward, the use value of objects becomes secondary to the fantasy they create, they are solely "ornaments." Mrs. Thornton's uptight preoccupation with shrouding her things to preserve them from the wear and tear of life signals her estrangement from the surroundings she herself created. If "to inhabit is to leave traces" (ibid.: 58, my translation), then this confirms Mrs. Thornton's position as a ghost in her own house. She carefully collects and aggregates the objects befitting her bourgeois status, but proves unable to use them.

Unlike Mrs. Thornton's immaculate carpets, the Hales's drawing room has a history: on the Milton house windows one can see the "dear old Helstone chintz curtains," one of numerous relics from the South. In spite of the surroundings being so different from the Southern village, the new Milton house throbs with the same interiority which characterized the old parsonage in which "the carpet was far from new" and "the chintz had often been washed" (NS, 23).

Reality erupts in Mrs. Thornton's drawing room when Margaret is brought in unconscious and bleeding after her confrontation with the assembled workers on strike. All the chairs, carpets, and sofas that Mrs. Thornton had sought to protect from the mill are suddenly marked by evidence of the violence and bloodshed going on right outside the door. The bleeding and fainting Margaret, on Mrs. Thornton's sofa, demonstrates that there is no containment strategy that can prevent the real outside world from colliding with the bourgeois inner sanctum. After Margaret is gone, Mrs. Thornton tries hard to erase all traces of the incident: "She went to the sideboard … and took out a duster … She had seen a drop of eau de Cologne on the polished arm of the sofa and instinctively sought to wipe it off" (NS, 186). The Cologne, which was used to bathe Margaret's wound, reminds Mrs. Thornton of Margaret's blood and—like the cotton-dust from the mill—it has to

be kept at a safe distance and leave no trace on the upholstery.

By putting the safe interiority of the bourgeois middle class in jeopardy, Margaret becomes a prey to two cooperating interpretive systems: on the one hand the bourgeois dictates of separation between classes, sexes, and public and private which will condemn her for breaking down these barriers, on the other hand the investigative police, interested in all inappropriate traces, that will later try to criminalize her behavior.

The neat but artificial separation between outside and inside which Mrs.Thornton strives for has her enmeshed in a vicious circle of inner contradictions. She considers her son as the head of the "hive of bees" and she boasts of being a true Milton person, but she tries hard to differentiate herself from the workers and her interior from the mill. What she dreads are potential modifications to the status quo she has so far painstakingly maintained. This unwillingness to part with her household world is brought to a crisis when she learns that her son intends to ask for Margaret's hand:

The newly married couple-to-be would need fresh household stocks of linen; and Mrs. Thornton had clothes-basket upon clothes-basket, full of table-cloths and napkins, brought in, and began to reckon up the store. There was some confusion between what was hers, and consequently marked G.H.T. (for George and Hannah Thornton), and what was her son's—bought with his money, marked with his initials. Some

of those marked G.H.T. were Dutch damask of the old kind, exquisitely fine; none were like them now. Mrs. Thornton stood looking at them long—they had been her pride when she was first married. Then she knit her brows, and pinched and compressed her lips tight, and carefully unpicked the G.H. She went so far as to search for the Turkey-red marking-thread to put in the new initials; but it was all used—and she had no heart to send for any more just yet. So she looked fixedly at vacancy; a series of visions passing before her, in all of which her son was the principal, the sole object— her son, her pride, her property. (NS, 209)

With an extraordinarily commonplace subject-matter treated in an unusual way, this short text seems to be already paving the way for modernism in its representation of women whose psyche is both reflected and fractured in every surrounding object.

Mrs. Thornton's musing begins as a projection into a future of which she feels certain. Her designation of John and Margaret as "the newly married couple-to-be" is indicative of her conflation of present and future as if the second should necessarily follow from the first. She delves into abundant piles of linen as into layers of family history and the "reckon[ing] up" in provision of what is to come is transformed into a stock-taking of the past. This time it is past and present merging as there is "some confusion between what was hers … and what was her son's." The reason for this "confusion" is not clear as the initials embroidered on the linen—"G.H.T. for George and Hannah Thornton" and presumably J.T. for John Thornton—are sufficiently dissimilar. The explanation lies in the fact that the "confusion" is not brought on by a difficulty in reading initials but by a blur in Mrs. Thornton's mind as to what has been and what is and will be. Instead of prompting her to look forward, her inventory irresistibly draws her back to a time when "Dutch damask of the old kind" was still available, before the mass production of cloth in industrial mills such as her son's. Nostalgia is now the predominant mood of this musing and it is reinforced by the use of the past perfect "had been" to mark the time "when she was first married" as very remote. In her article on "Bronte's *Villette* and the Art of Bourgeois Interiority" (Badovska 2005), Eva Badowska, using Walter Benjamin's Arcades Project, equates the art of bourgeois interiority with a form of homesickness, the longing for a place one thinks is lost. The traces of oneself that are visible in one's interior would be "a compensation for the losses borne by the subject" (ibid.: 1518). Home would be this place never reached, either because it is always already lost or never attained. Mrs. Thornton is this homesick near-bourgeois, maybe homesick because only near-bourgeois, as all bourgeois probably are. The industrial mills owned by her son have—in raising her to the middle classes—made a displaced person of her, condemned to permanently hover between what she now has

(a beautiful drawing room) but which does not constitute her interiority, and what she has almost completely lost (her son), and which already belongs to others.

That the initials have to be "unpicked" is tantamount to erasing the past, the old, a whole portion of her life, and it does not happen without an internal suffering that cannot be completely held in but must become manifest in "knit[ted] brows and compressed ... lips." She does not fight the odds when it so happens that the "Turkey-red marking-thread" is "all used" and instead of spelling out on the family linen the initials of the future, she indulges in "a series of visions." Mrs. Thornton's wandering contemplation of her household linen perfectly exemplifies her and her family's situation of precarious balance, standing as they do at the crossroads between past and present, tradition and modernity.

The cotton dust Mrs. Thornton painstakingly tries to keep at bay shrouds the whole town. Milton as a whole is under the spell of the material it transforms and the coal necessary to this transformation. Cloth is literally in the air, it is what the town breathes. The "unparliamentary smoke" from the factory chimneys is the first thing the Hales notice on arrival—it taints everything and chokes colors; it explains why Mrs. Hale finds it, as she says, "impossible to keep the muslin blinds clean ... above a week together" (NS, 82). Most importantly it will soon become synonym with her bad health and depressed spirits, her whole life having been emptied out of its former Southern homeliness. But if Mrs. Hale finds the smoke gets to her drawing room and indirectly tampers with her health, others find that the by-products of the cotton industry touch them much closer and much deeper.

With barely enough cloth to cover their bodies, Milton factory workers do not worry about protecting the little furniture they have against the invasive dust. Perversely, neither Bessy's body nor her home benefits from the finished product of the material she's transforming. The kind of wrapping, dressing, or protection which cloth can afford does not exist at the Higgins's lodgings: the only elements in their interior are an uncarpeted stone floor, a chair, and a squab with nothing to cover or allay their bareness.

Bessy has been working in the cotton mills from an early age, working, as she puts it, "her heart and life away … with the mill noises in my ears, until I could scream out for them to stop … and with the fluff filling my lungs, until I thirst to death for one long deep breath" (NS, 101). In Bessy's life, cotton exists first and foremost as raw material in the process of being transformed, and what this transformation brings about is a violation of the only thing she has got to call her own, which is her body. The extent to which cotton fluff operates an unhealthy symbiosis with the workers is attested when Bessy explains to Margaret how some workers opposed the creation of "a great wheel at the end of the carding-rooms, to make a draught and carry off the dust" because "it made them hungry … after they'd been long used to swallowing the fluff" (NS, 102). Fluff thus replaces both air and food and shows industrial transformation to bring about at least one condition of modernity, which is alienation. This pervasiveness, its scope and depth, should also be regarded as a sign of the age: the second industrial revolution made possible the production and distribution of goods in mass-quantities thanks to new machinery, the employment of a large and mostly unskilled workforce, and new means of transportation. Thus, if on the one hand the modern industrial system permitted a greater penetration of the market by the goods produced, it also allowed on the other hand a greater penetration of the human bodies enrolled in the production process.

Close to our skin and intimate, cloth is the familiar material on which all of our daily little revolutions get imprinted. In *North and South* it records Margaret's negotiation of Victorian dictates in terms of feminine appearance and behavior. Her instinctive, unmediated relation to what she does or does not wear stresses her refusal to have others represent and interpret her. Cloth in the narrative also allows the materialization of a complex network or feminine companionship and solidarity, mainly embodied in the friendship between Bessy and Margaret cutting across class and enduring beyond death. However, the mechanized production of cotton disrupts the privacy and homeliness of women's relation to cloth and to each other. The cotton dust created by carding penetrates everywhere and makes pregnant the alienating character of modern production processes and their devastating effect on both feminine interiors and female bodies.

North and South is not a political pamphlet and Elizabeth Gaskell does not propose a solution to the breach of human bodily integrity by the infiltration of machine-led industrial processes. The novel only seeks to make patent the relationship between the fabric of history and the fabric of intimacy, showing the traditional boundaries between them to be inadequate. In the face of an increasingly pervasive and volatile modernity, as embodied in cotton dust, *North and South* stresses the need for women not to withdraw inside a private space others delineated for them but rather to engage in and interact with the world at large.

Note

1.   Gaskell 1998, p. 12. All references are to this edition, noted as (NS, page number).

References

Badowska, E. 2005. "Choseville: Bronte's Villette and the Art of Bourgeois Interiority." *PMLA*.

Benjamin, W. 2000. "Paris, capitale du XIXème siècle." In *Oeuvres III*, p. 58. Paris: Gallimard.

Briggs, A. 1988. *Victorian Things*. London: B.T. Batsford.

Brown, B. "Thing Theory." *Critical Inquiry* 28(1), *Things* (Autumn 2001): 1–22.

Freedgood, E. 2006. *The Ideas in Things: Fugitive Meaning in the Victorian Novel*. Chicago and London: University of Chicago Press.

Gaskell, E. 1998. *North and South*. Oxford: Oxford University Press.

Marx, K. 1990. "The Fetishism of the Commodity and its Secret." In *Capital*, Vol. 1, pp. 163–77. London: Penguin.

Pollock, G. 2003. *Vision and Difference: Feminism, Femininity and the Histories of Art*, p. 124. London and New York: Routledge.

Shuttleworth, S. 1998. "Introduction." Gaskell, *North and South*, p. xxviii.

Trotter, D. 2008. "Household Clearances in Victorian Fiction." *19: Interdisciplinary Studies in the Long Nineteenth Century*, Issue 6.

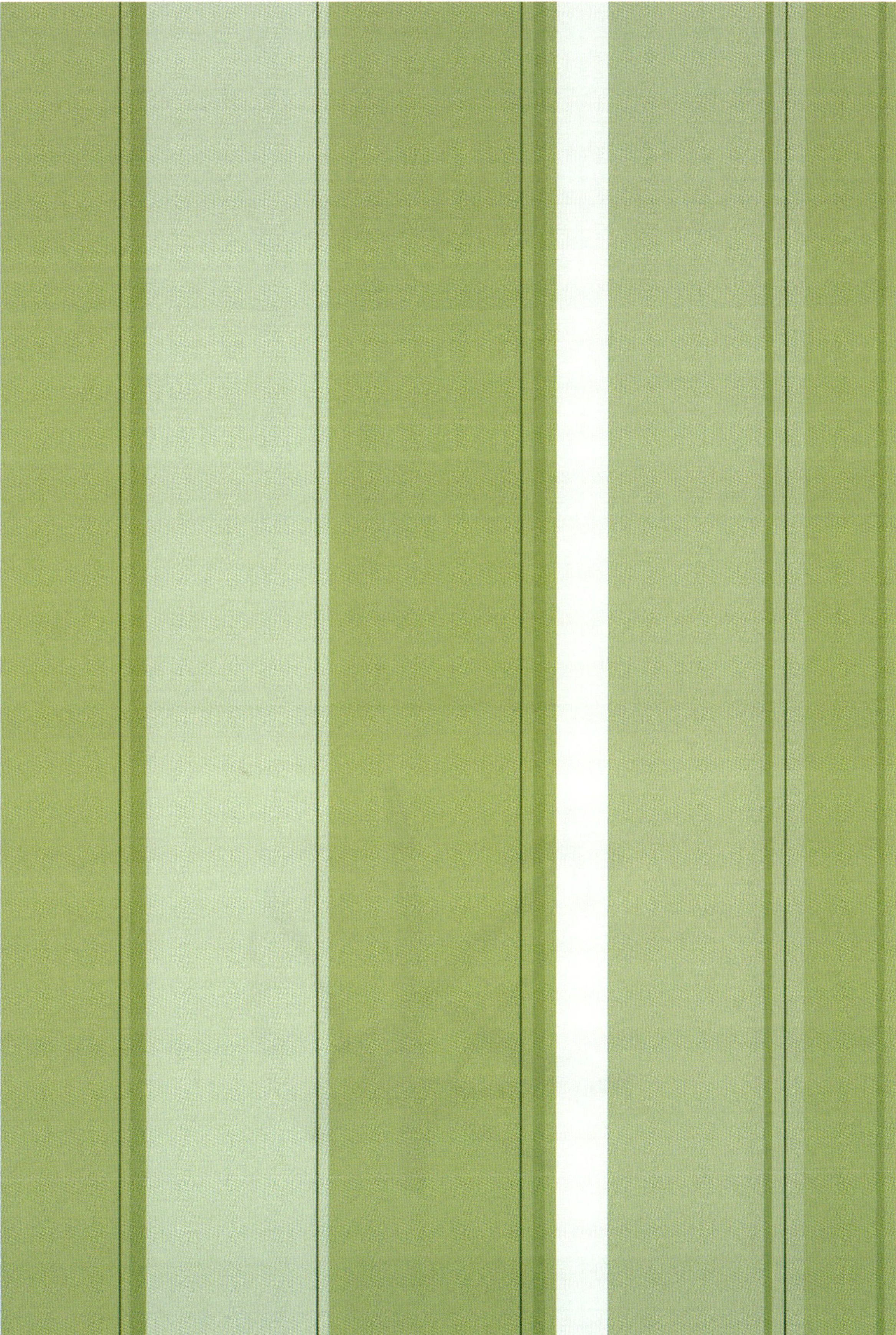

Art Museum Dust Collection: Wearing Away Museum Grounds—Dust Bunnies, White Lies, and New Measures

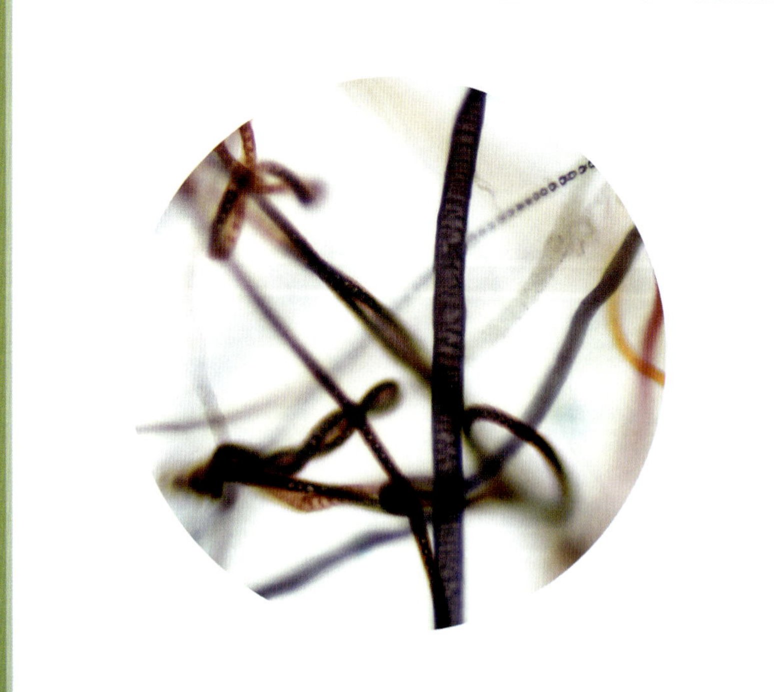

Abstract

This Dialog piece details the current collaborative work underway between Sean Miller's *Art Museum Dust Collection* and Kelly Cobb's textile-based studio project Garment/Research.[1] The *Art Museum Dust Collection* is an ongoing conceptual project that spans more than 13 years and includes dust from art museums worldwide. The *Art Museum Dust Collection* consists of a plethora of art-related activities and media, including a photographic series utilizing microscopy, dust-collecting actions in museums, dust-collecting equipment, performances, multiples, wearable art, and a miniature gallery featuring an art-museum dust montage mural.

Keywords: textile, conceptual, art, performance, museum, dust, jacquard, apparel, weaving, collection

KELLY COBB AND SEAN MILLER

Kelly Cobb is an Instructor of Fashion and Apparel Studies at the University of Delaware. Garment/Research, her studio moniker, is an umbrella term for cross-genre works, usually involving costume as a point of reference. In project-related works she merges Costume Design with Social Sculpture and Performance Art/Participation Art.

Sean Miller is an internationally exhibiting multimedia artist based in Gainesville, Florida. He is a cofounder of SOIL (Seattle, WA) and the founder/director of the John Erickson Museum of Art (www.jema.us). Miller serves as a Senior Lecturer at the University of Florida where he teaches the Workshop for Art Research and Practice.

Textile, Volume 8, Issue 3, pp. 286–303
DOI: 10.2752/175183510x12868938341448
Reprints available directly from the Publishers.
Photocopying permitted by licence only.
© 2010 Berg. Printed in the United Kingdom.

Art Museum Dust Collection: Wearing Away Museum Grounds—Dust Bunnies, White Lies, and New Measures

Introduction

The *Art Museum Dust Collection* was initiated by and is maintained by Sean Miller, the Director of the John Erickson Museum of Art (JEMA).[2] Over the years, the collection has attracted many valued admirers and collaborators. The *Art Museum Dust Collection* invites an interrelationship with craft, art, design, and contemporary culture via the participation of collaborators who work in a variety of disciplines and media.

Most recently, artist Kelly Cobb has prepared plans to tailor for Miller a museum director's suit woven of dust. In addition, Cobb has exhibited jacquard woven dust fabric in an international traveling exhibition organized by JEMA. Cobb and Miller will continue to collaborate and examine the parallels between textiles and dust to discover new ways to significantly complement Miller's diligent conceptual project.

JEMA Director Sean Miller Considers Clothes and Dust

If considered from the proper perspective(s), dust as it relates to textiles has the capability of invoking a sense of wonder. In order to fully consider the significance of dust in relation to textiles and clothing, it is helpful to move beyond familiar everyday associations with these materials and consider their properties, complexities, and the numerous ways they function, impact, and sometimes even intrude upon our lives. A quick survey of any bedroom closet reveals clothes hanging suspended, waiting to be worn and guided through daily activities. We become intimate collaborators with these hanging sculptures. It is not surprising that many individuals own a "lucky shirt" or other clothing item that allegedly provides comfort and even good fortune. If one were asked to define "clothing" to another life form that had no frame of reference, one might find oneself comparing clothes to architecture, sculpture, bedding, bandages, or some kind of tool. However, one's description would have to be crafted with words that conveyed notions of intimacy. Whatever clothing is, it is always close to us. It is like a friend or lover—always along for the ride during our ups and downs—and the meaningful, mundane, and pivotal moments that combine to form our trajectory through life's events.

Some of our most prized clothing items, despite the best of care, over time, become frayed, and wear thin. Old garments become clearly more lightweight, colors fade, and stitching threads fray. As if caught in the process of reductive sculpture, our clothes wear down like sanded wood or chipped marble. When we purchase or tailor an item recognizable to all as "blouse," "scarf," or "pants," what is actually acquired is a complex matrix of varied threads saturated with dye. The closer one observes any clothing item, the more clearly one understands the multiple components that make up the garment and how they are systematically arranged. Close inspection reveals cloth fibers as comparable to any carefully stacked pile of objects, such as stacks of firewood or bales of hay. The threads are arranged in such a way that they will hold their form. However, despite our best efforts, entropy will take a toll. The more we spin, shake, brush, rub, pat, sit on, and bounce the pile, the more pieces are going to fall away. The lint catcher in the dryer helps us measure our wardrobe as it slowly defects from our governance. As a child, my father used to tell my brother and me to quit pillow fighting and jumping on furniture because the dust aggravated his allergies. At the time the complexities of this playful battle were lost on me. However, as my brother and I played and fought—a literal rising storm of tiny airborne particles filled our living room. Waves of fibers and particles swept toward my father's nose and mouth, congesting his breathing and causing discomfort and irritation. Despite its varied and mysterious origins, dust always seems to have a stealthy, disruptive, and subversive quality.

Museum Grounds: Sean Miller Measures Art Museum Dust in Relation to "The White Cube"

An image comes to mind of a white, ideal space that, more than any single picture, may be the archetypal image of 20th-century art. And it clarifies itself through a process of historical inevitability usually attached to the art it contains. (O'Doherty 1986)

In an art museum, a viewer is disappointed by the presence of dust. Besides being physically bad for the collection, the elusive substance flies in the face of the unconscious desires and expectations art audiences hold for the transcendent "white cube" gallery or museum space. Dust must be removed to preserve the integrity and fallacy of the timeless objective white cube. In addition, typically and almost universally dust, as it relates to art, is a major distraction. The annoying substance infiltrates clean Plexiglas cases, framed artworks, and freshly painted varnish. It descends on sculptures and polished floors, and it attaches itself to photographic negatives, prints, and slides. It even settles on the documentation and record keeping of an art institution. File cabinets and computer keyboards slowly collect this at times elusive but ever-present material.

My fascination with dust as art subject originated thirteen years ago on the third and fourth floors of the Seattle Art Museum (SAM). Not that those floors are especially dusty places: rather, they were places where I was forced to confront art museum dust as a tangible, yet unwelcome, substance.

As an Exhibition Technician at SAM, one of my weekly duties included the careful removal of dust from the art displays. This tedious, solitary, and meditative task began to mold my thoughts in unexpected ways. The aura of the museum gave the task a performance art quality and the dust itself captured my imagination as a bewildering material. As if by magic, it reappeared each week, on schedule, like an unwanted subscription—an inevitable airmail delivery of the most boring gray junk mail imaginable. When I was hired to carefully regard the material and dutifully remove it in the hallowed halls of the museum, it became an obsession for me.

A pivotal moment with the museum dust occurred when I was cleaning around an African Mask display. I noticed a tiny fiber had fallen from one of the masks—too small to report—barely noticeable, actually. However, that minute fiber had a monumental impact on me. The fiber represented additive and reductive sculpture simultaneously, depending on where one perceives the prime location of the art. If one supposes the art resides in the mask then the fiber obviously becomes a reductive element. However, if one reverses one's thinking and considers the dust as the hypothetical site for the art, the fiber becomes an additive element.

In the end, I decided that the most progressive point of view was to consider the fiber as both additive and reductive sculpture, and furthermore, to perceive both the mask and the dust to be artworks in their own right. On this day, I decided art-museum dust has a hidden aesthetic value and conceptual significance. Since that day in 1996, my art has been collecting dust.

Art-museum dust is a hybrid of decaying art, the art institution, the art audience, artists themselves, and art administrators. Due to this synthesis, it may be the most pure and beautiful material present in many museums.

The *Art Museum Dust Collection* project started in 1996, and today includes over 80 museums worldwide and continues to grow. The original collection was started in collaboration with Seattle Art Museum Coworker Phil Stoiber. We formed a mail art project and began contacting museum employees around the U.S. and requesting dust samples and dusty white gloves for our collection. We displayed the collection, including white gloves with trace amounts of dust on the fingers and certificates with dust samples. Our early dust was hand-collected or given on permanent loan from various museum employees.

In 2002, I began using microscopy as a way to photographically document the dust. I was immediately amazed at the aesthetics of the dust—the fibers, colors, textures, and even the creatures that existed in a small pinch of the stuff. The resulting photographic documentation was inspiring to me, and in many ways I found the imagery had a clear dialogue with Modernist-style abstraction, especially Modernist abstract painting (Figures 1 and 2).

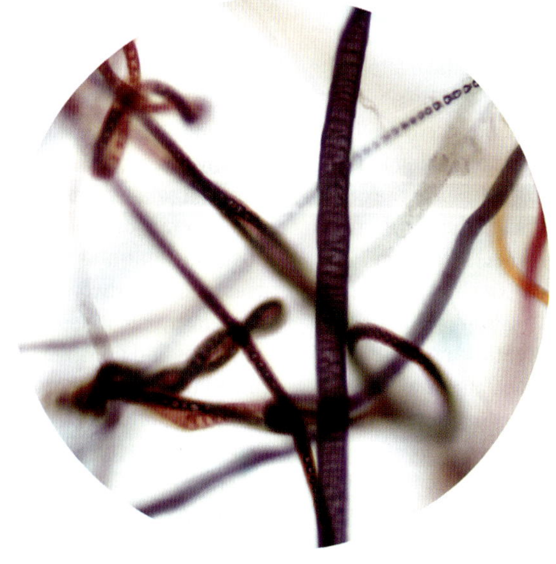

Figure 1
Sean Miller, *Art Museum Dust Collection* Microscopy (Musée du Louvre), 2009.

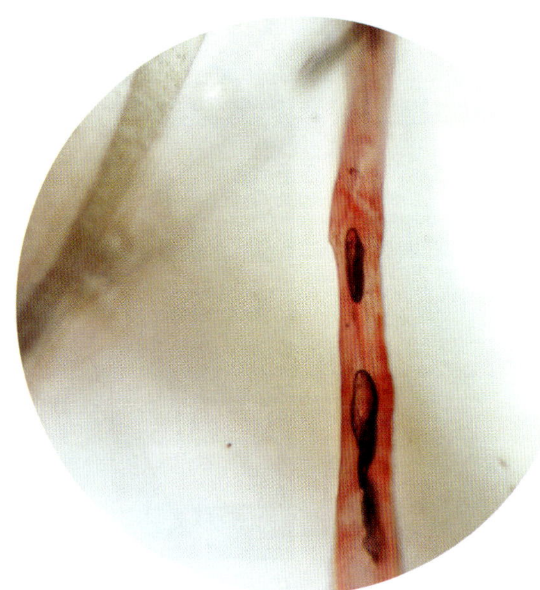

Figure 2
Sean Miller, *Art Museum Dust Collection* Microscopy (Modern Museum of Art, NYC), 2009.

In March 2003, at the Harn Museum of Art in Gainesville, Florida, during the symposium *Museum as Archive: Archive as Museum,* the *Art Museum Dust Collection* expanded further. I revealed new art-museum dust microscopy and I went so far as to claim all currently existing and future art-museum dust worldwide as a personal ready-made. Considering that universally museums are actively trying to rid themselves of this substance and have no use for it—I decided JEMA should accept responsibility for recognizing, designating, collecting, and claiming art-museum dust as a part of JEMA's growing permanent art collection. It is my hope that viewers will begin to recognize the presence of this rich material in art museums as an intentionally exhibited, on loan, artwork—not tiny bits of clutter.

Since its origins the *Art Museum Dust Collection* project has been maintained by a variety of artists, designers, and well-wishers. In 2004 San Francisco-based designer Connie Hwang began collaborating on the dust collection by assisting with design, archiving, and overall organization and branding of the collection.

LuLu LoLo has joined the Art Museum Dust Collection collaborators as an Art Museum Dust Collection Specialist (Figures 3 and 4). LuLu LoLo is a New York-based playwright, performance artist, and visual artist. She has worked to collect art-museum dust internationally and turn the process of dust collecting into a performance event.

In March 2009, LuLu LoLo and Sean Miller collected dust at a series of art museums in Genoa, Italy as part of a series of interventions curated by Caterina Gualco of UnimediaModern Contemporary Art (Genoa, Italy) (Figures 5 and 6). In addition to designing the textiles and garments for Art Museum Dust Collection, Kelly Cobb has been active as a Dust Collection specialist and researcher (Figure 7), most recently harvesting dust with curator Irene Hofmann at the Contemporary Museum in Baltimore, Maryland (Figures 8 and 9).

Art-museum dust probably interests audiences for different reasons. For me, there is a personal enjoyment in the absurdity of maintaining the collection. However, the dust additionally serves as a type of evidence against the museum. It is an indication and reminder of the power of nature, time, and entropy over the timelessness, the publicity, and the imposing nature

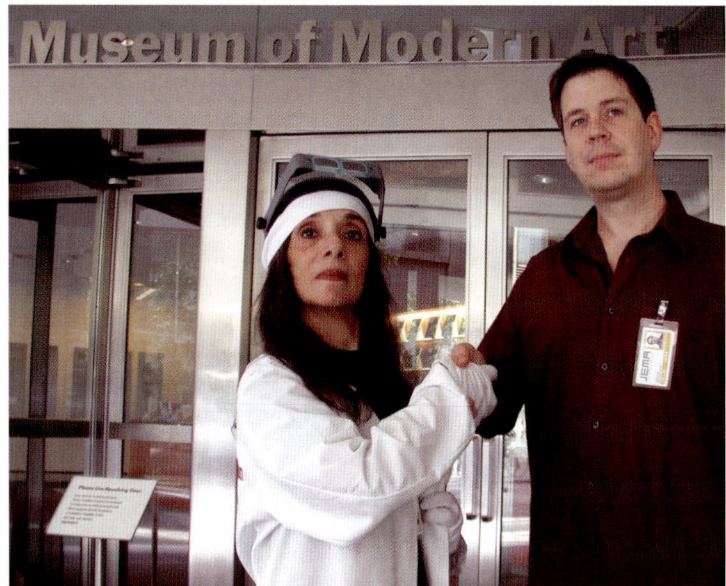

Figure 3
LuLu LoLo (JEMA's Art Museum Dust Specialist) and Sean Miller (Executive Director of JEMA) meet in person for the first time to collect dust at MoMA, September 2009. Photo by Bethany Taylor.

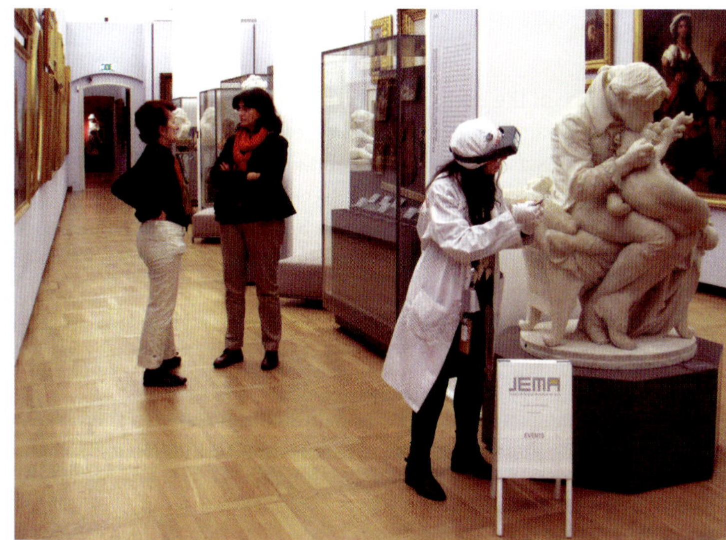

Figure 4
LuLu LoLo gathering dust at Galleria d'Arte Moderna in Genoa, Italy, 2009. Left-to-right: Caterina Gualco, Director of UnimediaModern Contemporary Art, Dott. Maria Flora Giubilei of the Galleria d'Arte Moderna, and LuLu LoLo. Photo by Sean Miller.

of many monumental museums. It also demonstrates the limitations as well as the dynamic possibilities of the human energy and ongoing activities that sustain and define the institution. The dust indicates the lived experience and social aspect of viewing, maintaining, exhibiting, and appreciating art. It seems vital, in considering the contemporary art museum, that the collective nature and collective action in the museum should be weighted heavily, especially in order to sublimate the flipside perceptions of art museums as timeless, hermetically-sealed, security-filled, geographically fixed, upper-class, esoteric, vaulted spaces. These latter

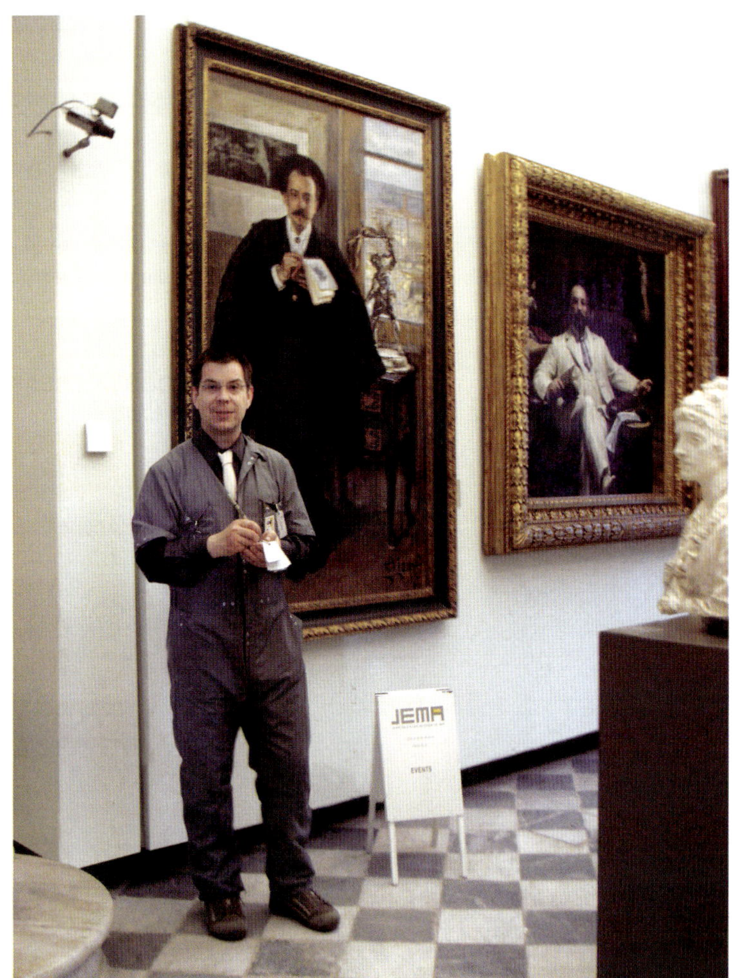

Figure 5
Sean Miller pauses from collecting dust at Galleria d'Arte Moderna in Genoa, Italy, March, 2009.

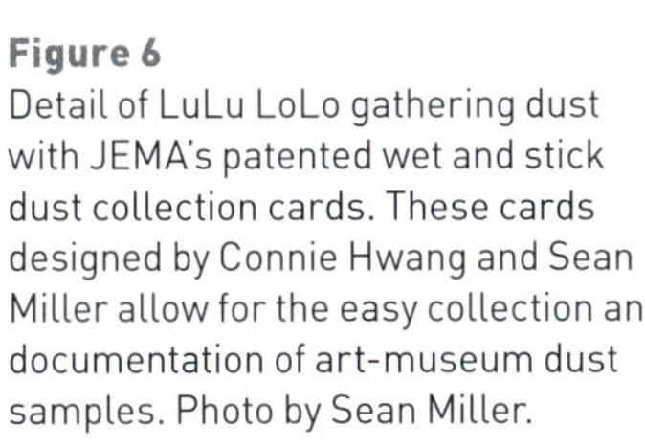

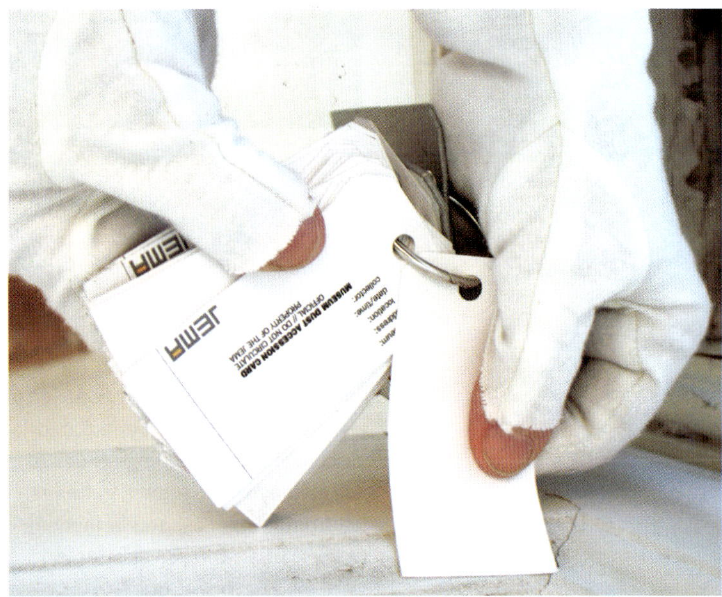

Figure 6
Detail of LuLu LoLo gathering dust with JEMA's patented wet and stick dust collection cards. These cards designed by Connie Hwang and Sean Miller allow for the easy collection and documentation of art-museum dust samples. Photo by Sean Miller.

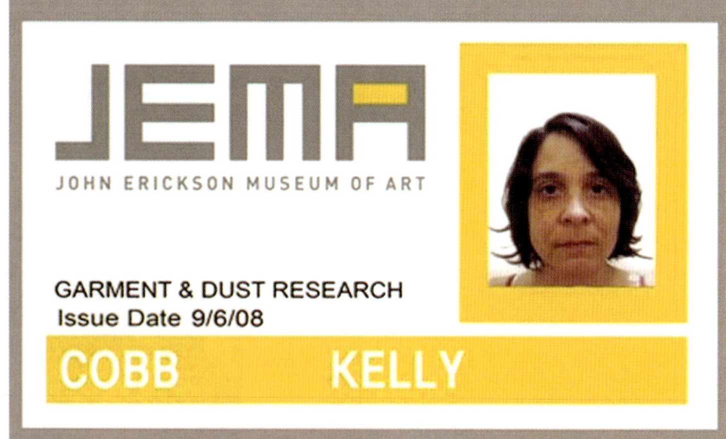

Figure 7
John Erikson, Museum of Art I.D.
Badge.

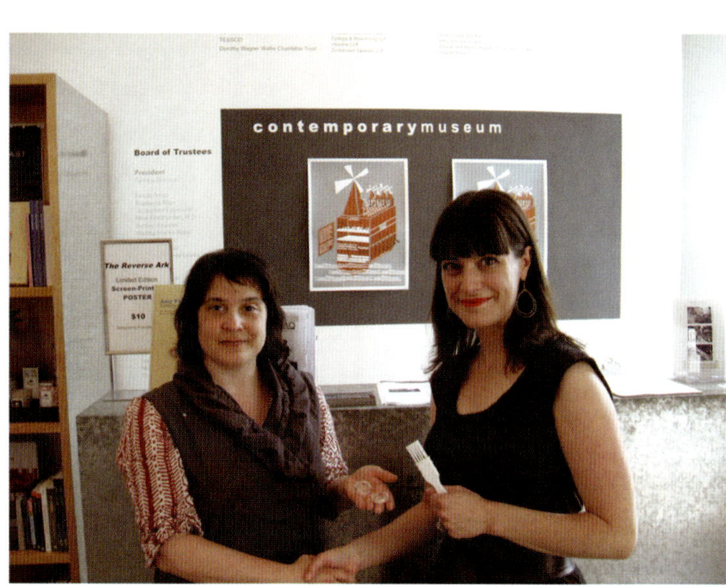

Figure 8
Kelly Cobb of JEMA's Garment & Dust
Research Division (left) and Irene
Hofmann, Executive Director of the
Contemporary Museum in Baltimore,
MD (right). Dust Harvest, 2009.

associations will not serve art museums well in the twenty-first century.

This remains a pertinent issue for contemporary art museums because, despite a never-ending slew of attempts to unconventionalize the methods of art display by museums, galleries, alternative spaces, and individual artists, Brian O'Doherty's "white cube" remains a foreboding presence in the public's collective consciousness in regards to art experience and practice. If one considers one's most stirring first-hand visual-art experiences, there remains a strong possibility that several of the artworks involved were somehow collaborating conspiratorially with the white cube of the gallery or other conventions

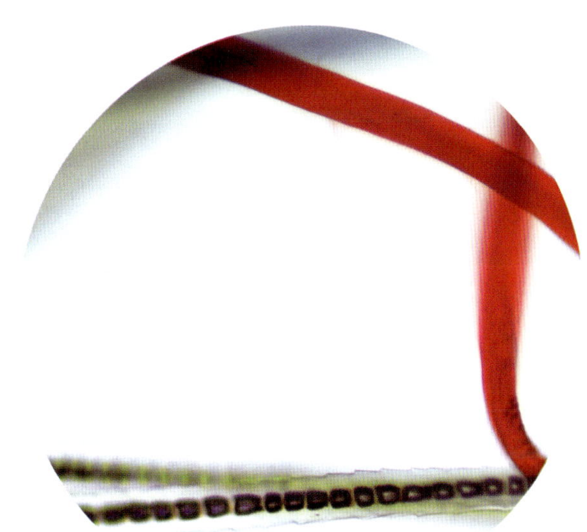

Figure 9
Sean Miller, *Art Museum Dust Collection Microscopy* (Contemporary Museum, Baltimore, MD), 2009.

associated with modernist art-display tactics. Many artworks remain framed and supported by stealthy bits of museum putty, track lighting, spackle, glossy wood floors, and various mathematical formulas (for proper placement in the gallery). These elements conspire together toward the seamless visual presentation of the art object to an art audience.

Sean Miller Imagines Various Art Museum Dust Scenarios

A museum promotes security to ensure a timeless, safe, and static environment for its permanent collection and special exhibitions. But it is also responsible for producing many other things. Alfred H. Barr, The Museum of Modern Art's first Director, touched on notions of museum production in a confidential report to the trustees. He stated:

Basically, the Museum 'produces' art knowledge, criticism, scholarship, understanding, taste ... once a product is made, the next job is distribution. An exhibition in the galleries is distribution. Circulations of exhibition catalogs, memberships, publicity, radio, are all distribution. (Barr 1933: 2)

It is not impossible that, unbeknownst to Barr, as he wrote this report, his arm rubbed briefly on his desk. This rubbing action detached several micron-sized dead skin particles and they went airborne (a micron is one twenty-five-thousandth of an inch). It is also not impossible that, due to a slight draft in his office, one skin particle floated upward and settled on top of a bookshelf. As it landed it commingled with a dust-sized portion of a Picasso assemblage, a microscopic bit of the Sahara Desert, and a piece of one of Frida Kahlo's eyelashes. Something was being produced in MOMA that Barr's report had omitted. A different collection was under way not only at MoMA but in art museums around the world. For generations of museum employees, this ongoing growing collection is a constantly and carefully regarded preoccupation. A tireless struggle continues as staff attempt to de-accession this unwanted collection and its components (Figure 10).

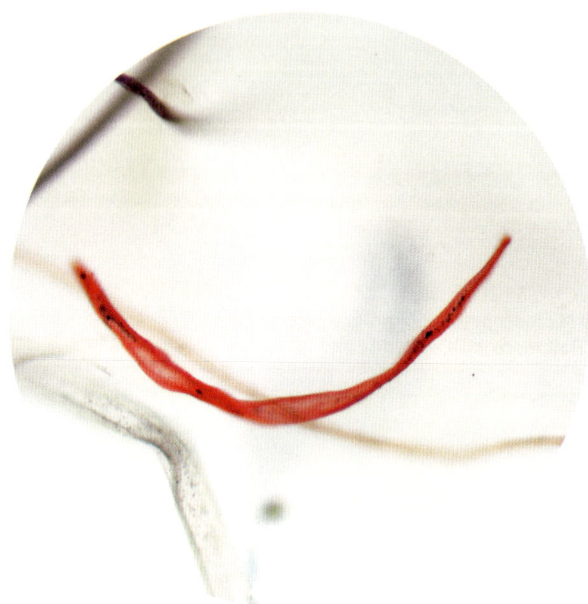

Figure 10
Sean Miller, *Art Museum Dust Microscopy* (Pergamon Museum, Berlin), 2009.

Kelly Cobb Considers Frida's Eyelash

Can you have one dust? Is it not perceptible until it's gathered together with other dusts?[3]

Dust gathers quite differently in relation to how patterns are bound in fabric, or even how fibers combine into weave. I never considered until first viewing Miller's microscopy that dust is essentially a textile; a spontaneous, tumbled non-woven; a collection of cast-offs, crumbs, spores, flakes of skin, ancient grains. As fluid as any material textile can be, dust is constantly shifting, shedding, or growing. The collective nature of dust is compelling. Rogue particles die alone; it is the disparate hair and flake in combination that become visible and particularly sublime as photographed microscopy.

Combinations further interpreted in varied twills and shaded satins are simultaneously intimate and epic.

The project teases out many variants of "the collection," as dust itself is a collection of smaller dusts—spontaneous bits and parts of people, places, and time. The curatorial suit and garment accessories form a sartorial collection. The gathering of museum dusts from collections around the world is exhibited as an art collection in its own right. The collective of many various types of art, artists, and ideas form a new hybrid collection.

Kelly Cobb Figures Stuff: Something from Nothing

The literature of historic textiles is replete with amazing examples of supplemental warp, damask, and Jacquard figured textiles.

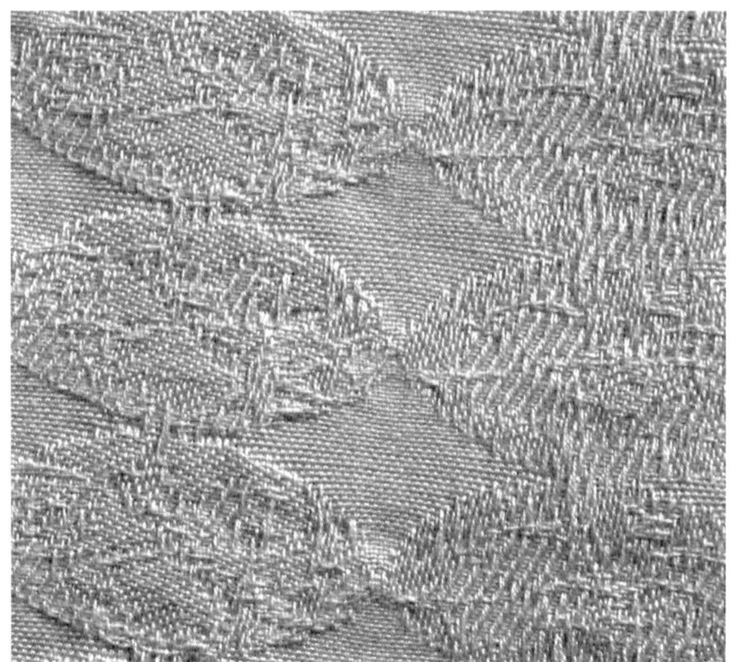

Figure 11
Dust Yardage, detail. Kelly Cobb, 2008.

Theories regarding symbolism of cloth abound. There is a palpable significance and power to an embedded symbol. Why do makers embed imagery into cloth? Why do we wear figured textiles? These questions are worthy of further investigation.

Turkish weavers weave secret "little gifts" or Boncugu[4] into their carpets as a wish, or for good luck. The details that exist in the embedded dust cloth recall these gifts. The notion of embedding the trace into cloth by way of pattern and structure is a central theme in *Art Museum Dust Collection*. The discovery of wondrous forms and compelling compositions and structures is also integral to the photographic documentation of the dust.

Burmese *acheik* figured textiles (Maxwell 1990) are inspired by natural phenomena such as cloud and water patterns. Similar to a cloud, the world of dust unfolds from seemingly nothing, from an aside or periphery. Dust teeters between something that is and something that once was.

Textiles embedded with power objects elevate the position or status of the wearer. Depictions of "animals of might" impart strength, mythical beasts ward off evil spirits. Petals, creepers, and flower heads promote fertility. Symbolic rhombs, motifs of legend, celestial nymphs, and romantic encounters are also embedded into cloth to articulate emotions and ways of being we would like to possess, but can't necessarily touch (Figure 11).

Textile Iconography morphs and shifts as regions mingle and as cultures are exposed to other symbolic registries. The power of the symbol, be it vapor, cloud, or dust, lies in the urge to touch the intangible, to make nothing something.

> *The physical forms assumed by clothing, like all of our artifacts, merge into and participate in a collective ordering and interpretation of the worlds "stuff". "Being formal" then becomes an activity that has a precise sartorial correlative, namely absorption by and into, a form.*[5]

Kelly Cobb on Being Formal

I learned to weave in 1990 through a process called woven imagery in a beginners' weaving class taught by Sandra Brownlee. We would warp our looms in black or white, and simply let a tactile story unfold. It was quite a sublime experience, which I had forgotten until I wove off my first dust sample at the Oriole Mill in North Carolina.[6]

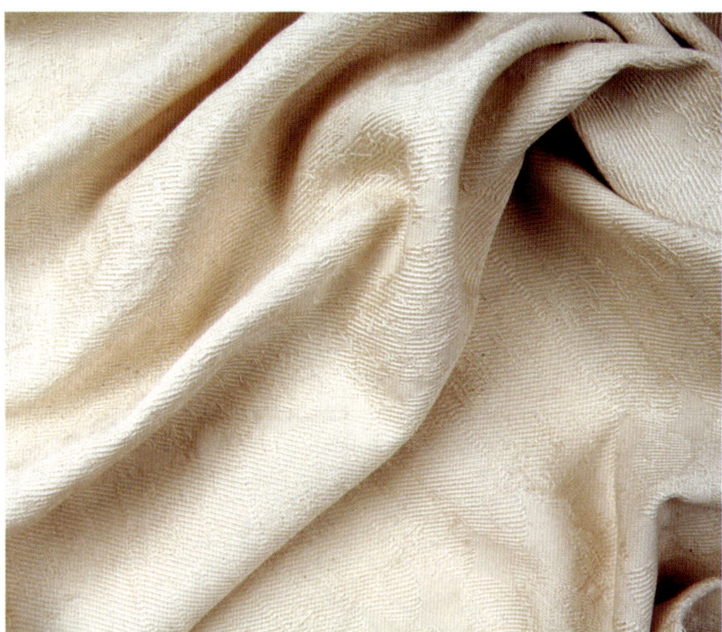

Figure 12
Dust Yardage, detail. Kelly Cobb, 2008.

The signature fabric in the *Dust Collection* is patterned with configurations and varied scale of dust microscopy. Dust is woven via the Jacquard process into dust cloth. There is a life and complexity to this fabric. Each patterned microscopy exists as a world in itself, each bit and flake and fiber has its own designated weave and in combination a tactile conversation. Gathered on a larger pliable plane, it seems a whole universe is unfolding (Figure 12).

In the summer of 2008, I visited The Jacquard Center[7] in North Carolina to explore the potential of utilizing Jacquard designed fabric for *The Dust Collection*. My time at The Jacquard Center was highly productive and the Jacquard process seems an ideal medium to elucidate dust. I worked closely with director Bethanne Knudson to develop repeat patterns that would complement textiles for the use of menswear, specifically a man's three-piece suit. JEMA has since extended the dust collection to include uniforms and garment accessories for curatorial assistants and dust researchers, as well as a floor treatment for the JEMA dust gallery.

Kelly Cobb on New Measures: Tailoring a Pliable Context

And you may carve a shrine about my dust. (Tennyson 2008)

Often, garments cut from figured cloth were worn as ritual garments or to mark status or special rank. Special clothing can articulate the wearer's position. My primary interest was in developing the design for a suit constructed out of custom dust figured cloth, the quintessential power garment (Figure 13).

The suit elucidates Miller's status as director and curator, and underscores Miller's ongoing commitment to unsettling viewers'

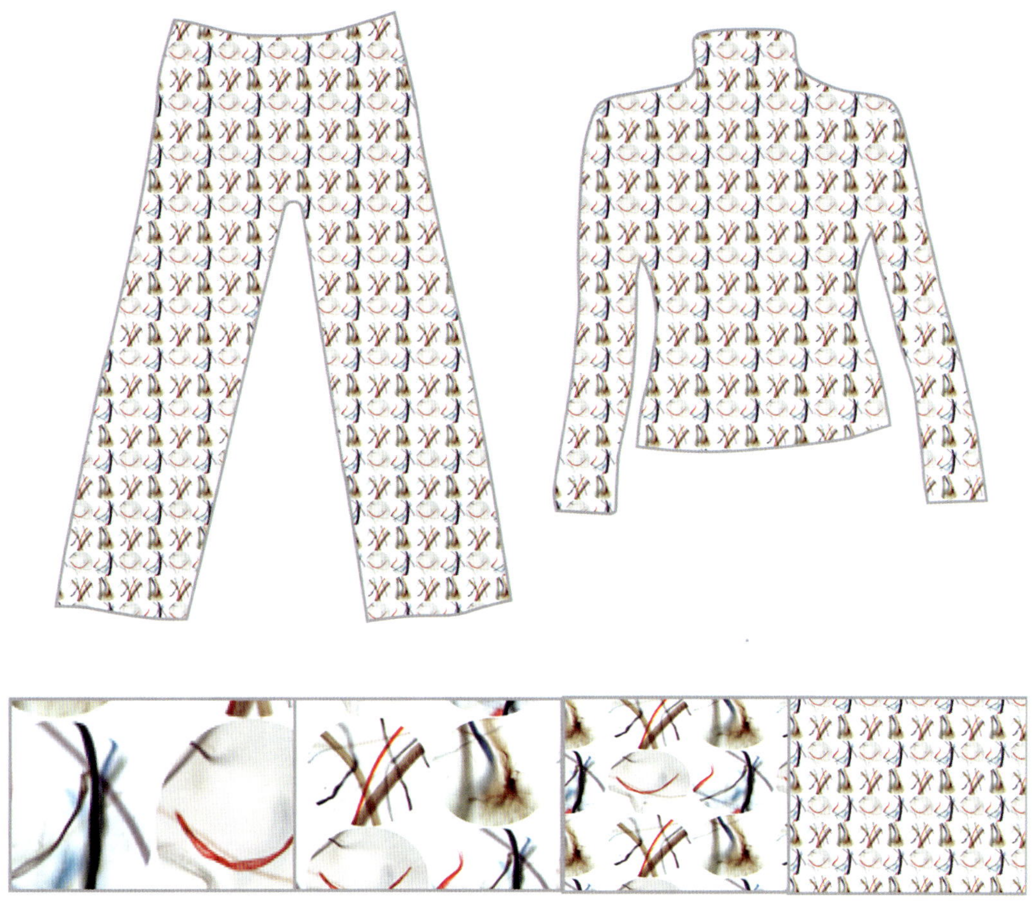

Figure 13
Designer flat, scale test #d003. Kelly Cobb, 2008.

preconceptions concerning the nature of the contemporary art museum. He will become stylishly adorned with the dust, and through his activities he will stir the dust, while simultaneously wearing it like a badge of honor (in the same way that a uniform symbolically legitimizes and reminds us of the importance of a judge or an officer of the law).

I like the notion of outfitting a process. The *Art Museum Dust Collection* project includes performances, such as dust harvesting, official proclamations, lecturing, and conversing with museum professionals, as well as many significant curatorial actions. Performative gestures are often hard to frame. In my experience, I have found that the garment provides an ideal frame and pliable context (Figure 14).

Sean Miller Discusses Connie Hwang and Kelly Cobb Exhibition at the John Erickson Museum of Art

As Kelly Cobb and I continue to collaborate on the *Art Museum Dust Collection* fabric I have also been proud to include it in exhibitions at JEMA. In 2008, Kelly Cobb and Connie Hwang began working independently with the microscopy images to create an exhibition for JEMA titled the *Art Museum Dust Collection* exhibition. Connie Hwang created an *Art Museum Dust Montage*, a wallpaper montage to cover JEMA's gallery walls. Kelly Cobb has transformed her first art-museum dust imagery into a digitally woven fabric to create her *Art Museum Dust Collection Weaving*. This material is exhibited in the JEMA galleries as a floor treatment.

JEMA opened Connie Hwang and Kelly Cobb's exhibition *Art Museum Dust Collection* in Genoa, Italy on March 12, 2009. In Genoa, Cobb and Hwang's exhibition was included as part of a series of museum interventions organized by Genoa-based curator Caterina Gualco of UnimediaModern Contemporary Art. Cobb and Hwang's *Art Museum Dust Collection* traveled to the following Genoa art institutions: Villa Croce Museo d'Arte Contemporanea, Museo di Strada Nuova, Galleria d'Arte Moderna of Genoa, Nazionale di Palazzo Spinola, l'Aula Magna dell'Universitàdi Genova, and UnimediaModern Contemporary Art.

Despite their working separately, the results of Cobb's and Hwang's efforts designing and producing work with the dust imagery yielded strong and cohesive results. Connie Hwang responded to working

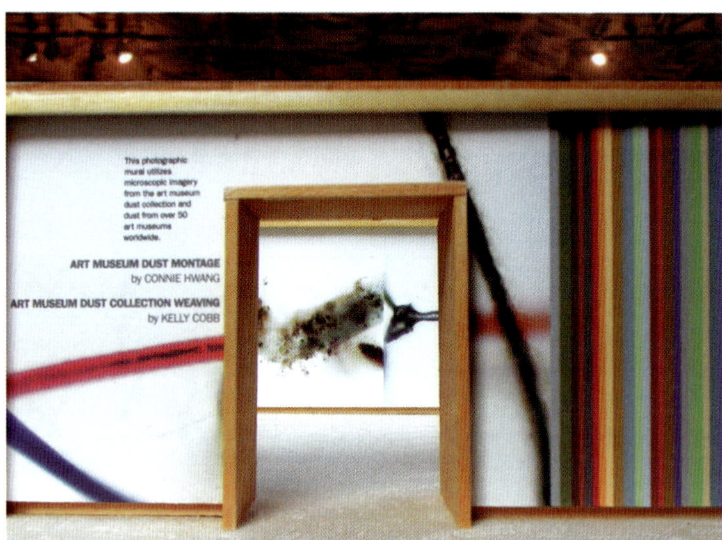

Figure 14
Installation view of Kelly Cobb and Connie Hwang's *Art Museum Dust Collection* exhibition at JEMA, Photo by Sean Miller.

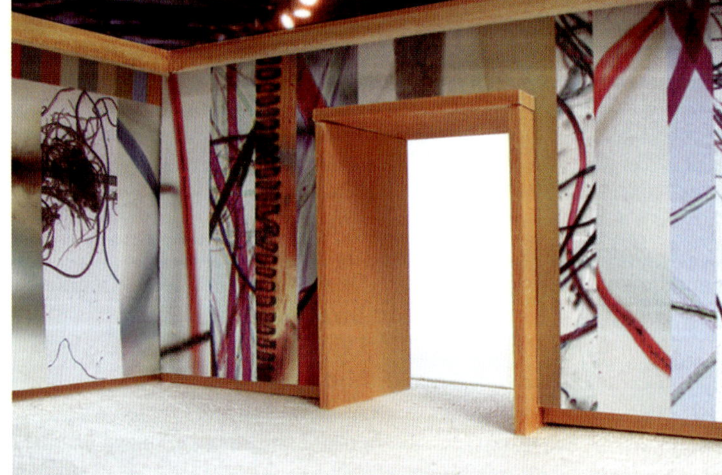

Figure 15
Installation view of Kelly Cobb and Connie Hwang's *Art Museum Dust Collection* exhibition at JEMA, Photo by Sean Miller.

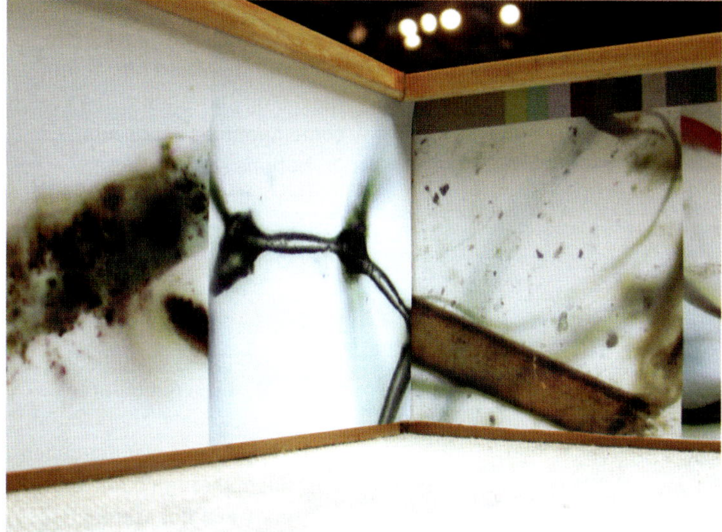

Figure 16
Installation view of Kelly Cobb and Connie Hwang's *Art Museum Dust Collection* exhibition at JEMA, Photo by Sean Miller.

with dust as a subject by stating: "Designing with dust interests me, because the dust particles relate to history, language, and/or text. Designing with the dust touches the power of storytelling—from trailing the dust to making space for it—or sometimes I think it may be something else entirely?" (Figures 14, 15, and 16).

Conclusion

Contemporary art audiences generally understand the artifice of museum display; they know where to look for art in a museum, and they know what to ignore. Contemporary museum-goers wisely hedge any perceptual or intellectual overload by telling themselves an ongoing stream of "white lies" in order to observe the socially inscribed cues from the museum which dictate what is institutionally endorsed as "art object." In an art museum, art could be anywhere or claimed to be anywhere, but most contemporary viewers dutifully follow these culturally inscribed visual cues. This creates an aesthetic climate whereby many contemporary art audiences still wander through exhibition spaces like Arctic explorers lost in a white-out blizzard, looking for any recognizable forms that may lead them to safety or bring them in from the cold.

Could it be that the contemporary art museum is wasting space? Even worse, not perceiving space in a contemporary context—or fully progressive or creative manner? Artists, directors, and curators should have the vision to redesign the contemporary art museum. The twenty-first-century art museum should go far beyond furniture showrooms, poster shops, magazine stands, window displays, office buildings, design centers, and airports.

The digital age has afforded us new increments by which to measure the material world and new mechanisms for viewing and perceiving it. In a digital, social-networked society, which benefits from continual scientific updates, technological breakthroughs, and new theories regarding the nature of time and space, it seems that massive changes may lie in store for our culture, and therefore also for the contemporary art museum. With so many artists worldwide struggling to "find a space" to exhibit their work, hopefully projects like JEMA and the *Art Museum Dust Collection* offer some inspiration and two possible small alternative models.

As museums and galleries are struggling to expand in size and offer space for new exhibitions, art-museum dust may remind some viewers of the near-infinite amount of space already available. It will be interesting to measure the progress of artists, museums, curators, and audiences as they continue to redefine and explore the ways art may occupy space in our contemporary social context. Much more is possible in the ways spaces for art are creatively utilized.

A desire to exhibit (and soon wear) art-museum dust is one small way to simultaneously contribute critical possibilities, aesthetic insights, style, and humor into the dialog surrounding the contemporary art museum.

Notions such as these motivate the maintenance and expansion of the *Art Museum Dust Collection*. This substance—art-museum dust—is a literally like a ghost that silently follows us ... hovering ... invading our air space. It is a reminder to us that our museums' "permanent collections" are never permanent. Dust floats through outer space and fibers of it float through the air in our atmosphere, eventually settling in our homes and on our possessions. Our clothes and our bodies contribute to it. By looking closely at dust we can envision a whole world of possibilities within a tiny circle.

Notes

1. Garment/Research: http://www.garmentresearch.org/wpress/
2. John Erikson Museum of Art: http://www.jema.us/
3. From a conversation with the artist and artist/curator Judith Leeman.
4. *Boncugu* was introduced to me by workers at a Turkish rug importer's shop, where I worked as a design assistant in 1996. They used *boncugu (bonjuk)* to refer to intentional surprises or symbolic gifts which Turkish weavers embedded into carpets. Upon further reading, I found that *Nazarlik* is officially the word and means "charm used against the evil eye." It can also be referred to as *kem nazar, nazar Boncugu, goz* (Landreau, 1983).
5. Georg Simmel. *Clothes and Fashion*, quoted in Carter (2003: 64).
6. http://www.theoriolemill.com/
7. http://www.thejacquardcenter.com/who.htm

References

Barr, A. H. 1933. "Present Status and Future Direction of the Museum of Modern Art," p. 2. MoMA Archives: AHB Papers (AAA: 3266; 122).

Carter, M. 2003. *Fashion Classics from Carlyle to Barthes*. Oxford and New York: Berg.

Landreau, A. N. 1983. *Flowers of the Yayla: Yörük weaving of the Toros Mountains*. Washington, DC: Textile Museum.

Maxwell, R. J. 1990. *Textiles of Southeast Asia: Tradition, Trade, and Transformation*. New York: Oxford University Press.

O'Doherty, B. 1986. *Inside the White Cube: the Ideology of the Gallery Space*. Santa Monica, CA: Lapis Press.

Tennyson, A. "St. Simeon Stylites." In the readprint digital library, http://www.readprint.com/work-1411/St-Simeon-Stylites-Lord-Alfred-Tennyson (accessed July 15, 2008).

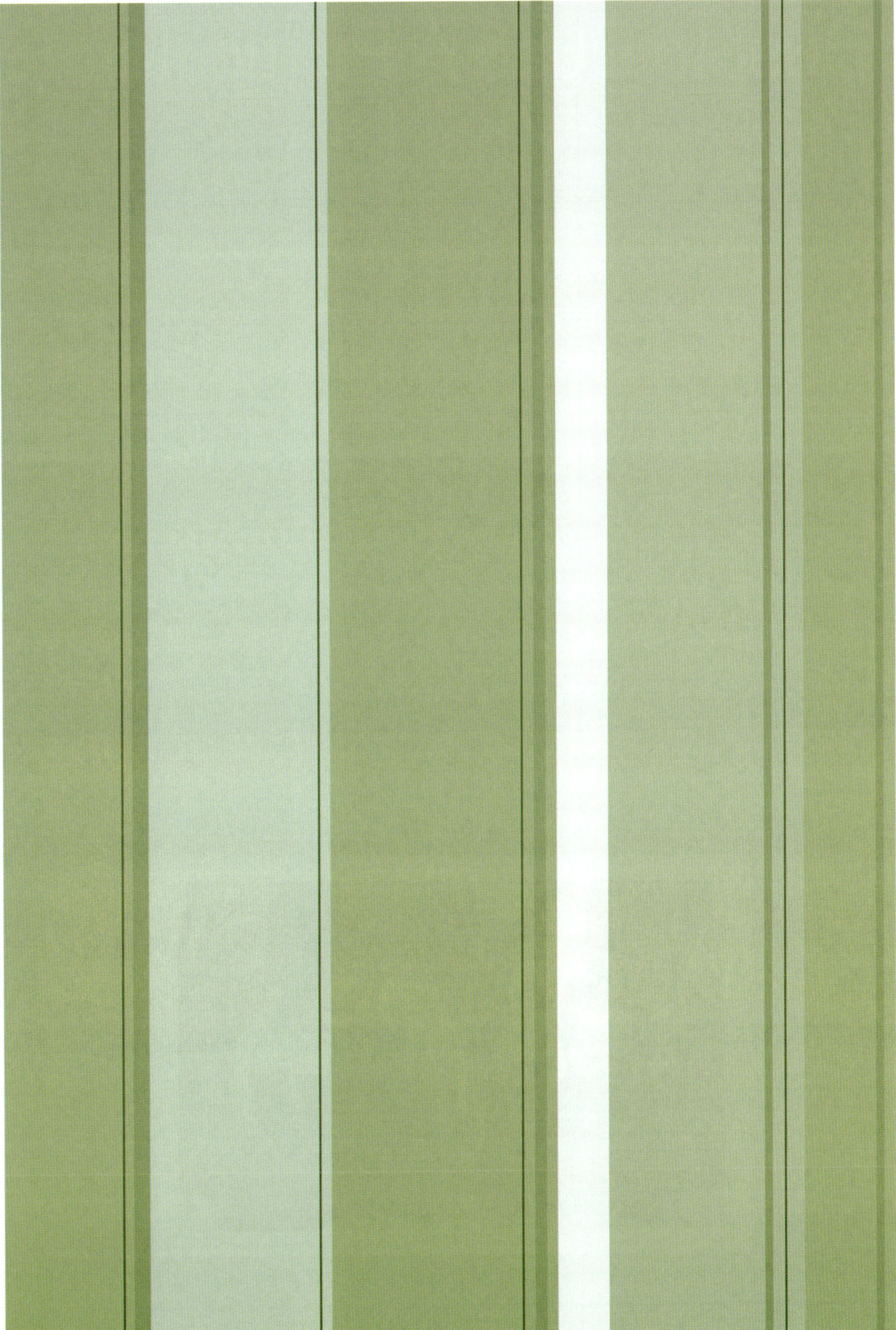

Dust to Dust: A Particular History of Khaki

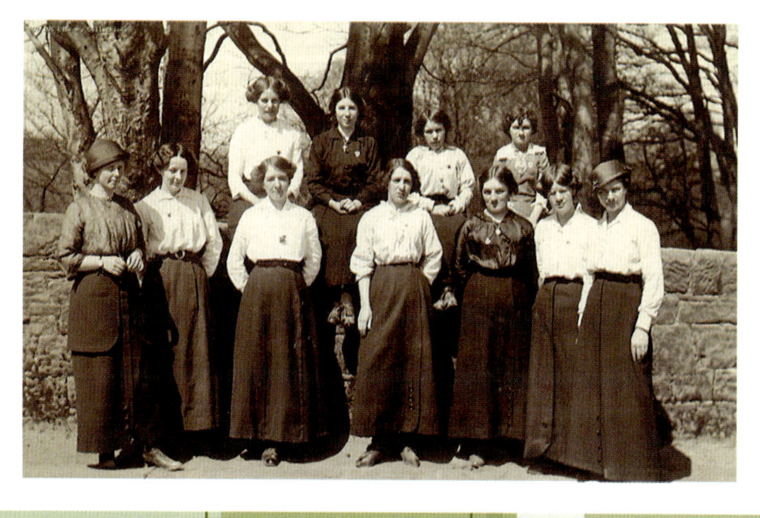

Abstract

This article explores the word "khaki" in various contexts, focusing on its etymological association with dust. It is not a technical textile history, though elements of process, production, and consumption are discussed as critical to the formation of what khaki means. The article emphasizes the associative power of khaki—in production, in use, and on disposal and dispersal—from the late nineteenth century to the Second World War and in a variety of European and international contexts. Focusing on ideas of the particle and processes of fragmentation, it is a teasing out of what might be described as khaki's poetics.

Keywords: dust, khaki, military uniform, dyeing, recycling

CATHERINE MORIARTY

Catherine Moriarty is Curatorial Director of the University of Brighton Design Archives and Principal Research Fellow in the Faculty of Arts. Between 1989 and 1996 she was the founding research coordinator of the National Inventory of War Memorials at the Imperial War Museum, London. Completing her doctorate at the University of Sussex in 1995, she has published widely on commemoration and figurative sculpture after the First World War. In 2008 she was awarded the University of Melbourne Macgeorge Fellowship for her research on the sculptor Paul Montford.

Textile, Volume 8, Issue 3, pp. 304–321
DOI: 10.2752/175183510x12868938341484
Reprints available directly from the Publishers.
Photocopying permitted by licence only.

Dust to Dust: A Particular History of Khaki

This article is an exploration of the word "khaki" in various metonymic contexts, each touching on its etymological association with dust and ideas of the particle. It is not a technical textile history, though elements of process, production, and consumption are, as we will see, critical to the formation of what khaki means. It is, therefore, in terms of both approach and content, a particular history. Its focus is the associative power of khaki—in production, in use, and on disposal and dispersal—and it is this that creates the structural basis that sustains forays into what might be described as khaki's poetics. Conventional textile studies might focus on what khaki is: this article argues that to suggest what khaki means involves an exploration of the symbolic and the emotional alongside the material, the technical, and the political.

While some research paths have predetermined routes, this one did not. Instead, it could be described as a series of unfoldings. Rather than aspiring to comprehensiveness, this article is based on a variety of encounters and takes the form of a commentary. It derives from an art historical approach to representation, be it visual or textual, a longstanding interest in cultures of commemoration, and two particularly powerful experiences of place, in Benghazi, Libya and in the Yorkshire mill town of Batley. Integral to this article are the images that accompany the text. They are not those one might expect since they are not illustrative in a conventional sense. Beginning and ending with images of women involved with the making and pulling apart of khaki, they are components of the actual and representational transformations that are the subject of this study.

Origins

Soldiers of the British Army engaged in the military activity that accompanied imperial expansion were fully aware of the disadvantages of wearing red tunics. Rather than textbook battles fought on a field at an arranged hour, the nature of warfare on the margins of colonial incursion was much more unpredictable. The terrain, enemy, timing, and temperature were all unfamiliar. Set piece engagements were replaced with ongoing border policing and the repression of insurrections. Having led extensive campaigns in India and Africa throughout the 1870s and 1880s, Viscount Wolseley endorsed the need for service dress of a subdued hue, "the soldier should not be clothed in tissues of glaring colour visible at great distances, and which furnish to the enemy convenient targets" (quoted in Lavisse 1906: 71).

It was in the Afghanistan region of the North West Frontier, in 1848, that Lieutenant-General Harry Burnett Lumsden issued his soldiers with uniforms dyed a yellowy-brown that resembled the color of the dusty terrain in which they fought. The idea originated with his second in command Major W. S. R. Hodson. As Colonel Younghusband put it later in his 1908 publication *The Story of the Guides*, a tribute to this irregular force comprising both cavalry and infantry raised largely from the Punjab:

> *Following out the principle that the corps was to be for service and not for show, the time-honoured scarlet of the British Army was laid aside for the dust-coloured uniform which half a century later, under the now well-known name of* khaki, *became the fighting dress of the whole of the land forces of the Empire.* (Younghusband 1908: 5)

According to one account, Hodson had contacted his brother in England asking him to send out cloth for nine hundred men of a color that would make them "invisible in a land of dust" (Hodson Pressinger 2000: 3). Yet, as is often the case with the detail of military lore, there are various competing accounts that in themselves speak of the storytelling practices embedded in regimental rivalry. Certainly, however the cloth was sourced, whether imported or bought from the local bazaar, the name used to describe it remains a legacy to its origin on the North West Frontier and the Punjabi troops who first wore it. A direct appropriation of the Urdu word *kāki*, meaning dust-colored, stemming from the

Persian *kāk*, meaning dust, the word itself is inextricable from its geographic and linguistic contexts and the colonial prerogative of commandeering that deemed useful: and khaki did prove useful, in all subsequent wars of the British.

Other early attempts to change the color of uniforms in order to make troops less conspicuous appear to have involved ad hoc experiments in dyeing. Some sources recount that during the Indian Mutiny in 1857–58, British regular soldiers had used office inks to turn their standard-issue uniforms of unlined white tunic and trousers a dull light brown: other sources recount the use of cow dung, tea, and berry juice (Theis 1903: 2). Following these early experiments in the field, various units incorporated khaki uniform to varying degrees and in various ways. Undoubtedly, the move was pragmatic and, as Tomas Abler notes, the post-Mutiny British infantry began to resemble increasingly their irregular native counterparts epitomized by Lumsden's Guides (Abler 1999: 111–29). Moreover, dramatic advances in firearms technology in the last decade of the nineteenth century—the introduction of the magazine-fed Lee-Enfield rifle, the employment of the machine gun, and developments in long-range artillery—meant that, though it was no longer any guarantee of relative security, remaining out of sight would be increasingly significant.

The military demand for khaki-colored cloth meant that it was soon being manufactured in quantity in British mills. In 1884 Frederick Albert Gatty of

Preston lodged the first "khaki patent" (it was also registered in India), followed a year later by printed specifications that can still be found in the regional archives near the centers of textile manufacturing.[1] Gatty's timing was well judged, for 1885 saw the uniforms of the British Army in India change officially to khaki. The patent of 1884 (no. 11456) was followed by another two years later specific to the dyeing of wool, and here too Gatty was well placed. In 1902, khaki serge became the fabric adopted by the British Army for home service dress, "finally banishing the traditional scarlet to a ceremonial role" (Newark et al. 1996: 14). Yet despite some formalization as to what khaki should be, these strictures appear not to have unified the color entirely, for just as the color of the earth's dust changes in different regions, so khaki had to modify. Writing in 1903, Dr Freidrich Carl Theis described khaki as "a range of shades" that varied from "grey to olive, and from olive to brown" (Theis 1905: 5). The purpose of his publication, entitled *Khaki on Cotton and other Textile Material*, was to set out a variety of approaches to khaki-dyeing and it included samples of cloth colored with dyes manufactured in both Germany and Britain. Constituting a guide and a dye recipe book, Theis's text distinguished between "true" khaki achieved by "compounding on the fibre certain metallic oxides" derived from chromium and iron, and its "artificial" counterparts produced by synthetic dye stuffs, "the so called 'sulphur colors' in particular." Theis compared the advantages and qualities of each approach in the production of this "modest and serviceable hue." While arguing that the "original" processes remained preferable for dying canvas, specifically that for tents, the practical advantages of their synthetic equivalents for the industrial production of uniforms for mass armies was clearly beyond doubt.

Khaki adapted well, though British troops did not, to the particularities of the war against the Boers in South Africa at the turn of the century. By this time the word was used widely, beyond its direct connection to cloth, as an adjective to denote military association. The 1900 General Election, when pro-war sentiment returned Lord Salisbury's Conservative government with an increased majority, became known as the Khaki Election; a *Khaki Alphabet* was published for children illustrating the military leaders and famous battles of the Boer War (Powles 1901); and "khakiism" was coined to describe a militant spirit or policy. Just over a decade later, the scale of the production of khaki cloth would escalate hugely in response to the demand for uniforms for those enlisting, and later conscripted, in the world's first industrial war. A war with its focus in Western Europe meant, inevitably, that the shade of khaki adopted for the fabric of service dress became less sandy in color and, in fact, greener.

The First World War

During the First World War mostly men wore khaki, though it was also worn by women in both voluntary and official support services: the First Aid Nursing Yeomanry wore khaki soon after their formation in 1907 and the Women's Army Auxiliary Corps adopted it in 1917.[2] Khaki cloth—chiefly serge but also other types for different components of uniform and kit—was produced in British mills, increasingly by women, especially as the numbers of male textile workers enlisting swelled. The gender division between spinning, a male domain, and weaving, where women comprised the bulk of the workforce, became more fluid as men joined up and women were required to step in, though as Gail Braybon has pointed out with regard to the woolen industry, "men still did the night work and set the machines" along with other key supervisory and technical roles (Braybon 1981: 64; see also Carter 1915; Singleton 1994; and Zimmern 1918). Trades associated with the manufacture of uniform were also affected. Just two months into the war, the long hours and low wages of women making khaki thread at Ainsworth & Sons at Cleator Mills, Cumbria had raised comment, the workers resorting to strike action in 1915 (Figure 1).[3] Recruitment in Lancashire and Yorkshire was particularly high and many male textile workers joined Pals battalions, named so because their formation enabled colleagues and friends to serve together. The news of losses in these units had a devastating impact on the communities from which they came. Those of the Accrington and Leeds Pals at the Battle of the Somme in 1916 epitomize the mass slaughter of the First World War.[4]

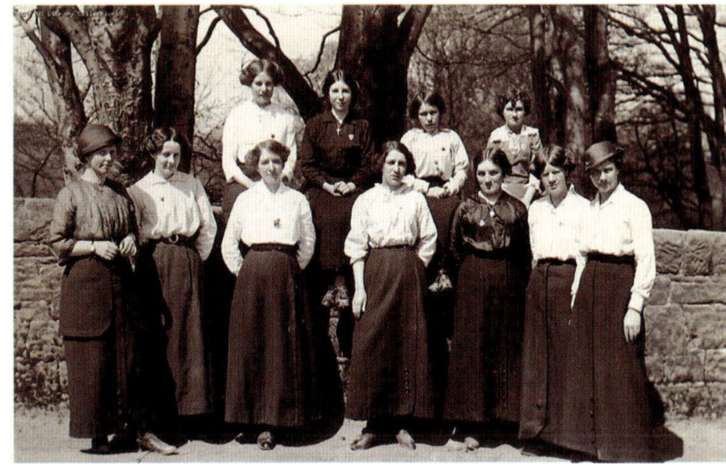

Figure 1
Cleator Mills Strike Committee, 29 April 1915. These textile workers were paid 7–9 shillings per week for 60 hours' work. 250 women—who were members of the National Federation of Women Workers—and 20 boys came out on strike. After 6 weeks, the company conceded their demands for a 10 percent war bonus and agreed full recognition of the union. TUC Library Collections, London Metropolitan University.

As well as being intimately involved in the manufacture of khaki, to women also fell the task of encouraging men to wear it. One recruiting poster addressed to the "Young Women of London" demanded: "Is your 'Best Boy' wearing Khaki? If not don't <u>YOU THINK</u> he should be?" Recruiting campaigners used the word khaki in a range of approaches and the term "in khaki" was commonly understood as a metaphor for serving with the armed forces (Figure 2). Yet the surge of recruits in the first months of the war meant that there was not enough khaki cloth to meet demand. In November 1914, Lord Kitchener was so concerned about the shortage of woolen khaki that he suggested cotton mills convert to woolen spinning and weaving (Singleton 1994: 606). The British government, in order to stimulate dye production, invested in plant infrastructure, began to train more chemists, and revoked enemy patents, for Germany had been a major exporter of dye stuffs to Britain, the United States, and elsewhere (*Encyclopaedia Britannica* 1949: 806–7). Yet, in the early years of the war, as Peter Simkins described it, "the fact remained that, until the clothing industry as a whole had geared itself to cope with the demands of a mass army, there was precious little khaki to be had anywhere." For many, the shortage of uniforms was a disappointment and short-term compromises in different colors were extremely unpopular—khaki was what was required (Simkins 1988: 256–77). For as well as being desired by the men themselves as a sign of distinction, it also made them attractive to others. As music hall star Marie Lloyd teased her audiences, "I didn't like you much before you joined the army, John, but I do like you, cockie, now you've got yer khaki on" (Collins and Leigh 1916; Woollacott 1994: 325–47).

Though originating as a hard-wearing drill, canvas, or worsted serge for trousers, tunics and shirts, the color was adopted for knitted items such as socks, under-garments, and headwear, in heavy wool for greatcoats, and as paint, it could cover military objects of all sizes. Be it the high-quality cloth selected by Savile Row tailors to make up the bespoke uniforms of officers (Ugolini, 2007: 159), or the rougher, mass-produced and often ill-fitting kit distributed to other ranks, this enveloping khaki matériel, as a sign of the military body and as an immediate identification of those who were part of it, was employed to denote both the collective and its component parts. Though the original purpose of khaki was to render the soldier inconspicuous, away from battle it made his association with the armed forces distinct. In 1916, a leaflet was published for men about to be called up entitled "First Day in Khaki: what to do." It made no bones about the significance of dressing in uniform. In the section about joining one's regiment, the recruit was told that he would receive a free traveling warrant, and was advised to "wear your oldest clothes and take paper and string to do them up in a parcel to send home" (Great Britain, Army 1916). Divested of civilian clothing, the recruit was ready to be re-dressed.

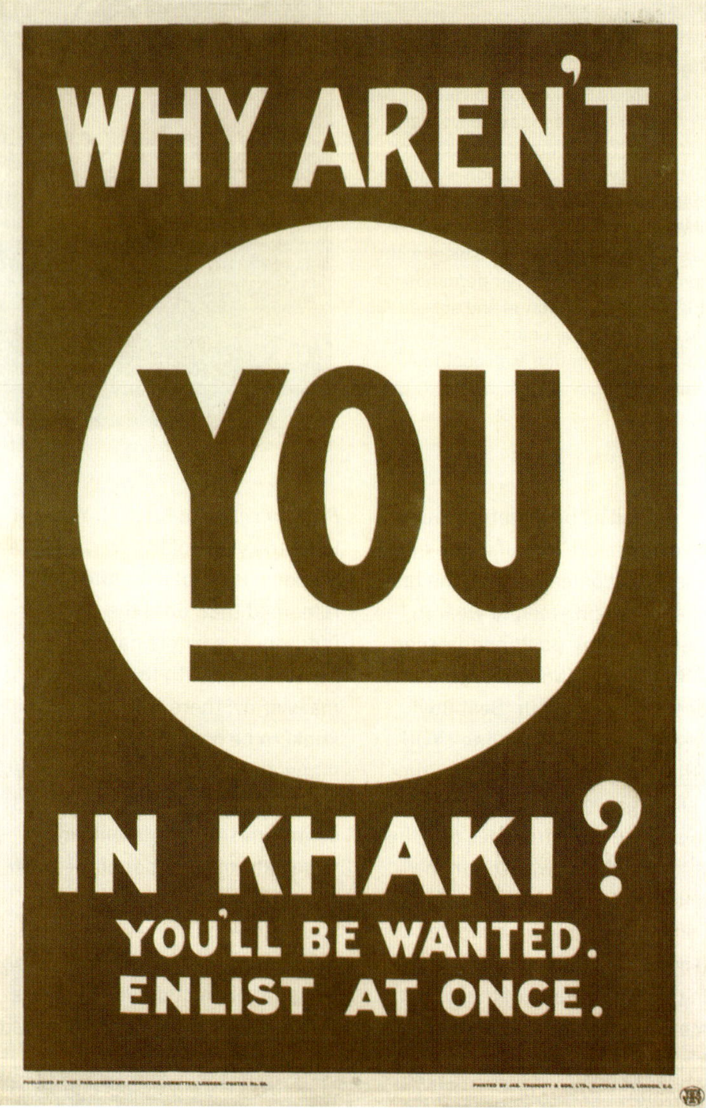

Figure 2
Parliamentary Recruiting Committee
poster *Why Aren't You in Khaki?*, 1915.
Imperial War Museum.

The paintings of the war artist Bernard Meninsky, commissioned by the Ministry of Information in 1918, represent groups of troops at points of departure or arrival (Figure 3). While there is formal interest in the compositional arrangement of these men as a group, the most compelling aspect of these works is Meninsky's sustained exploration of the color khaki, particularly its enveloping capacity, its tonal cohesion, and its dullness. Other painters would go on to engage with this color in similar or very different ways. By covering the body of soldiers entirely in khaki, bonnet to puttee, Meninsky stresses the united body of these men. Those whose faces are discernable are as anonymous as those whose

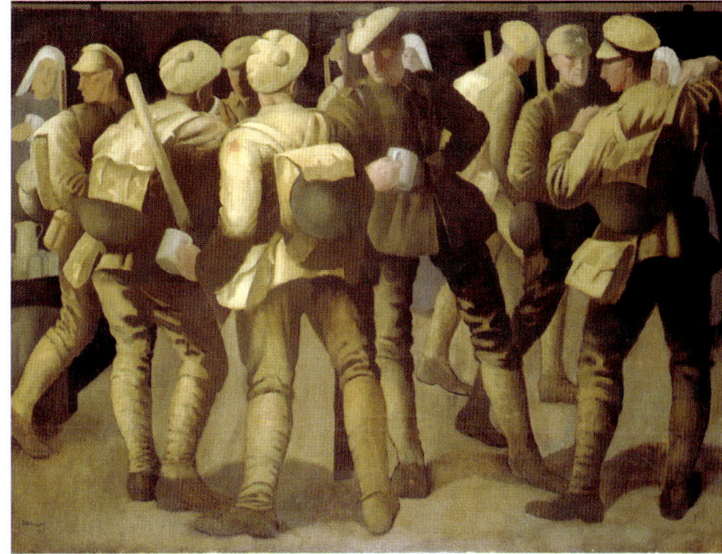

Figure 3
Bernard Meninsky, *The Arrival*, 1918.
Oil on canvas 762 mm × 1019 mm.
© Crown Imperial War Museum.

faces are turned away, and the subdued tonal range nullifies any distinctive features. For those soldiers required to wear khaki from head to toe, the color became indicative of being subsumed in a mass. While the red of the British soldier before 1850 was associated with distinctiveness, those covered entirely in the color of dust were meant to be less visible in battle by means of its remarkable cohesiveness. Dust, originating in the earth, implies a sandy, dry component of the terrain, the meaning that Lumsden would have inferred in the mid-nineteenth century—one that indicates the warmer climates of colonized countries. Yet it assumes a different form and meaning in Western Europe where the cooler and wetter environment turns loose earth to mud. In the twentieth century, the paler sand-colored cotton drill that had been issued to the soldiers fighting in the dusty wars of India, the Sudan, and South Africa while retained for desert kit, was adapted for wars that would

be fought in the temperate marine climate of Western Europe. Theis's 1903 textbook on khaki included samples of the *feldgrau* (field grey) preferred by the German government for its soldiers, and the olive drab chosen by the United States. Theis advocated, presciently, the greater suitability of a darker khaki than that which the British used hitherto, and indicated the shade he meant precisely, "the colour of plumage of the common sky-lark [alauda arvensis], a dark grey-brown" (Theis 1903: 2).[5] Soon enough, this innocent avian association would be literally blown apart. The colors of field grey and khaki, now produced by the industrial embracement of organic chemistry, would be ranged against each other covering mass armies, either side of trenches, all battling—certainly in France and Flanders—with the mud as much as with each other. As one combatant wrote, "mud is the great enemy ... nothing can keep it from your hands and face and clothes" (Bartlett 1917: 37–42).

While the darker shades of khaki were adapted for combat in Europe, paler khaki on lighter cloth was issued as desert kit for the warmer arenas of the world war, for troops in Palestine, Egypt, and the Middle East. During the Second World War clothing for this geographic range was extended with the introduction of an even darker green for campaigns in Asia where jungle warfare brought another climatic zone in which troops had to fight.

The development of camouflage by the French in 1915, closely followed by the British, the Americans, and the Germans, focused primarily on the disguise of artillery emplacements, tanks, other large items of equipment and structures of strategic significance. Avoiding observation from the air called for considerable ingenuity, and artists were called upon to work alongside engineers in the development of camouflage techniques. In Britain efforts to disguise battleships by way of "dazzle" patterns to disrupt their outline engrossed students at the Royal Academy of Arts (Black 2009). It was the German Army that developed the only application of camouflage for personal use during the First World War. It issued to its storm troopers a version of the *Stahlhelm* (steel helmet) painted with a disruptive pattern that had first been used to disguise aircraft. Its origins might be seen to derive from the Germanic legacy of forest hunting and the long-range shooting expertise and stealth of Jäger light infantry units who understood well the benefits of effective cover. Their green uniforms had inspired later British units, specifically The 6oth King's Royal Rifle Corps, known better as the Green Jackets. Effective disguise in wooded environments deriving from hunting traditions, though informing a very particular military conduit, would lead before long to the wide-scale development of camouflage fabrics for service dress, yet during the First World War and indeed for most of the Second World War, khaki remained the foundation fabric of military uniformity (Newarket al. 1996: 8–27).

Dust, Paint, and Fragmentation

At this point, having established an overview of the military appeal of khaki, it is time to consider khaki's associative power. Let us turn to Pozières, on the Western Front, in July 1916. Here, the Australian war correspondent Charles Bean wrote a disturbing description of the experiences of the Australian troops:

> One knew that the Brigades
> which went in last night were
> there today in that insatiable
> factory of ghastly wounds.
> The men were simply turned

> in there as into some ghastly
> giant mincing machine. They
> have to stay there while shell
> after huge shell descends
> with a shriek close beside
> them—each one an acute mental
> torture—each shrieking tearing
> crash bringing a promise to each
> man—instantaneous—I will tear
> you into ghastly wounds—I will
> rend your flesh and pulp an arm
> or a leg—fling you half a gaping
> quivering man (like these that
> you see smashed around you
> one by one) to lie there rotting
> and blackening like all the things
> you saw by the awful roadside,
> or in that sickening dusty crater.[6]

In ways maybe similar to, or different from, Bean's description of fragmentation, servicemen in khaki merged with the battlefield, sometimes field, but also with deserts, swamps, forests, and beaches. Official war artists painted this blurring of matter, of men and land—be it dry or wet—at a distance, or up close and in death. George Washington Lambert painted Australian troops merging with the landscape in his depictions of Gallipoli, while C.W.R. Nevinson's *Paths of Glory* of 1917 is a well-known instance of a muddier death on the Western Front.[7] During the Second World War, war artist Ivor Hele painted Australian troops in the dry rocky terrain of North Africa and then in the damp of New Guinea (Figure 4). In death, the dead were sometimes buried, sometimes not, their bodies decaying, and submerged uniforms disintegrating within the earth itself. Thus the men became not simply covered in dust-colored cloth but dust themselves. From

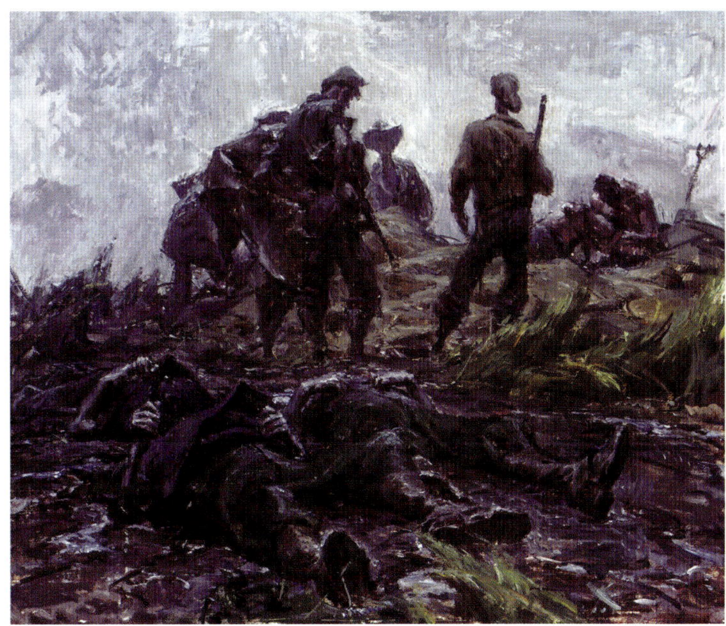

Figure 4
Ivor Hele, *Battlefield Burial of Three NCOs*, 1944. Oil on canvas 763 mm × 916 mm. Australian War Memorial ART22560.

a distance, the analogy of dust may have provided comfort, as one headstone to an RAF pilot shot down in 1942 in the Commonwealth War Graves Commission Cemetery in Tobruk, Libya is inscribed, "Dust thou art, to dust returnest, was not spoken of the soul" quoted from Longfellow's *A Psalm of Life*. Another next of kin selected Tennyson to mark the grave of a soldier killed later that year in Benghazi, it reads: "Thou wilt not leave us in the dust."[8]

True khaki, as Theis defined it, was achieved by immersing cloth in a solution of metallic oxides, and though rapidly superseded as a process, there remains nonetheless an analogy with the painter and the suspension of pigment (derived either from minerals or clay earth) in oil. In each case, similar organic substances are inherent to particular color transformations. It is with this in mind that the portraits of Ambrose McEvoy,

resulting from his commission to paint portraits of eminent naval commanders and Victoria Cross winners during the First World War, warrant particular attention. While the representation of each subject is achieved in a manner that would not have tested convention, it is his treatment of uniform, particularly khaki uniform, that concerns us here. His portraits of *Brigadier-General B.C. Freyberg, VC, DSO*; *Commander W.M. Le C. Egerton, DSO, RNVR*; *Major-General C.E. Lawrie, CB, CMG, DSO*; and *Commander D.M.W. Beak, VC, DSO, MC, RNVR* (Figure 5), all of 1918, reveal a sustained interest in the substance of paint and the margins of the represented body. While obliged to depict the appropriate insignia on the chests of his sitters, the remainder of their khaki jackets created space for investigation—of paint, its pigment, and its ability to cover or not, the canvas to which it is applied. The interest

lies in obscuring, revealing, or disintegrating the subject within the space that surrounds him, and the nature of the paint itself.[9] While tones of khaki were crucial to the ordonnance of Meninsky's contemporaneous paintings, McEvoy rejected cohesion and instead explored ideas of fragmentation and dissolution, both materially and symbolically.

Matter suspended also fascinated sculptors. While serving on the Western Front, the Scot Alexander Carrick created a model of a soldier from the most readily available material—the mud of the trenches. This was cast in plaster behind the lines by a Belgian artist and finally in bronze on Carrick's return home (McGinlay 1992).[10] We might imagine the dust-colored uniforms, intended originally for the drier climes of India and Africa, turned to slurry in the damp of Northern France and Flanders, and this coagulation of

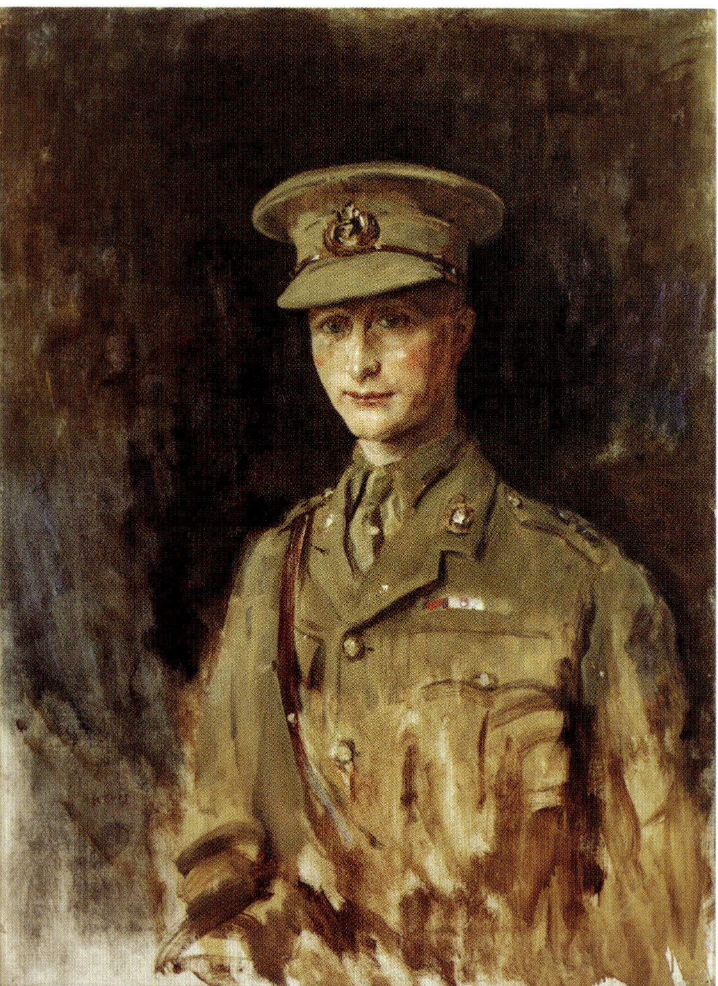

Figure 5
Ambrose McEvoy, *Commander D.M.W. Beak, VC, DSO, MC, RNVR*, 1918. Oil on canvas 1019 mm × 762 mm. © Crown Imperial War Museum.

matter producing the modeling substance for the sculptor. Carrick's sculpture of one who had fought, cast in permanent form, would achieve a stasis more enduring than either cloth or flesh, this being the fundamental aim of monumental objects of many kinds, and figurative representations explicitly. General Sir Ian Hamilton was clearly aware of this connection when he unveiled the war memorial at Batley, West Yorkshire, on 27 October 1923 (Figure 6). It takes the form of a statue of a soldier wearing a greatcoat that would have been made originally of khaki cloth but now, in sculpted representation, is the green of oxidized bronze. The General was required to pull a cord that, as the local newspaper described, "caused the Union Jack to flutter down in the breeze and expose the dignified, khaki-clad figure in mourning pose ..." Addressing the huge crowd before him, he declared:

The men went forth into battle: the women wove khaki. Miles

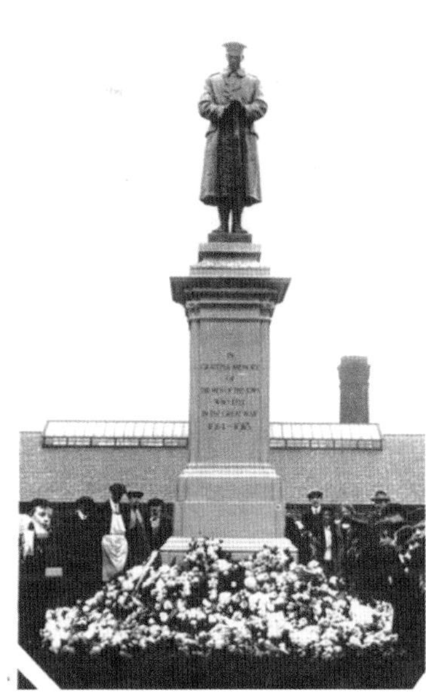

Figure 6
Batley War Memorial, West Yorkshire,
1923. Batley Community Archive.

*and miles of khaki cloth poured
out of Batley and the fighting
men wore it, fought in it, died in,
and were buried in it. So here
today we have unveiled a figure
of one of those brave Yorkshire
fighters.*[11]

Re-use and Restitution

Batley had attained particular
significance as a mill town in the
West Riding Heavy Woollen District
during the second half of the
nineteenth century. As Christopher
Malin's research shows, it was the
center of the shoddy trade with
over thirty mills engaged in the
recycling of woolen rags and their
reweaving into blankets, carpets,
and uniforms. The reclamation
of uniform as men died, or were
injured, was organized through the
War Office, and an army clothing
salvage scheme was set up in

the Batley and Dewsbury area in
1916. By 1917, approximately 45
million separate woolen articles
had been recovered from the front
lines (Malin 1979; Zimmern 1918;
Davies and Morley 1999: 351). In
the procedures that followed, the
fibers of khaki were fragmented
as the rags were ground apart.
Whether the uniforms from which
they derived were purchased
originally from an officer-class
metropolitan tailor, perhaps with
some ceremony and certainly due
attention, or simply handed over
in a bundle from a perfunctory
quartermaster at a regional depot,
the grinding process established
an equivalence, a release from
the complex relations attached
through fabrication, distribution,
and use. Indeed, the process itself
was described by Samuel Jubb, in
his 1860 text on the subject, as
"kicking up a dust," a dust known
as "devil dust," unpleasant to work
with, a menace to health, and a
sign of the transformation under
way (Jubb 1860: 20–4). And even
the dust was reused, traditionally
for tillage and in the manufacture of
flock wallpaper. The now separated
khaki fibers were ready to be
recombined, rewoven, recut, and
redistributed. As Jubb asserted:

> *Not a single thing belonging to
> the rag and shoddy system is
> valueless, or useless; there are
> no accumulations of mountains
> of debris to take up room,
> or disfigure the landscape;
> all—good, bad and indifferent—
> pass on, and are beneficially
> appropriated.*

Significantly, cloth for military
purposes was produced in Britain
for overseas government contracts

and rags had long been imported in
quantity from foreign and colonial
sources, though domestic supplies
became more critical during the
war. Thus uniforms produced to
delineate national allegiance,
through recomposition, traversed
national boundaries, and in all
likelihood, that between friend and
foe. Such unknowable connection
between individual bodies had
previously been commented
upon in terms of class or race: the
thought of the rags of the poor,
or those of gypsies, covering the
backs of the better-off was intended
to induce a frisson of revulsion.
For the servicemen and women
of the First World War, wearing
the "reincarnated" cloth of dead
comrades, or indeed, that of the
enemy, was a distinct possibility.
Yet herein lies the possibility of
a different reading, one founded
on a comfort in common threads
perhaps, or a delight in the
albeit temporary confusion of
the signifying power of uniform
that fragmentation through
grinding brings about: these
ideas inextricable from the very
technologies of mass production
fired by the compulsive drive of
a war economy.[12] Indeed, it was
Mary Douglas who described with
great elegance (Douglas 1966: 198)
the disassociated formlessness
of dust and the new beginnings
possible through disintegration,
when things return to their "true
indiscriminable character."

Processes of uniform reuse
continued in subsequent wars, and
a photograph from the Australian
War Memorial, Canberra suggest
powerfully the mournful process of
contact with khaki fibers (Figure 7).
Uniforms no longer serviceable

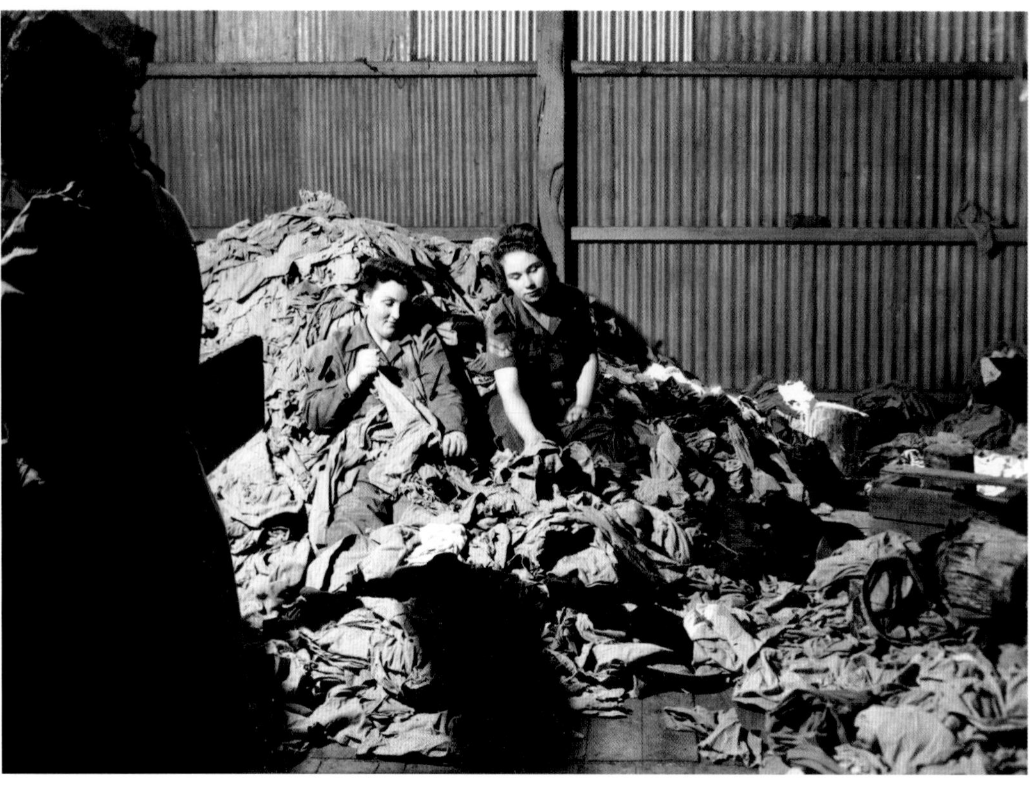

Figure 7
Members of the Australian Women's Army Service (AWAS), converting unserviceable khaki drill uniforms into rags for cleaning, at 3 Army Salvage Depot, Melbourne, in 1944. Another member of the AWAS sorts the rags at a nearby table after they have been torn up by those who are seated amid a large pile of the uniforms on the floor. Australian War Memorial.

were torn into rags for cleaning by the Australian Women's Army Service during the Second World War, the process creating its own dust and an anonymous contact with those who had worn these garments, some dead, some alive perhaps in North Africa, New Guinea, or closer to home. This renting and pulling-apart achieves its pathos as an enactment of the violence of war played out by women, for, however it is performed—by hand or, more emphatically, by the teeth of industrial grinding mechanisms— tearing is always destructive. In his 1915 survey *Clothing the Allies' Armies*, G.R. Carter insisted that the quality of khaki cloth produced in Britain had not deteriorated as a result of increased demand and that this was all the more important "in view of the severe strain upon clothing equipment in the 'trench and siege' warfare", he continued:

The normal severe tests for Government cloth are maintained. Khaki must weigh 1 lb. 4½ oz. to 1 lb. 5½ oz. per yard. Samples taken from any part of the piece pulled against a dead weight must stand a pull of 430 lbs. across the warp and 2½ ins. Across the weft. (Carter 1915: 101)

Yet however durable khaki cloth might be—over time, in different military situations, and in a range of climatic zones—the conditions of modern battle could sunder cloth and flesh instantaneously. In the museum at El Alamein, Egypt, examples of the khaki uniforms worn by the combatants of the North Africa campaigns are displayed. Be they those of German, Italian, or Commonwealth troops, the variations in the color, type, and quality of cloth are clearly discernable at close range, yet upon the sand and rocks of the desert all would have merged with their surroundings. At the cemetery where the Free French troops who were killed at Bir Hakeim in 1942 are buried is a translation of the commemorative poem written by the Révérend Père Charles Alby:

O wind of the desert,
Blow a little of the sand that sticks
to their bones
And carry it over the sea, over the
mountains and the valleys,
So that the great soldiers of France
can see it,
This powder.[13]

Thus, while the donning of uniform signalled and enabled allegiance to the military body, in death the disintegration of the body and its trappings could achieve significance of a similar kind. The gravestone in Lone Pine cemetery, Gallipoli, to the Australian Private Thomas Henry Bright does not mark his actual grave. Instead, it states that his body is believed to be buried somewhere in the cemetery

and that he died between August 6 and August 11, 1915. This suggests there was not much of him left, and it is unlikely that he had a burial service where the familiar line "earth to earth, ashes to ashes, dust to dust" was intoned. However, his next of kin did have the opportunity to select the inscription on his gravestone. It reads:

HE HAS CHANGED
HIS FADED COAT OF BROWN
FOR ONE OF GLORIOUS WHITE

Though highly apposite to this article, such textual individuations need to be considered in context. The appearance of incorporation that khaki brought about, and the apparent uniformity and leveling that the building of a mass citizen army required, achieved a parallel in the commemorative structures, both bureaucratic and physical, that were designed to honor its vast casualties. For the grave of Private Bright looks like many of the others built by the Imperial War Graves Commission around the world after both the First and Second World Wars. Regardless of rank or belief, all those with a known grave were given a headstone or grave marker that en masse, and from a distance, appeared the same. Rather than blending with their surroundings, the white headstones of these cemeteries clearly punctuate the landscapes of battle, the political wish for long-term visibility in counterpoint to the military operational imperative of obscurity.[14]

Acknowledgement

Various people with expertise in areas where I claim none have commented on drafts of this article. I would like to thank Paul Cornish, Catherine Harper, Amy de la Haye, Lou Taylor, Michele Walker, Terry Weston, and the anonymous peer reviewers for their constructive criticism. Val Asquith of the Batley Community Archive suggested some important published sources and kindly permitted the reproduction of Figure 6 from the project's digital image library. This article is dedicated to my Australian friends with whom I traveled in North Africa in October 2008.

Notes

1. Lancashire Record Office holds the patents and related papers of F A Gatty & Co. Ltd. DDX 1325/1/4 1884 to 1885.
2. Formed in January 1917, the Women's Army Auxiliary Corps recruited the first women into the British Army to serve in a non-nursing capacity. It was renamed the Queen Mary's Army Auxiliary Corps in 1918. By providing catering, clerical, storekeeping, and vehicle maintenance services, more men were available for combat. Though most remained in Britain, around 9,000 WAACS served abroad, many close to the front line. Manchester Art Gallery holds a WAAC uniform that belonged to Olive K Jordan, whose rank was Acting Administrator. It comprises a khaki wool gabardine suit with a beige silk shirt supplied by Geo. B Ashford Ltd of Birmingham, and a khaki felt hat. Accession number 1947.2536/10. Ewing (1975) remains a useful source.

3. Labour History Archive & Study Centre, LP/WNC/7/1/9/47–8.

4. Singleton (1994) points out that Pals battalions from the centers of textile manufacturing were not comprised solely of textile workers.

5. The forces of other European countries opted for dark blue, dark grey, black, and green uniforms, and the French madder-red trousers.

6. Charles Bean's diaries are held at the Australian War Memorial, Canberra. AWM 38, 3DRL606/54 Diary July–August 1916, pp. 109–10.

7. See Lambert's *Anzac: the Landing 1915* painted in 1920–22, and *The Charge of the 3rd Light Horse Brigade at the Nek, 7 August 1915*, of 1924.

8. The Imperial War Graves Commission, established in 1917, was renamed the Commonwealth War Graves Commission in 1960. See Longworth 1985.

9. Two portraits by McEvoy's contemporary at the Slade, Sir William Orpen, bear comparison, where the textured brown background of the canvas support stands in as the khaki of his subjects' jackets: *Field-Marshall Haig* and *Major-General Trenchard* of 1917, Imperial War Museum.

10. In 1918 Carrick's statuette was exhibited at the Royal Scottish Academy. On figurative sculpture after the First World War see Moriarty 1995 and on the greatcoat in particular, Moriarty 2004.

11. The report commented on the fact that the figure wears a cap bearing the badge of The King's Own Yorkshire Light Infantry. *Batley News*, 3 November 1923, p. 8. The memorial, commemorating 783 dead, was the work of Messrs Wright & Sons Ltd. of Bradford and cost £2,000. See also the National Inventory of War Memorials, Imperial War Museum, record 2131. A comparable commemorative association formed part of the unveiling of the war memorial in the Lancashire mill town of Crompton in April 1923. A lead casket was placed inside the monument, containing in addition to the usual coins and a copy of the local newspaper, three cops of spun cotton and a length of cloth manufactured in the district. See Public Monuments & Sculpture Association record MROLD061 accessible via the Visual Arts Data Service http://vads.ahds.ac.uk/.

12. As Malin 1979 explains, up until 1917 the use of recovered wool was permitted in greatcoat cloth, for blankets and horse rugs, and for fulfilling overseas orders and for the uniforms of British territorial units. After this date, renewed fears of shortages encouraged the War Office to allow a percentage of shoddy in khaki serge, shirting flannels, and other cloth. See also Carter 1915, p. 98 and for a view from the United States see "What Comes Out of the Rag Bags: Woolen Clips and Old Clothing Which Find Their

Way to the Mills Again." *New York Times*, Sunday 9 June 1918, p. 38.

13. Transcribed from the English translation of the poem displayed at the Free French cemetery, Tobruk, October 2008.

14. The Commonwealth War Graves Commission maintains the graves and memorials of almost 1.7 million Commonwealth servicemen and women who died in the two world wars. These include the graves of more than 935,000 identified casualties and almost 212,000 unidentified individuals. The names of almost 760,000 people can be found on memorials to the missing. The headstones at Gallipoli differ from those elsewhere; taking the form of tablets mounted on low plinths they were designed to better withstand earthquakes and the extreme conditions of the peninsula.

References

Abler, T. 1999. *Hinterland Warriors and Military Dress*. Oxford: Berg.

Anstey, H and Weston, T. 1997. *The Anstey Weston Guide to Textile Terms*. London: Weston.

Bartlett, V. O. 1917. *Mud and Khaki: Sketches from Flanders and France*. London: Simpkin, Marshall & Co.

Black, J. 2009. "A Few Broad Stripes: Perception, Deception and the 'Dazzle Ship' Phenomenon of World War One." In N. J. Saunders and P. Cornish (eds) *Contested Objects: Material Memories of the Great War*, pp. 190–202. London: Routledge.

Braybon, G. 1981. *Women Workers in the First World War*. London: Croom Helm.

Carter, G. R. 1915. "Clothing the Allies' Armies." *Economic Journal* 25(97), March: 97–103.

Collins, C. and Leigh, F. W. 1916. *Now You've got yer Khaki on*. London: Star Music Publishing Co.

Davies, S. and Morley, B. 1999. *County Borough Elections in England and Wales, 1919–1938: A Comparative Analysis: Barnsley-Bournemouth*. London: Ashgate.

Douglas, M. 1966. *Purity and Danger: An Analysis of Concept of Pollution and Taboo*. London: Routledge and Kegan Paul. Reprint, London: Routledge, 2002.

Dupree, M. 1996. "Foreign Competition and the Interwar Period." In M. B. Rose (ed.) *The Lancashire Cotton Industry: A History Since 1700*, pp. 265–70. Preston: Lancashire County Books.

Eliade, M. 1958. *Patterns in Comparative Religion*. London and New York: Sheed and Ward.

Encyclopaedia Britannica. 1949. Chicago: University of Chicago Press.

Ewing, E. 1975. *Women in Uniform*. London and Sydney: Batsford.

Great Britain, Army. 1916. *First Day in Khaki: What to Do. ABC Guide for Attested and Unattested, etc.* London: Temple Press.

Hodson Pressinger, S. 2000. *Khaki Uniform First Introduction 1848 (Battle Use 1849) & Hodson's Memorial*. London: Sandilands Press.

Jubb, S. 1860. *The History of the Shoddy-trade: Its Rise, Progress and Present Position*. London: Houlston and Wright. On-line version accessible at http://www.archive.org/details/historyshoddytroojubbgoog

Lavisse, É. C. 1906. *Field Equipment of the European Foot Soldier*. Washington: US War Department. First published in Paris, 1902.

Longworth, P. 1985 [1967]. *The Unending Vigil: A History of the Commonwealth War Graves Commission 1917–1984*. London: Leo Cooper. Reprint, 1985.

Malin, J.C. 1979. *The West Riding Recovered Wool Industry, ca. 1813–1939*. PhD thesis, University of York.

McGinlay, J. 1992. "Sculptor Supreme." *Scots Magazine* 137(8), November: 844–51.

Milner, L. 1991. *Leeds Pals: A History of the 15th (Service) Battalion (1st Leeds), the Prince of Wales's Own (West Yorkshire Regiment), 1914–1918*. London: Leo Cooper.

Moriarty, C. 1995. "The Absent Dead and Figurative Sculpture." *Transactions of the Ancient Monuments Society* 39: 7–40.

Moriarty, C. 2004. "Remnants of Patriotism": The Commemorative Representation of the Greatcoat after the First World War." *Oxford Art Journal* 27(3): 291–309.

Newark, T., Newark, Q., and Borsarello, J.F. 1996. *Brassey's Book of Camouflage*. London: Brassey's.

Powles, L.D. 1901. *The Khaki Alphabet*. London: Edward Arnold.

Simkins, P. 1988. *Kitchener's Army: The Raising of the New Armies 1914–1916*. Manchester: Manchester University Press.

Singleton, J. 1994. "The Cotton Industry and the British War Effort, 1914–1918." *Economic History Review* 47(3), August: 601–18.

Theis, F.C. 1903. *Khaki on Cotton and other Textile Material*. Berlin: M. Krayn and London: Heywood & Co.

Turner, W. 1986. *The "Accrington Pals": the 11th (Service) Battalion (Accrington), East Lancashire Regiment*. Preston: Lancashire Library.

Ugolini, L. 2007. *Men and Menswear: Sartorial Consumption in Britain 1830–1939*. Aldershot: Ashgate.

Woollacott, A. 1994. "'Khaki Fever' and Its Control: Gender, Class, Age and Sexual Morality on the British Homefront in the First World War." *Journal of Contemporary History* 29(2), April: 325–47.

Younghusband, G.J. 1908. *The Story of the Guides*. London: Macmillan.

Zimmern, D.M. 1918. "The Wool Trade in War Time." *Economic Journal* 28(109), March: 7–29.

Websites

Australian War Memorial, www.awm.gov.au/

Imperial War Museum, www.iwm.org.uk/

National Inventory of War Memorials, www.ukniwm.org.uk/

Visual Arts Data Service, www.vads.ac.uk

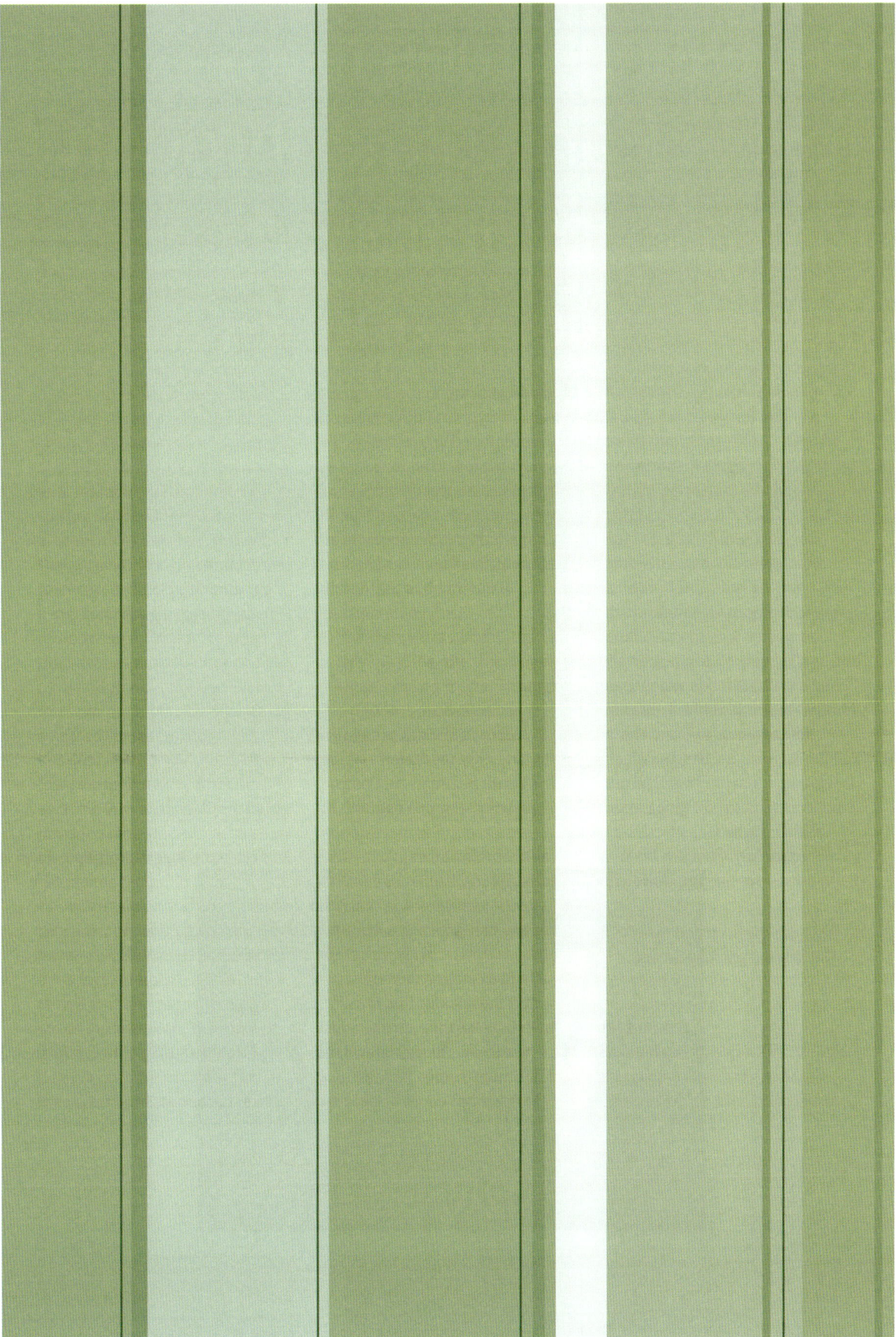

Revealing Clues from Textile Particulate through Microscopy, Infrared Spectroscopy, and X-ray Microanalysis

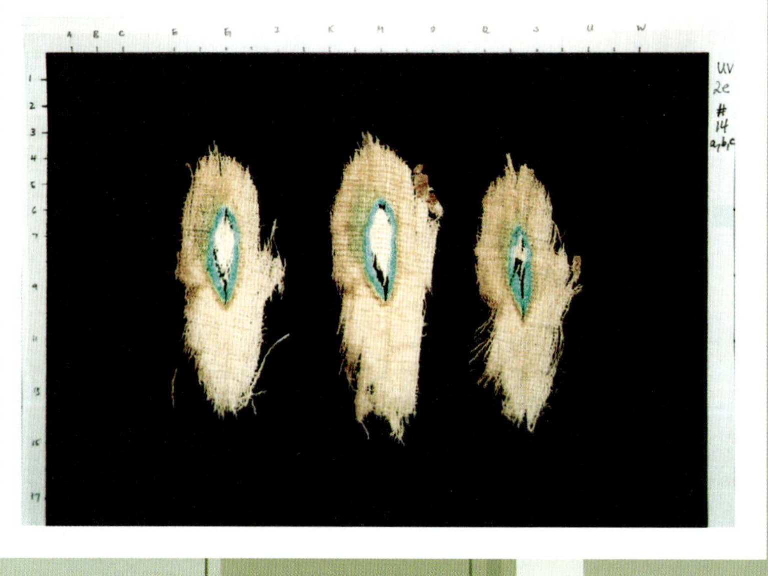

Abstract

Textiles found in prehistoric sites in eastern North America often are brittle fragments. Many appear brown or black in color due to degradation and staining; most display no evidence of color or pattern. These degraded fragments readily shed particulate matter. Although typically discarded, study of the particulate provides a wealth of information. Based on work with comparative materials, optical microscopy, infrared spectroscopy, and X-ray microanalysis have been shown to be useful in classifying fibers, providing evidence for dye and pigment coloration, characterizing the type of degradation incurred, and providing evidence for mineralization. From the study of textile particulate, inferences can be made concerning plant and animal use for fiber production; technology of fiber-processing and coloration; characteristics of the burial context; resource use and exchange; time and effort costs in collecting and processing raw materials; and the potential social structure of the community in which these products were manufactured and used. The results reported and inferences drawn serve as examples of the types of information that can be gleaned through the study of the seemingly inconsequential particulate.

Keywords: textiles, charred, plant fiber, animal fiber, microscopy, infrared spectroscopy

KATHRYN A. JAKES, AMANDA J. THOMPSON, AND CHRISTEL M. BALDIA

Kathryn A. Jakes holds a Ph.D. in textile and polymer science from Clemson University. She is a professor of textile and fiber science in the Department of Consumer Sciences, College of Education and Human Ecology, Ohio State University. Contact information: 1787 Neil Avenue, Columbus, OH 43210-1295, jakes.1@osu.edu.

Amanda Thompson holds both the M.S. and Ph.D. in Textile Science with a minor in Anthropology from Ohio State University and a B.A. in Anthropology from Brigham Young University. She is currently an assistant professor at University of Alabama in the Department of Clothing, Textiles, and Interior Design, College of Human Environmental Sciences. Contact information: Box 870158, 306D Doster Hall, Tuscaloosa, AL 35487-0158, amanda.thompson@ua.edu.

Christel Baldia holds both M.S. and Ph.D. in Textile Science with a minor in Anthropology from Ohio State University. She received her B.S. in Archaeology from Weber State University and Medical Laboratory Technology from Cologne, Germany. She currently works as a forensic scientist for the New York Laboratory of U.S. Customs and Border Protection at 1100 Raymond Blvd., Room 561 Laboratory, Newark, NJ 07102, christel.baldia@dhs.gov

Textile, Volume 8, Issue 3, pp. 322–341
DOI: 10.2752/175183510x12868938341529
Reprints available directly from the Publishers.
Photocopying permitted by licence only.

Revealing Clues from Textile Particulate through Microscopy, Infrared Spectroscopy, and X-ray Microanalysis

Introduction

Textiles found in prehistoric Native American sites in eastern North America often are brittle fragments rather than large intact objects. Because the moist conditions of the burial context are not conducive to preservation of organics as are the dry conditions of the southwest, the textiles that are recovered are small in size and few in number. These fragments have not been studied extensively because most are barely large enough to display the yarn interlacings that permit definition of their fabric structure. With such small fragments, the intended end use of the fabric product can only be speculated. Many of these small surviving fragments appear brown or black in color due to degradation and staining. On first appraisal, these fragments display no evidence of color or pattern. In addition, these degraded fragments readily shed particulate matter, which is evidence of their degraded state, and which provides cause for concern when an analyst handles the object. The little bits that fall away are rarely preserved or examined.

Textiles have gained a place as an important artifact class along with ceramics and lithics in the study of prehistoric technologies and lifeways (e.g. Power 2004). Until recently little research has been done with prehistoric remnants such as the black and brown fragments from eastern North America beyond a description of their twined fabric structure. As we began to study the fabric fragments, determining protocols for appropriate examination and learning the types of information that could be garnered, we recognized the value of the particulate that was shed from these textiles as an avenue to understanding the fabrics themselves. This article focuses on the study of the particulate shed from degraded fabrics and explores the wealth of information that this particulate holds. Examples taken from research with textiles from the Seip Mound Group in Ohio are given; the concepts are applicable to other fragile textiles and the particulate matter that they shed.

The Site and Its Textiles

The Seip Mound Group is a Middle Woodland period site in Ohio affiliated with the Hopewell Cultural Complex (*c.*100 BCE–400 CE) (Prufer

1964; Brose 1978), defined by a network of ideological and material exchange that extended from New York to Florida. This "sphere of influence," sometimes called the "Hopewell Interaction Sphere" (Struever and Howart 1972; Brose 1978; Carr and Case 2006), is defined by the similarity of artifacts recovered from burial mounds and earthworks as well as the structure of these sites. Large geometric earthworks and associated burial mounds containing a multitude of artifacts, including many produced from imported materials, are characteristic of Hopewell sites. The sites, however, are not "culturally homogeneous" (Pacheco 1996: 18); Ohio Hopewell groups often are distinguished from other Hopewellian sites by the uniqueness and size of the earthworks and the variety of artifacts found (Greber 1979). Greber (1996) also recognized the distinctive deposits recovered from Seip Mound in particular that distinguish it from other Ohio Hopewell sites. Coon (2009) proposes that distinctions can be made that separate the sites in south central Ohio (Seip Mound Group and Hopewell Mound) from the Turner and Fort Ancient sites in southwestern Ohio. He states that the former two sites display evidence of an exclusionary power strategy—i.e. one in which alliances are made with outside distant groups which provides support for leadership. In addition, these sites show evidence that the people held special knowledge concerning the production of crafts. Thus, the vast number of artifacts recovered from elaborate mounds indicates complex societies

and trade across distances, sophisticated technologies used in artifact manufacture, and complex ideologies and cultural patterns as shown in highly decorated artifacts and in evidence for extensive rituals.

The Seip Mound group was first excavated by Mills (1909) and later by Shetrone and Greenman (1931). The site yielded more textile evidence than any other Hopewellian mound site; over 200 of these textiles are curated at the Ohio Historical Society in Columbus, Ohio. The fabrics are fragmentary, ranging in size from a few millimeters to about 3 cm, with a few pieces as large as 20 cm. No association with specific site locations was noted when these materials were recovered, and the field notes from the 1908–1909 excavation have been lost. The Shetrone and Greenman excavations were supported by the Ohio Historical Society so the recovered materials were held therein soon after their recovery. However, some textile fragments were sent to schools and museums across the country, mounted in glass cases and labeled with the statement "Textile from Seip Mound." In more recent years these glass plates were returned to the Ohio Historical Society, to rejoin the other textile fragments that were housed in storage boxes.

First examined by Willoughby (1938), the fabric structures are twined in different ways to produce loose open constructions and compact dense constructions. Church (1984) described the twined fabric structures and proposed that the textiles from Hopewell sites including Seip provide evidence of

high social status of the individuals associated with them; the yarns employed in textiles from Seip are finer that those seen in fabrics from other mound sites. Hinkle (1984) and White (1987) also describe twined fabric structures in Ohio Hopewell textiles. Song (1991; Song et al. 1996) examined particular fiber samples noting their fineness, the presence of both bast fiber and rabbit hair, and the apparent color differences. Thompson (2003) examined the charred materials from five Ohio mound sites including Seip. The fine yarns from Seip are made with plant-stem fibers and provide evidence that extensive processing was conducted in order to yield bast fiber with no associated plant-stem material. These fine yarns reflect a craftsperson's knowledge of the location and collection of appropriate plant materials and processing methods to release the fibers from the remainder of the stem materials. Knowledge included the allocation of the time needed for these procurement activities and the scheduling of these activities for the appropriate times of the year when the plants are mature (Jakes, Chen, and Sibley 1993; Jakes, Sibley and Yerkes 1994; Jakes 1996; Jakes and Ericksen 1997).

Thompson and Jakes (2005) present a model that shows how textiles that were associated with burning rituals at Ohio Hopewell sites were protected from complete combustion and could have been included in the mound with other artifacts. Mills (1907, 1909, 1916) reports that burned remains were smothered with dirt in order to stop the combustion process. Thompson and Jakes (2005) propose that such a process would quench smoldering and allow organic materials to survive the ceremonial treatment. In fact, these charred materials may be more significant than uncharred ones because they are known to have been associated with burning. Since there are no records from the excavations and no provenience for the textile fragments, it cannot be assumed that they were associated with burials of human remains but may have been part of some other ceremony in which burning occurred. Thompson (2003) and Baldia (2005) each observed patterns of gradation in shades of black in the patina on some of the charred fragments from Seip that are suggestive of chemical differences. The sharply defined and repeated patterns also indicate that the materials had to have been colored in patterns before they were burned.

As was first noted by Shetrone and Greenman (1931), the textile evidence from Seip Mound is particularly notable because the fabrics are colored in patterns. Willoughby (1938) describes the dark maroon, clear yellow, and black designs. Song (1991; Song et al. 1996) found colored fibers in the yarn samples studied. Both Wymer (2004) and Wimberley (2004) commented that they observed colored textiles in association with copper artifacts from Seip. Baldia (2005) conducted an extensive study of all of the fabrics from Seip that are curated at the Ohio Historical Society with particular emphasis on uncovering evidence for coloration. After grouping the fragments into categories based on apparent color, she used a variety of photographic methods to explore whether evidence of coloration or chemical difference could be accentuated by different types of illumination and forensic photographic techniques (Baldia and Jakes 2007a). Because differences in areas of the fabrics are revealed by the photography and these differences are not obvious in ordinary viewing conditions, the photographs can be used to indicate locations for future sampling from the textile so that samples may be representative of areas with chemical difference. Baldia, Jakes, and Baldia (2008) provide results of the photography and subsequent optical microscopy of particulate material from selected Seip textiles. Techniques of optical microscopy, conducted using a Zeiss Axioplan Research microscope, include brightfield, darkfield, polarized light, and differential interference contrast techniques. Even the fragments that appeared to be of simple construction on first appraisal were shown to be more complex as they were turned over and multiple layers and colors were seen. There is evidence for decorative enhancement of the textiles as well, including fringe and a leatherlike material attachment. Baldia and Jakes (2007b) explore the inorganic and organic colorants that could have been used in these materials. Pigment particles are larger in molecular size than dyes, and in general are applied to a fabric surface using a binder such as plant resin. Dye molecules interact chemically with the fiber substrate resulting in a thorough saturation of the fiber with color (Adrosko 1971; Aspland 1997). Evidence for both dyes and pigments are present in the Seip textiles.

Jakes, Baldia, and Thompson (2007) discuss the infrared spectra of charred, mineralized, dyed, and pigmented comparative plant and animal fibers; they compared these to the infrared spectra of fiber samples of textiles from the Seip Mound Group and those from Etowah Mound, a Mississippian period site in Georgia. These spectra were obtained using a Perkin Elmer Spectrum 2000 Fourier Transform Infrared spectrometer, equipped with a deuterated triglycine sulfate detector (64 scans, 4000–400 centimeter^{-1}, resolution of 4 centimeter^{-1}, baseline corrected). They found that they could distinguish protein and cellulose fibers in the infrared spectra of experimentally prepared charred examples. Because charred materials that retain some structure are not completely burned to carbonaceous char or white ash, some organic composition is retained and this is apparent in the infrared spectra. They also present a flowchart by which subgroups of plant fibers in the Comparative Plant Fiber Collection can be separated according to lignin and oxalate composition. Infrared spectra of an unknown fiber, then, might be used to classify fibers from archaeological textiles into subgroups. The presence of significant amounts of oxalate, for example, distinguishes bast fibers obtained from woody plant species from those that belong to herbaceous species. Subsequent determination of the types of lignin present, based on their infrared absorbances, allows further separation of the woody species into those with lignin typical of softwood and those with lignin typical of hardwood. Since

oxalates associated with plant fibers survive through charring, they may be useful as an avenue for classification even in material which retains little distinctive organic composition.

Infrared spectra also are useful in distinguishing copper minerals in mineralized fibers. This identification could lead to a better understanding of the archaeological context and the process by which copper ions can be transported within the fiber wherein inorganic deposits are formed, replacing the internal structure and taking the external shape of the fiber eventually forming pseudomorphs. Jakes and Howard (1986a; 1986b) provide a discussion of the mechanism of pseudomorph formation; their presence has been noted on objects from around the world (e.g. Vollmer 1975; Jakes and Sibley 1984, 1989; Chen et al. 1998; Unruh 2003).

Conditions of pH and oxidation potential allow available inorganic corrosion products to migrate along with ground or rainwater to impregnate the fibers. As conditions change, sulfate, acetate, or carbonate compounds are formed. Green encrustations on a mineralized fiber from an Etowah, Georgia site were identified as similar to malachite, while green stains on a Seip textile appeared to be similar to verdigris (Jakes et al. 2007).

In addition to mineralization products of copper, iron oxide can be identified by its infrared spectral characteristics even in charred pigmented fiber samples. Iron oxide is a significant component of ocher, a common pigment material. Absorption bands typical of iron oxide were seen in the spectra

of a cellulosic sample from Seip indicating the possible use of ocher pigment (ibid.). Additional inorganic pigments could also be identified by their infrared spectra.

While it was not possible to identify dyes through the infrared technique, some spectral differences between undyed and experimentally dyed fibers were noted, indicating that infrared spectra may be useful as a component of a set of analyses conducted to identify dyes. The additional use of Raman spectroscopy would provide complementary information and could be applied to the same samples used in infrared spectroscopy without additional sample preparation. A large comparative database of inorganic pigment spectra has been developed (Bell et al. 1997; Clark 2007). More recent development of a surface-enhanced Raman technique has shown promise in identification of organic pigments and dyes (Chen et al. 2007).

The Seip textiles are very degraded and little bits readily flake off. Despite storage in stable museum conditions, loose bits can be found in the boxes in which the materials are stored. This is the case even in those that were housed between glass plates, despite the protection they were intended to provide. When Baldia photographed selected Seip textiles, she collected this particulate reasoning that this material might serve as an ideal sample on which to test analytical techniques. While it is possible that some stray material might contaminate the samples she collected, it was assumed that the majority of this particulate was representative of the textile with which it was associated. Certainly, a spurious fiber or contaminant could be disregarded, while the majority of the particulate is likely to have come from the fabric fragment.

While Jakes et al. (2007) report some foundational work on the infrared spectra of comparative materials and Baldia et al. (2008) report some optical microscopy results in examination of fibers from Seip textiles #4, 10, 31, 30 and 32, this article presents some new IR spectra (Seip #5, 14, and 37), summarizes the results of microscopic examination of particulate materials from Seip textiles, and provides an exploration of the implications of the findings of the accumulated body of analytical work for the inference of culture and history of the prehistoric people who created and used the textiles. This article reports on the exploration of the types of information available from microscopic examination of the particulate from degraded, charred, or mineralized archaeological textiles complemented by elemental and chemical compositional analysis. Do these materials retain recognizable chemical or physical structures? Are there useful clues provided by examination of this material that would otherwise be thrown away? What inferences may be drawn from the evidence provided in the examination of particulate?

Experimental Methods

Methods for development of comparative materials, including dyeing with representative dye plants and pigment painting are reported elsewhere (Thompson 2000; Thompson and Jakes 2002; Baldia 2003; Jakes et al. 2007). Rabbit hair (*Lagomorpha* order) and milkweed fiber (*Asclepias syriaca* L.) were used as models of animal and plant fibers, bedstraw (*Galium* species) and sumac (*Rhus* species) as dye-plant examples (Jakes and Ericksen 2001), and iron oxide as an example of ocher pigment. Methods of charring and mineralizing comparative materials are also reported in other studies (Srinivasan 1993; Srinivasan and Jakes 1997; Thompson and Jakes 2005). Samples from the archaeological textiles were obtained by collecting particulate shed by the materials and found in the glass cases and storage boxes.

Small samples of the comparative materials and of the archaeological textile particulate were each mounted on microscope slides with Permount (Fisher Scientific) and examined with a Zeiss Axioplan research microscope using brightfield, darkfield, polarized light, and differential interference contrast techniques. Images were collected using a Progres camera and Zeiss Axiovision software.

To prepare samples for infrared spectroscopy, small amounts (about 2–5 milligrams) of each of the comparative examples or the particulate were ground with a mortar and pestle, mixed with potassium bromide and pressed into a pellet (Jakes et al. 2007). The pellets were examined using a Perkin Elmer Spectrum 2000 Fourier Transform Infrared spectrometer, equipped with a deuterated triglycine sulfate detector (64 scans, 4000–400 centimeter $^{-1}$, resolution of 4 centimeter $^{-1}$, baseline corrected). The infrared spectra of the materials provide information about the chemical composition of the samples, since organic groups each absorb infrared radiation in characteristic "bands" or wavelengths. Thus an infrared spectrum provides some chemical information that is not available in microscopic examination.

A Jeol JSM-820 scanning electron microscope (SEM) and an Oxford Analytical eXL energy dispersive X-ray analyzer (EDS, EDAX, EDX) were used to examine planchette-mounted samples of the particulate, after each was carbon-coated in a Denton Vacuum Desk II coater. Energy dispersive analysis of X-rays provides information about the elemental composition of the fibers and any surface deposits; this information, complementary to the infrared spectra, can be gathered from very small samples.

Results of Seip Particulate Analysis

Table 1 provides a summary of the results of microscopic and infrared spectroscopic examination of fibrous particulate from the Seip textiles. Optical microscopic

Table 1

Optical microscopy and infrared spectroscopy of fibers and deposits

		Optical Microscopic Examination	Infrared Spectroscopy
Charred Textiles, Case #5, #36, #37, #39			
Fibers	Color	Fiber surface structure cracked, uncolored areas graphite-like and shiny; in dark field, surface looks like burned wood; edges of fiber reddish; identified as bast; many fiber bundles;	#5 Similar to charred rabbit hair/protein; #36 similar to charred cellulose
Deposits	Adhering*	Encrustations; red deposits	#5, #36 Iron oxide
	Non-adhering	Some mineral-like material	
Other		Due to charring, no internal structures visible; Brightfield examination shows black rods and some deposits	
Yellow/brown Textiles, Case #4, #10, #31			
Fibers	Color	Red, yellow, green color inside rabbit hair fibers. dark brown, red-brown, yellow inside rabbit hair fibers, brown bast	#10 appears mineralized; #4 looks like rabbit hair/protein
Deposits	Adhering*	Encrustations, some deposits observed in darkfield do not coincide with color	
	Non-adhering	Light blue, white, 2 or more different deposit types	
Other		Unidentified bast fibers not milkweed or Indian hemp	
Turquoise/white Textiles, Case #14, #23			
Fibers	Color	Bast fibers with strong polarization colors, looks like milkweed. #23 includes an unidentified yellow/brown bast; no colors within the fibers	#23 not like malachite, but is like verdigris
Deposits	Adhering*	Blue granules, uncolored smaller granules, small red granules	
	Non-adhering	Mineral, isotropic	
Other			

*Adhering deposits are associated with fiber fragments, non-adhering deposits are loose particles not associated with fiber fragments.

examination of the Seip particulate showed that the charred fragments and those from the yellow/brown category (Figure 1) are made of bast and rabbit-hair fibers. The fabrics with the distinctive turquoise and white patterns (Figure 2) contained bast fibers. None of the infrared spectra from Seip samples displays the bands typical of oxalates. Either the fibers are ones which do not deposit large amounts of oxalate, e.g. the herbaceous plant fibers, or they are woody species of fibers that were very well cleaned of all associated plant material. It is most probable that the fibers that were used in the Seip textiles were obtained from herbaceous plants and not woody species (Jakes et al. 2007) not only because they have limited oxalate but also because these plants yield very fine fibers (Jakes et al. 1994).

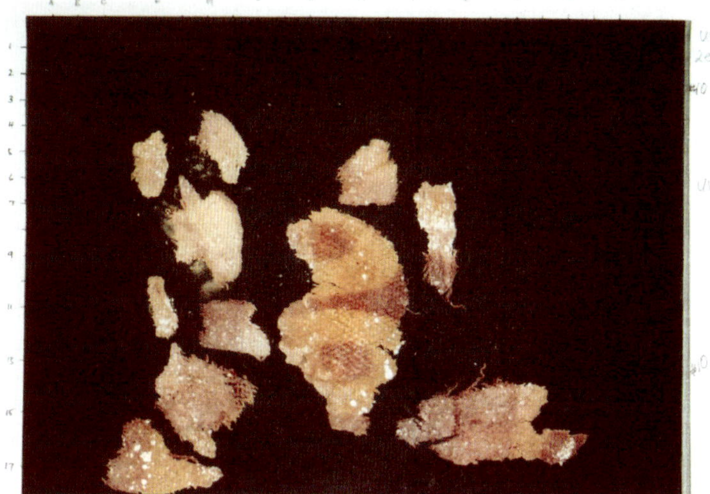

Figure 1
Example of a yellow and brown textile, Seip #10.

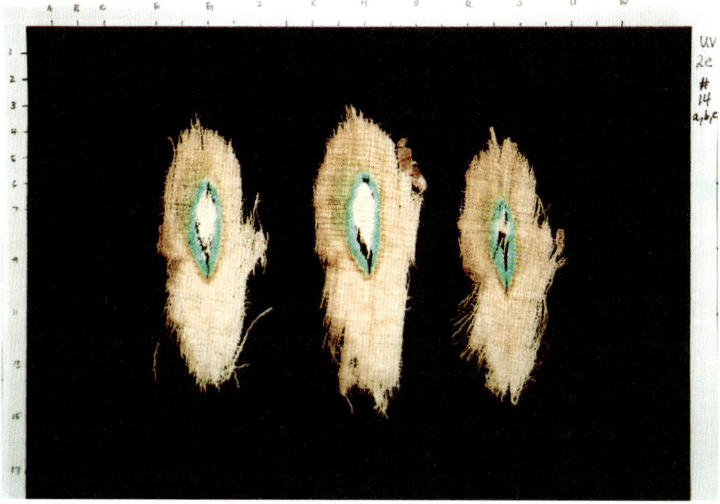

Figure 2
Example of a textile with turquoise and white coloration, Seip #14.

Although specific types of lignin were found to be useful in separating groups of fibers from woody and herbaceous species of plants in the Comparative Plant Fiber Collection (Jakes, Baldia, Thompson 2007), no lignins were found in the charred Seip materials. While this result was not unexpected, the potential usefulness of differences in lignin types must be considered in other plant fiber textiles. In examination of bast fiber samples from a later period site, for example, lignin types typical of herbaceous dicots were discernable (Jakes et al. 2007).

Charred Textiles

The charred textiles contained both bast and rabbit-hair fibers. The fibers are cracked due to extreme dehydration; they are graphite-like and shiny in color. In some the edges look reddish, indicative of ocher pigmentation. The infrared spectrum of the particulate recovered from the charred black Seip #5 displays some similarities to that of charred rabbit hair (Figure 3). The spectrum reflects the proteinaceous nature of the fiber while also showing evidence of dehydration and oxidation. In addition, the absorbances at 594 centimeter $^{-1}$ and 465 centimeter $^{-1}$ in the Seip #5 sample indicate the presence of iron oxide, the major component of ocher which was a common pigment used on fabrics and as body paint by the Hopewell people. This is corroborated by the EDS data that shows high iron content in samples of the particulate from these textiles.

Yellow/Brown Textiles

Samples in this group (#4, #10, and #31) contain dark brown, red brown, green, and yellow-colored rabbit hair, as well as some unidentified bast (Figure 1). The fibers are thoroughly saturated with color, indicating that they were dyed rather than pigmented on their surfaces (Figure 4). The infrared spectra of the particulate obtained from Seip #4 (Figure 5) confirm its proteinaceous composition, corroborating microscopic identification of rabbit hair. The infrared spectrum of the particulate from Seip #10, however, doesn't look like protein (Figure 6) nor is it typical of cellulose. In fact, the sharp peaks appear more like a material that has been mineralized. While EDS showed that all of the Seip fibers in the yellow/brown category contained significant amounts of copper, and their preservation is likely to have been supported by impregnation with copper ions, the particulate from Seip #10 is mineralized to a greater

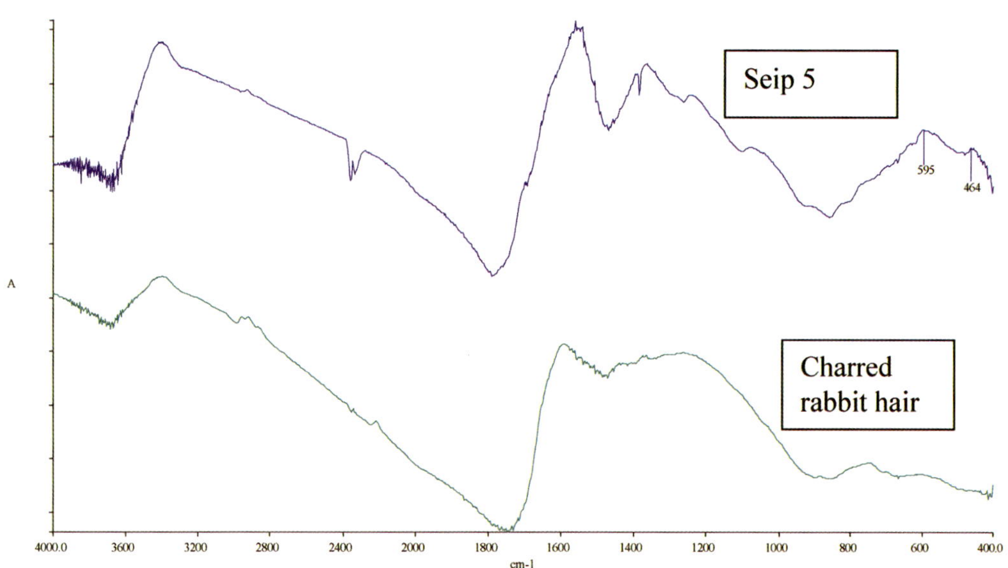

Figure 3
Infrared spectra of dust from Seip #5 compared to charred rabbit hair.

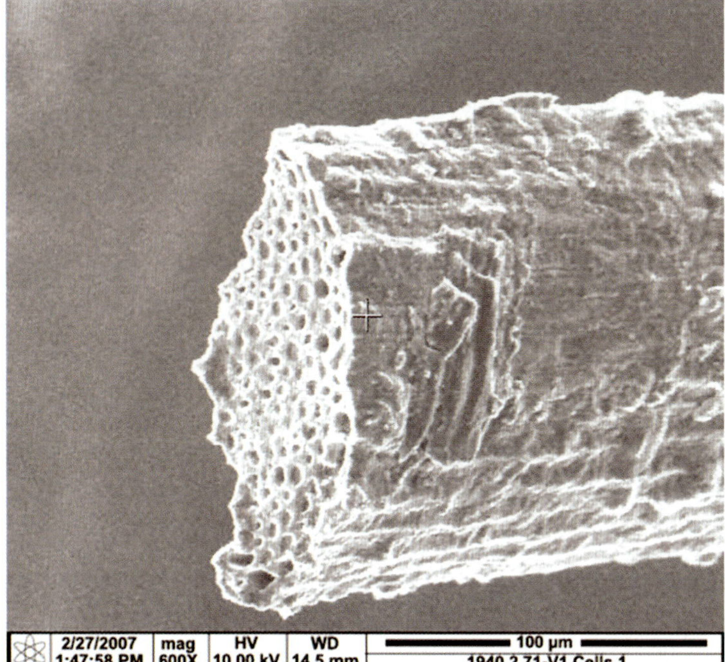

Figure 4
Red, yellow, and brown rabbit-hair fibers from Seip #10.

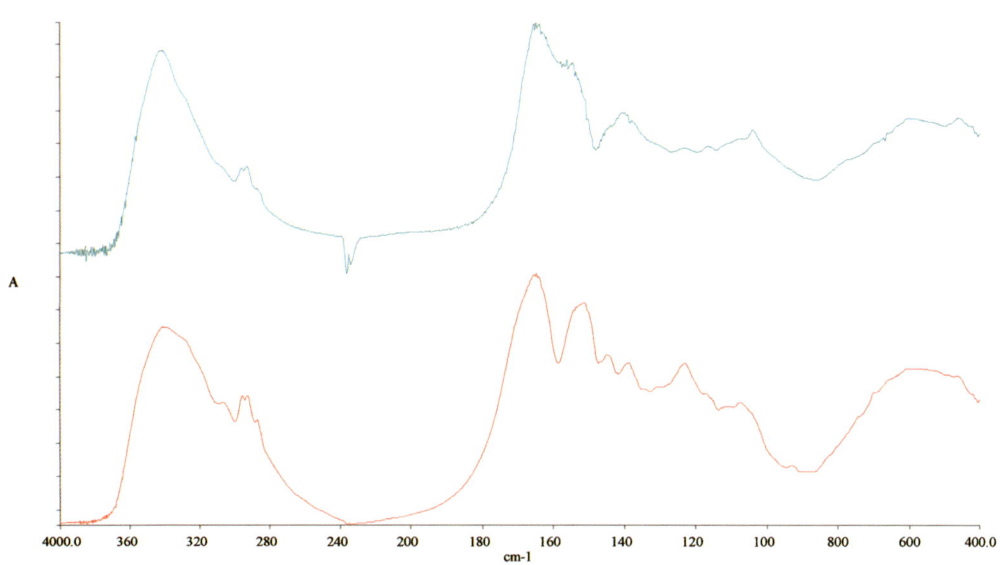

Figure 5
Infrared spectrum of particulate from Seip #4 compared to wool.

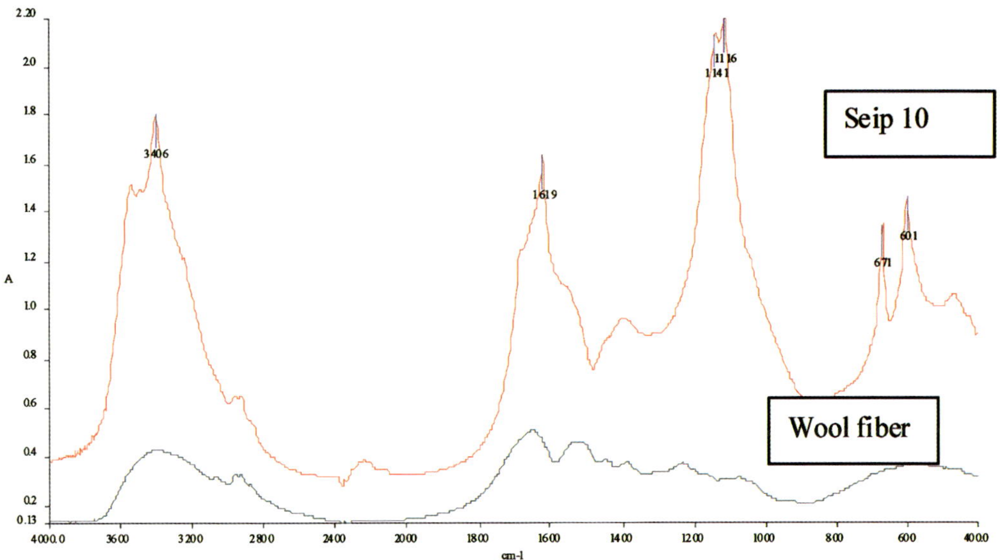

Figure 6
Infrared spectrum of particulate from Seip #10 compared to wool.

extent than sample #4. Surface deposits including some that are blue in color were seen on the fibers in the yellow/brown category. These deposits are likely to be copper-containing salts formed in the burial context due to close association of the materials to corroding copper. Thus the Seip #10 particulate sample must be composed of a considerable proportion of the copper mineral surface deposits.

There is no significant difference in the elemental composition between the yellow, brown, and green fibers. The only difference that existed between the fibers and the deposits adhering to the fibers is in the amount of carbon, indicating that the deposits are primarily inorganic while the fibers retain considerable amounts of organic components. Since there is a difference in color and yet there are no differences in heavy elements, it must be concluded that the difference in colors of the yellow/brown group are due to organic components, e.g. dyes. Many different plants could have been the source for these colorants. Flavonoid dyes from plants such as oaks (*Quercus* species), onion (*Allium* species) or yarrow (*Achilla* species) could have provided dyestuff for the color yellow (Adrosko 1971; Densmore 1974[1928]; Baldia and Jakes 2007b). Brown colors could have been produced by quinones found in plants such as walnuts (*Juglans* species) and the red color could have come from sorrel (*Rumex* species) or from bedstraw (*Galium* species). Examples of native North American plants that yield a green color are common reed or cane (*Phragmitis* species). Similar to the collections and databases for textiles colorants that have been produced in Europe and the Middle East, a dye-plant collection should be established and the procedures developed for extraction of colorant from fibers and comparison to the comparative materials. In its absence, however, the observation that these fibers are dyed and some others are pigmented is useful for understanding craftsmanship of the past.

Turquoise/White Textiles

Seip #14 is a textile in the turquoise and white group (Figure 2). Overall the fabric is light tan in color with green- or turquoise-colored stains in circular patterns. The fabric in the center of these patterns is whiter than the areas surrounding them.

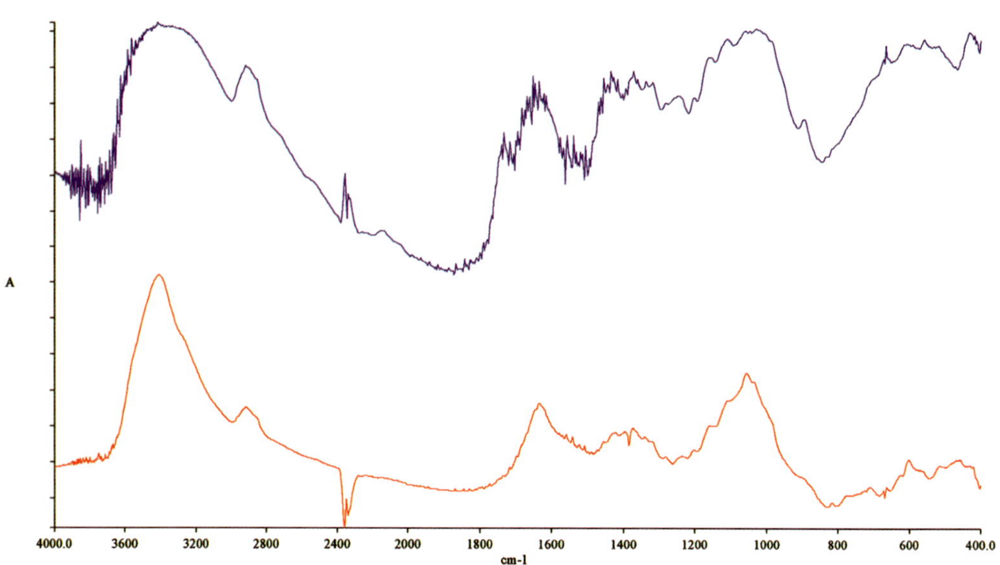

Figure 7
Infrared spectrum of Seip #14 compared to that of common milkweed.

As observed under the microscope, the fibers are not saturated with color, and therefore are not dyed. Rather, the fibers display different shades of green and blue material on their surfaces. The EDS of the fibers and deposits show significant amounts of copper. The infrared spectrum of the particulate sample did not look like verdigris, malachite, or azurite and in fact are not sharp as one would see in a mineralized fiber. The similarities of the Seip #14 fiber to that of common milkweed (Figure 7) reflect the fact that the infrared spectrum represents the entire fiber, which although encrusted with copper mineral products, is not thoroughly mineralized. The white-colored center of the turquoise and white textiles could be coated with a kaolin-type white clay. The EDS of this area shows significant quantities of aluminum and silicon typical of clay; such clays are abundant in southern Ohio.

Implications for Seip and Other Archaeological Textiles

The poor condition of the textile fragments from some sites hinders their study. They are fragile and small, they are stained brown due to degradation and, to date, the types of evidence they provide was considered limited. However, because fabric manufacture and use is such an integral part of society, these fragments must be studied if we want to learn more details about prehistoric cultures. In an effort to preserve the fragments, we suggest the use of the particulate that has been shed from them for garnering information prior to site-specific sampling from the fragments themselves. A vast amount of information can be gained and more will be possible as new technologies allow us to determine more information with smaller and smaller quantities of material.

Fiber Evidence

Examination of the particulate can show the classes of fiber that were employed in making the fabric. Even charred fibers provide some overall morphology that can indicate whether they are plant or animal, while other degraded fibers display morphology that can allow further classification. The presence of both plant and animal fiber in the particulate is indicative of a blended yarn or composite fabric. Plant fibers with clean surfaces reflect more extensive processing than fiber bundles with associated plant cells remaining on their surfaces. The presence of oxalate inclusions also aids classification of plant genera, while the use of infrared spectra and elemental analysis provides corroboration of the composition of these inorganic inclusions.

The condition of the fibers also informs the analyst about the condition of the entire fabric fragment. The fiber particulate is representative of the "worst case"—i.e. the most degraded areas of the material, because the particulate has been shed from the fabric. Not only will the fiber reflect desiccation through cracks and disrupted morphology, the fiber condition can also reflect the burial context, e.g. with evidence of mineralization. Thus, by looking at the particulate, the conservator has knowledge prior to employing any conservation treatment of the fabric.

Coloration of the fibers found in the particulate can indicate dye or pigment use. In cases where fibers are colored throughout, a dyeing process is likely to have been employed, whereas when fibers are observed with colored particles on their surfaces, some sort of pigment could have been involved. The particulate would form a useful set of trial samples for dye-identification procedures by a combination of Raman spectroscopy (Chen and Van Dinh 2007; Clark 2007), infrared, and visible spectroscopy (Martoglio et al. 1990; Jakes et al. 1990).

Surface particulate and encrustations are also indicative of conditions of the burial context. For example, if materials are buried in association with copper and if other conditions of the site are suitable, the copper-containing salts can encrust the surface of the fiber, or replace organic constituents within the fibers as these begin to mineralize, eventually transitioning into pseudomorphs. Use of infrared spectra and elemental composition can provide corroboration of these processes, depicting sharp peaks of mineral composition that stand out distinctly from the remaining organic structures of the fibers.

Given these findings, one could begin to hypothesize about the people who produced the fabric and used it.

Resource Use and Exchange

In the case of the Seip textile examples, the fibers found in the particulate are typical of plants and animals that are readily available locally. Similarly, the identification of iron oxide, a component of ocher, on some of the fibers and

of the white clay in the turquoise/white group reflects the use of resources that are found in soil deposits throughout the area. In fact, the mineral-rich colored soils of the area resulted in the name of the region's Paint Creek. The fact that locally available materials were used for textile production and decoration implies that the Ohio Hopewell communities operated independently in matters of crafts production. If in further study a unique component is found, comparable to finding obsidian or sea shells at these burial sites in Ohio, it might provide additional support for exchange which is already known to have occurred with other materials among the Hopewell peoples.

Use of local resources reflects knowledge of the location of those resources and of their maintenance. Plant stands, though wild and not cultivated, must be monitored each year, and cleared of secondary growth that might encroach and overtake them (Jakes and Ericksen 1997). Specific plants might be selected for premium textile production; for example, although fiber yield for nettles (*Urtica* sp.) is not as high as that of Indian hemp (*Apocynum cannabinum*), the fineness of the fiber achievable might lead the craftsperson to undertake the greater amount of work required in processing this fiber for yarns and fabrics.

Although textiles were made from locally available materials, one must be aware of possibilities for exchange of textiles, even if only as the bags in which other traded goods were held. Textiles provide an infrastructure that might be overlooked in preference to more durable artifacts, yet their presence in day-to-day life is essential.

Technology

Finding clean-surfaced plant fibers that are well separated from the remainder of the plant material is indicative of significant knowledge held by the people who created the fabrics from which the particulate was shed. Not only must the plants be collected but they must be handled in certain ways to release clean fibers that are strong and fine enough to be made into fine yarns. Densmore (1974[1928]), for example, describes a method of boiling plants with wood ash to aid in fiber extraction.

Considerable technological knowledge is required in coloration of the fabrics. There are different plant and mineral sources for dyes and pigments readily available locally, but their use represents considerable experimentation since the plants do not necessarily display the color that will be imparted to the fibers in the dyeing process. For instance, bedstraw roots, a cousin to the madder plant, yield dull red colors but the roots themselves do not appear colored. The mechanism of application and binding these colorants to plant and animal fibers is rather compli-cated and not necessarily the same among plant or animal-based fibers. In the case of dyeing, a mordant may be required and a procedure of cooking the fabrics with the colorant materials is likely (Adrosko 1971; Densmore 1974[1928]). In applying a pigment some sort of binder must be used and its source must also be identified. Thus colored fibers reveal technological sophistication and special knowledge even when larger contiguous fabrics are not available.

Social Structure

Knowing the fiber composition of the particulate, and thereby the composition of the textile fragment, leads to an understanding of the scheduling of activities by the craftspeople who must collect raw materials at appropriate times of the year. They knew where the stands of plants and the pockets of mineral pigment were located, and the effort required in their collection. They had to plan these activities, and organize the groups that would collect the resources. Collection activities must be scheduled to take advantage of plant-fiber maturity; at the prime time for collection, many individuals may be needed to collect and process the plants. Similarly, in collection of animal hairs, appropriate handling will allow collection and processing of skins to yield useable, spinnable fiber. These steps can be costly in time and labor (Jakes and Ericksen 1997).

For fibers to be spun into yarn they must be aligned. Although spindle spinning is faster than thigh spinning when short fibers are used, the long bast fibers are efficiently spun by a thigh spinning process which is the likely method for making yarn from plant-stem fibers (Tiedemann 2001; Tiedemann and Jakes 2006). The mechanism by which rabbit hair was combined with bast fibers in the yarn has not been demonstrated. Yarns are then twined into fabric. This can be achieved without a loom and using only a holding cord (Sibley et al. 1991). Finally the fabric can be dyed or painted. Since these activities are very time consuming, it is possible that the crafts specialists who conducted these tasks were freed of other duties in the community.

Although the status or class of specific individuals buried with the textiles cannot be determined since provenience is not known, one can infer that individuals at Seip are of a high status due to the large number of textiles recovered, the elaborate coloration, and the complex blending of plant and animal fibers observed.

Recommendations/Conclusion

It is important to save the particulate shed from seemingly nondescript fabric fragments. Forensic techniques (Robertson 1992; Petraco and Kubic 2004) include collection with tape as well as the use of small vials. As analytical methods progress, in fact, even more will be achievable from the examination of very small amounts of material. Examination of the particulate is a path to uncovering the past that does not incur damage to the small fragments that remain from prehistoric sites. With work conducted on the particulate, the analyst will have obtained knowledge of the textile without having taken a sample for destructive analysis. Subsequently using the forensic photography protocol developed by Baldia (2005; Baldia and Jakes 2007a), very small samples could be removed from the textile and subjected to testing that has been previously shown to be effective on the particulate.

References

Adrosko, R. 1971. *Natural Dyes and Home Dyeing*. New York: Dover.

Aspland, J.R. 1997. *Textile Dyeing and Coloration*. Research Triangle Park: American Association of Textile Chemists and Colorists.

Baldia, C. 2003. *Prehistoric Textile Materials: Technology of Dyeing with Bloodroot*. Master's thesis. Ohio State University, Columbus, OH.

Baldia, C. 2005. "Development of a Protocol to Detect and Classify Colorants in Archaeological Textiles and its Application to Selected Prehistoric Textiles from Seip Mound in Ohio." Ph.D. Dissertation, Ohio State University, Columbus, OH.

Baldia, C. and Jakes, K.A. 2007a. "Photographic Methods to Detect Colorants in Archaeological Textiles." *Journal of Archaeological Science* 34: 519–25.

Baldia, C. and Jakes, K.A. 2007b. "Toward the Classification of Colorants in Archaeological Textiles of Eastern North America." In M.D. Glascock, R.J. Speakman, and R.S. Popelka-Filcoff (eds) *Archaeological Chemistry: Analytical Techniques and Archaeological Interpretation*, pp. 15–43. Symposium series 968. Washington,D.C.: American Chemical Society.

Baldia, C., Jakes, K.A., and Baldia, M.O. 2008. "Coloration and Fabric Structure of Selected Polychrome Textiles from the Seip Mound Group." *Midcontinental Journal of Archaeology* 33(2): 197–220.

Bell I.M., Clark, R.J.H., and Gibbs, P.J. 1997. "Raman Spectroscopic Library of Natural and Synthetic Pigments (pre~1850 AD)." *Spectrochimica Acta A* 53: 2159–60.

Brose, David S. 1978. "An Interpretation of the Hopewellian Traits in Florida." In D.S. Brose and N. Greber (eds) *Hopewell Archaeology*, pp. 141–9. Kent, OH: Kent State University Press.

Carr, C. and Case, D.T. (eds). 2006. *Gathering Hopewell: Society, Ritual, and Ritual Interaction*. New York: Springer.

Chen, H.L., Jakes, K.A., and Foreman, D.W. 1998. "Preservation of Archaeological Textiles Through Fibre Mineralization." *Journal of Archaeological Science* 25: 1015–22.

Chen, K, Leona, M., and Van Dinh, T. 2007. "Surface-enhanced Raman Scattering for Identification of Organic Pigments and Dyes in Works of Art and Cultural Heritage Material." *Sensor Review* 27: 109–20.

Church, F. 1984. "Textiles as Markers of Ohio Hopewell Social Identities." *Midcontinental Journal of Archaeology* 9: 1–25.

Clark, R.J.H. 2007. "The Scientific Investigation of Artwork and Archaeological Artefacts: Raman Microscopy as a Structural, Analytical and Forensic Tool." *Applied Physics A* 89: 833–40.

Coon, M.S. 2009. "Variation in Ohio Hopewell Political Economies." *American Antiquity* 74(1): 49–76.

Densmore, F. 1974 [1928]. *How Indians Use Wild Plants for Food, Medicine, and Crafts*. New York: Dover. Originally published as "Uses of Plants by Chippewa

Indians," Forty-fourth Annual Report of the Bureau of American Ethnology, pp. 275–397.

Greber, N. 1979. "Variations in Social Structure of Ohio Hopewell Peoples." *Midcontinental Journal of Archaeology* 4: 35–75.

Greber, N. 1996. "A Commentary on the Contexts and Contents of Large to Small Ohio Hopewell Deposits." In P.J. Pacheco (ed.) *A View from the Core: A Synthesis of Ohio Hopewell Archaeology*, pp. 152–72. Columbus, OH: Ohio Archaeological Council.

Hinkle, K. 1984. *Ohio Hopewell Textiles: A Medium for the Exchange of Social and Stylistic Information*. Master's thesis. Ohio State University, Columbus, OH.

Jakes, K.A. 1996. "Clues to the Past: Further Development of the Comparative Plant Fiber Collection." In M.V. Orna (ed.) *Archaeological Chemistry: Organic, Inorganic and Biochemical Analysis*, pp. 202–22. American Chemical Society Symposium Series 625. Washington, D.C.: American Chemical Society.

Jakes, K.A., Baldia, C., and Thompson, A. 2007. "Infrared Examination of Fiber and Particulate Residues from Archaeological Textiles." In M.D. Glascock, R.J. Speakman, and R.S. Popelka-Filcoff (eds) *Archaeological Chemistry: Analytical Techniques and Archaeological Interpretation*, pp. 44–77. American Chemical Society Symposium Series 968. Washington, D.C.: American Chemical Society.

Jakes, K.A., Chen H.L., and Sibley, L.R. 1993. "Toward the Development of a Classification System for Plant Fibers." *Ars Textrina* 20: 157–79.

Jakes, K.A. and Ericksen, A.G. 1997. "Socioeconomic Implications of Prehistoric Textile Production in the Eastern Woodlands." In P. Vandiver, J. Druzik, J.F. Merkel, and J. Stewart (eds) *Materials Issues in Art and Archaeology, V.*, pp. 281–6. Materials Research Society Symposium Proceedings, Vol. 462. Pittsburgh, PA: Materials Research Society.

Jakes, K.A. and Ericksen, A.G. 2001. "Prehistoric Use of Sumac and Bedstraw as Dye Plants in Eastern North America." *Southeastern Archaeology* 20: 56–66.

Jakes, K.A. and Howard III, J.H. 1986a. "Formation of Textile Fabric Pseudomorphs." In J. Olin and J. Blackman (eds) *Proceedings of the 24th International Symposium on Archaeometry*, pp. 165–78. Washington, D.C.: Smithsonian Institution.

Jakes, K.A., and Howard III, J.H. 1986b. "Replacement of Protein and Cellulose Fibers by Copper Minerals and the Formation of Textile Pseudomorphs." In H. Zeronian and H. Needles (eds) *Conservation and Characterization of Historical Paper and Textile Materials*, pp. 277–87. Advances in Chemistry Series No. 212. Washington, D.C.: American Chemical Society.

Jakes, K.A., Katon, J.E., and Martoglio, P.A., 1990. "Identification of Dyes and Characterization of Fibers by Infrared and Visible Microspectroscopy: Application to Paracas Textiles." In E. Pernicka and G. Wagner (eds) *Archaeometry*

90, pp. 305–15. Proceedings of the 27th International Symposium on Archaeometry. Basel: Birkhauser Verlag.

Jakes, K.A. and Sibley, L.R. 1984. "An Examination of the Phenomeneon of Textile Fabric Pseudomorphism." In J.B. Lambert (ed.) *Archaeological Chemistry III*, pp. 403–24. Advances in Chemistry Series 205. Washington, D.C.: American Chemical Society.

Jakes, K.A. and Sibley, L.R., 1989. "Evaluation of a Partially Mineralized Fabric from Etowah." In Y. Maniatis (ed.) *Archaeometry 88*, pp. 237–44. New York: Elsevier.

Jakes, K.A., Sibley, L.R., and Yerkes, R.W. 1994. "A Comparative Collection for the Study of Fibers Used in Prehistoric Textiles from Eastern North America." *Journal of Archaeological Science* 21: 641–50.

Martoglio, P., Bouffard, S.P., Sommer, A.J., Katon, J.E., and Jakes, K.A. 1990. "Unlocking Secrets of the Past: The Analysis of Archaeological Textiles and Dyes." *Analytical Chemistry* 62 A1123–8.

Mills, W.C. 1907. "Explorations of the Edwin Harness Mound." *Ohio History* 16: 113–93.

Mills, W.C. 1909. "Explorations of the Seip Mound." *Ohio History* 18: 269–313.

Mills, W.C. 1916. "Explorations of the Tremper Mound." *Ohio History* 25: 263–398.

Pacheco, K. 1996. "Ohio Hopewell Regional Settlement Patterns." In P.J. Pacheco (ed.) *A View from the Core: A Synthesis of Ohio Hopewell Archaeology*, pp. 18–35. Columbus, OH: Ohio Archaeological Council.

Petraco, N. and Kubic, T. 2004. *Microscopy for Criminalists, Chemists, and Conservators*. Boca Raton: CRC Press.

Power, S.C. 2004. *Early Art of the Southeastern Indians: Feathered Serpents and Winged Beings*. Athens, GA: University of Georgia Press.

Prufer, O. 1964. "The Hopewell Complex in Ohio." In J.R. Caldwell and R.L. Hall (eds) *Hopewellian Studies*, pp. 37–83. Springfield, IL: Scientific Papers (Illinois State Museum), Vol. 12.

Robertson, J. 1999. "Protocols for Fibre Examination and Initial Preparation." In J. Robertson and M. Grieve (eds) *Forensic Examination of Fibres*, pp 116–34. London and Philadelphia: Taylor and Francis.

Shetrone, H.C. and Greenman, E.F. 1931."Explorations of the Seip Groups of Prehistoric Earthworks." *Ohio History* 40: 343–509.

Sibley, L.R., Swinker, M.E., and Jakes, K.A. 1991. "The Use of Pattern Reproduction in Reconstructing Etowah Textile Remains." *Ars Textrina* 15: 179–202.

Song, C.A. 1991. "Variations in Fiber Morphology of Prehistoric Textiles from the Seip group of Mounds: A Model of Explanation." Ph.D. dissertation, Ohio State University, Columbus, OH.

Song, C.A., Jakes, K.A., and Yerkes, R.W. 1996. "Seip Hopewell Textile Analysis and Cultural Implications." *Midcontinental Journal of Archaeology* 21(2): 247–65.

Srinivasan, R. 1993. "Exploration of the Effects of Carbonization on *Apocynum Cannabinum* Fibers." Master's thesis, Ohio State University.

Srinivasan, R. and Jakes, K.A. 1997. "Optical and Scanning Electron Microscopic Study of the Effects of Charring on Indian Hemp (*Apocynum Cannabinum L.*) Fibers." *Journal of Archaeological Science* 24: 517–27.

Struever, S. and Howart, G.L. 1972. "An Analysis of the Hopewell Interaction Sphere." *Anthropological Papers, Museum of Anthropology, University of Michigan* 46: 47–79.

Thompson, A.J. 2000. "Experimental Replication of Dyeing: Toward an Understanding of Dyeing Processes Used in Prehistoric Eastern North America." Master's thesis, Ohio State University, Columbus, OH.

Thompson, A.J. 2003. "Textiles as Indicators of Hopewellian Culture Burial Practices." Ph.D. dissertation, Ohio State University.

Thompson, A.J. and Jakes, K.A. 2002. "Replication of Textile Dyeing with Sumac and Bedstraw." *Southeastern Archaeology* 21: 552–7.

Thompson, A.J. and Jakes, K.A. 2005. "Textile Evidence for Ohio Hopewell Burial Practices." *Southeastern Archaeology* 24(2): 137–41.

Tiedemann, E.J. 2001. "Characterization of Prehistoric Spinning Technology: Toward the Determination of Spinning

Practices Employed in Mississippian Textiles." Ph.D. dissertation, Ohio State University, Columbus, OH.

Tiedemann, E. and Jakes, K.A. 2006. "An Exploration of Prehistoric Spinning Technology: Spinning Efficiency and Technology Transition." *Archaeometry* 48: 293–307.

Unruh, J. 2003. "Severely Degraded Textile on Archaeological Artifacts at the Agora Excavations in Athens, Greece." *Textile Specialty Group Postprints 12*, pp. 25–35. Washington, D.C.: American Institute for Conservation.

Vollmer, J. 1975. "Textile Pseudomorphs on Chinese Bronzes." In P.L. Fiske (ed.), Irene Emery Roundtable on Museum Textiles: 1974 Proceedings. *Archaeological Textiles*, pp. 170–4. Washington, D.C.: Textile Museum.

White, E.P. 1987. "Excavating in the Field Museum: Survey and Analysis of Textiles from the 1891 Hopewell Mound Group Excavation." Master's thesis, Sangamon State University, Illinois.

Willoughby, C.C. 1938. "Textile Fabrics from the Burial Mounds of the Great Earthwork Builders Ohio." *Ohio State Archaeological and Historical Quarterly* 47: 273–87.

Wimberley, V.S. 2004. "Preserved Textiles on Hopewell Copper." In P.B. Drooker (ed.) *Perishable Material Culture in the Northeast*, pp. 69–85. Albany, NY: New York State Museum Bulletin 500.

Wymer, D. 2004."Organic Preservation on Prehistoric Copper Artifacts of the Ohio Hopewell." In P.B. Drooker (ed) *Perishable Material Culture in the Northeast*, pp. 45–68. Albany, NY: New York State Museum Bulletin 500.

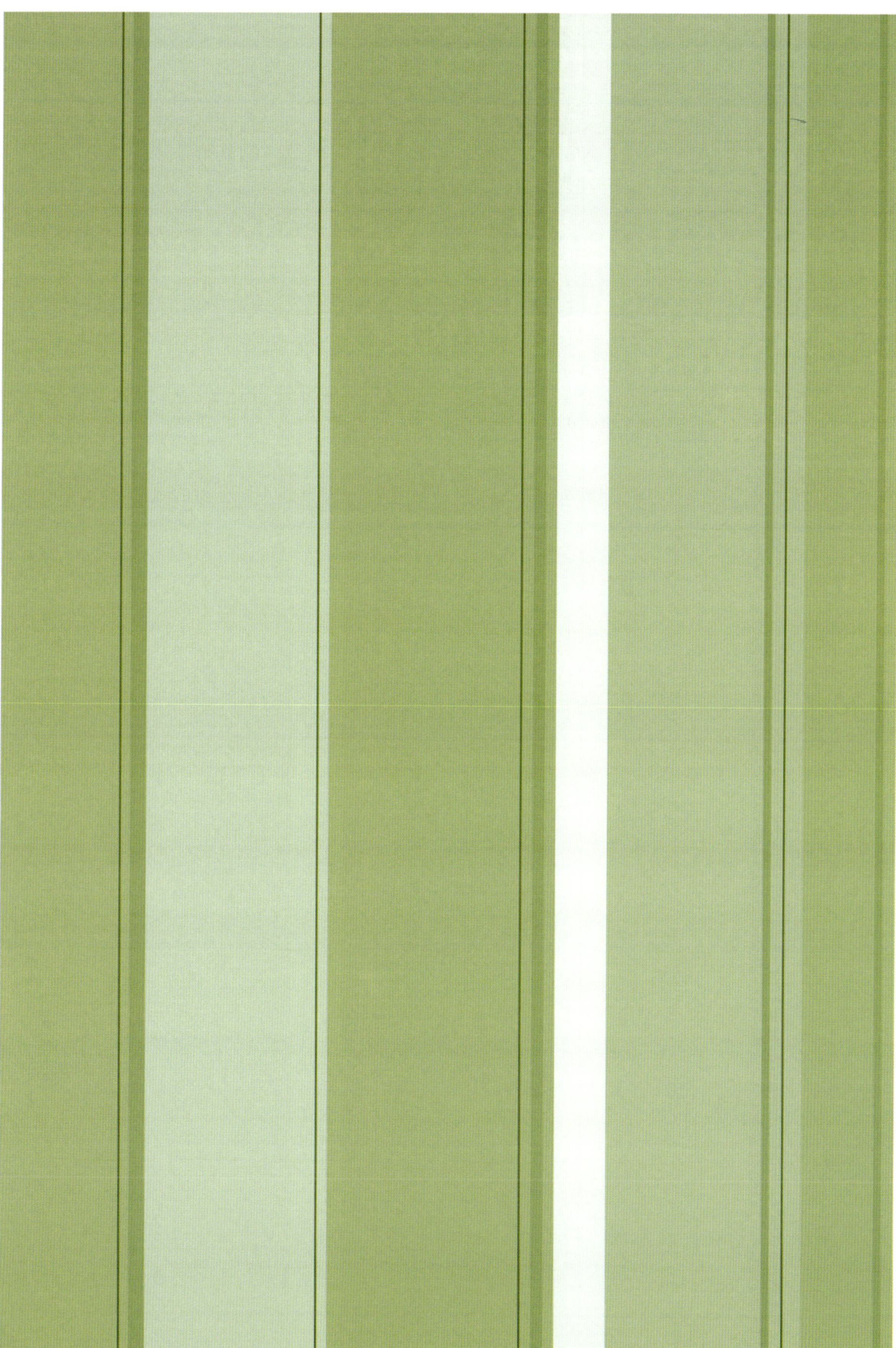

Smart Dust: Sci-Fi Applications Enabled by Synthetic Fiber and Textiles Technology

Abstract

In the field of materials design research there is an increasing interest in an amalgamation of the disciplines of science, technology, engineering, and maths in order to focus upon smart fiber and textile innovation for human and environmental applications. What may seem *sci-fi* solutions for a raft of different problems have at the core innovative man-made textiles and technologies, and are becoming the zeitgeist of many international research and development sectors with the promise of as yet unknown applications and commercial opportunities. In 2007 Ohmatex's White Paper on Smart Textiles reported that in 2005 smart and interactive fabrics were worth US$340 million with a compound growth rate of 28.3 percent per year which became US$642 million in 2008 and has continued to rise. Today there is a paradigm shift in research activity due to technical developments in miniaturization at nano-scale, coupled with improved sensor networks and the creation of new composites to enable the creation of smart technologies for integration into soft engineering products for the body and the built environment. These innovations are enabled in many cases by traditional textile design thinking and product development such as the creation of synthetic nano fiber polymers, to incorporate ubiquitous computing into textiles which have immediate applications that include health-monitoring, active insulation, personal communication, environmental sensors, and security. The enhancement of integral nano-innovations such as self-cleaning, water repellence, thermal regulation, "breathability," and materials that stiffen on impact or change shape are part of the textile future. *Smart Dust* is in this vanguard area, where the combination of synthetic textile polymer and pervasive and adaptive computing knowledge is emergent and highly technical in relation to applications. Here the objective is to move toward seamless invisible integration of technology, thereby producing products and services which are responsive to the external and human environment and which may ultimately contributing to wellbeing.

Keywords: ubiquitous computing, nanotechnology, polymers, smart textiles, sci-fi

JOAN FARRER

Dr. Joan Farrer RCA is Reader in 3D Design and Materials Practice at the University of Brighton and is a sustainable fashion textiles consultant, and member of the Pervasive Adaption (PerAda) research program, which is part of the EU FET Framework 7 European Coordination Action PANORAMA. J.Farrer@brighton.ac.uk

Textile, Volume 8, Issue 3, pp. 342–347
DOI: 10.2752/175183510X12868938341565
Reprints available directly from the Publishers.
Photocopying permitted by licence only.
© 2010 Berg. Printed in the United Kingdom.

Smart Dust: Sci-Fi Applications Enabled by Synthetic Fiber and Textiles Technology

In many ways it is the textiles and fashion industry that have informed consumers' understanding of the word *natural* as being related to nature and *synthetic* as being made artificially by chemical synthesis (especially so as to resemble a natural product) and not genuine[1]. Particularly in the last five decades *natural* fabrics (silk, cotton, wool, and linen) have been equated to *good* and *sustainable*, while *synthetics* became synonymous with *bad*. In the early twenty-first century, however, it can be argued that the development of synthetic fibers in the textile industry is at the forefront of a second Industrial Revolution, facilitating engineering concepts and fabric applications, leading developments in health, communication, security, and environmental sustainability. Smart-textile product development is at the heart of transdisciplinary engagement, embedding and facilitating ubiquitous technologies such as *Smart Dust*, which is an example of how the centuries-old textiles sector, far from being traditional and covered in dust, is playing a vital role in the development and commercialization of leading-edge blue-sky technology that has broad applications including human well-being.

The idea of *Smart Dust* has existed since 1964, when it was mentioned in the science-fiction novel *The Invincible* by Stanislaw Lem, who was the first to proffer the notion of a network of tiny mechanical robots. These mechanical robots could display simple and complex behaviors when triggered externally. Later, the hypothetical concept of *Smart Dust* was described for the layman in J. Storrs Hall's essay "Utility Fog: The Stuff that Dreams Are Made Of" (1993).[2] The robots (Foglets) described by Storrs Hall were microscopic with extending arms reaching in several directions. Grabbers at the end of the arms would allow the robots to mechanically link to one another and share both information and energy, enabling them to take form as a continuous substance with mechanical and optical properties. Importantly, in the age of computer networking each would have substantial computing power and would be able to communicate with its neighbors. In 2001 Kristopher S.J. Pister, working at the University of California (Berkeley), introduced the science of *Smart Dust*.[3]

Smart Dust engages with the concept of *ubiquitous computing* (in the sense of discreet seamless technology which is present everywhere and invisible) through the development of very tiny objects that interact with each other. These Micro Electrical Mechanical Sensors (MEMS) are devices (or tiny machines) that communicate with each other via wireless sensor networks (WSN), and are able to detect and report such variables as temperature, vibration, and light. In addition to funding, key challenges in the development of *Smart Dust* included reducing the size of the machine particles in the sensor networks (from current millimeter to micrometer scale), developing suitable carriers and commercialization of affordable technology. Liwei Lin, Professor of Mechanical Engineering and head of the international research team at University of California (Berkeley), developed microscopic nanofibers, which can convert energy from mechanical stresses into electricity (nanogenerators), using electrospun fibers made of block copolymers (in this case combinations of different polymer types) that self-assemble (into a collection of concentric cylinders) within the fiber. This has been made possible by a coaxial version of electrospinning technology that the research group under Rutledge developed and reported on in 2004, and which could create "wearable power" by combining electrodes and electrolytes into individual fibers and fabrics.[4]

Although the Mayans developed natural polymer applications from rubber tree sap for balls for children in the sixteenth century, the first semi-synthetic polymer produced was Bakelite™ in 1909 followed by the first synthetic fiber extrusions: rayon (1911), polyester (1935), and nylon (1938). The twentieth century saw a plethora of fiber and textiles polymer innovations, in conjunction with research and development in the chemical industry, to design molecular recipes for a variety of performance textile applications such as Kevlar™ (1971), created to be bulletproof and withstand temperatures up to 300°C. Simply, a compound is made into a polymer by the addition (condensation) of smaller molecules through a chemical reaction, where molecules (or monomers in the case of textiles) form a chain. These chains of beads can be designed to work in a variety of combinations to perform in different ways. The application of textiles know-how to the challenges involved in the realization of *Smart Dust* technologies was a natural progression given this chainlike structure of polymer fusions in relation to the nanorobotics (ranging in size from 0.1 to 10 micrometers and constructed of nanoscale molecular components) used in *Smart Dust*.

As a result of the application of these textiles technologies, Wireless Sensor Networks incorporating *Smart Dust* are now being used across a range of civilian and military applications. Current applications include monitoring (industrial processes, machine health, environment, habitat, and human activity), healthcare applications, traffic control, and battlefield surveillance. All of these have implications for the future of smart- and technical-textiles research and development. At the core of this concept is the exciting vision of minute, inexpensive, robust, networked processing devices distributed throughout everyday life and oblivious to the user to enable a better existence for humanity. For instance, this technology has the broad application potential to sense and react when a person enters a room in order to switch on lighting, manage patient or prisoner movements, activate cooling or heating imperceptivity to conserve energy, or alert producers of stale food.

"Despite being considered a traditional sector, the textile industry has been one of the pioneers in commercialising [*sic*] products incorporating nanotechnology."[5] Textiles knowledge, such as that of fiber spinning, blending, and production, has been instrumental in the growth of the nanotechnology sector: particularly due to the development of electrospinning[6] of polymer fusions into fibers.[7] The ongoing development of natural and synthetic polymers into nanofibers, surface coatings, and fabrics is producing new opportunities for transdisciplinary engagement, beyond the chemical and textiles sectors, in industries such as engineering and computing. The opportunity for fashion-textiles design is that fiber appears destined to become the carrier of new technologies, including energy-harvesting tools and ubiquitous computing applications. *Smart Dust* is one such application.

Notes

1. "Encarta Dictionary" (on-line). http://encarta.msn.com/

encnet/features/dictionary/
dictionaryhome.aspx
(accessed 12 June 2010).

2. John Storrs Hall is involved
in the field of molecular
nanotechnology, author of
*Nanofuture: What's Next for
Nanotechnology*, a fellow of the
Molecular Engineering Research
Institute, and Research Fellow
of the Institute for Molecular
Manufacturing. In 2009, Hall
was appointed president of the
Foresight Institute.

3. "Smart Dust, Design
and Engineering"
(on-line). *Wikipedia:
The Free Encyclopedia*
http://en.wikipedia.org/wiki/
Smartdust (accessed 12 June
2010).

4. HSU, T., "'Nanofiber' project
aims to turn clothes into
generators" (on-line) Physorg.
com science: physics: tech:
nano: news http://www.
physorg.com/news193558885.
html (accessed 12 June 2010).

5. Conde, J., Keles, Y., Escolano,
C., Morales, A., and Bax, L.H.
2009. "Observatory NANO
Economical Assessment/
Textile Sector Final Report
June 2009." Bax & Willems
Consulting Venturing,
Barcelona, Spain.

6. Gregory C. Rutledge is
Lammot du Pont Professor
in the Department of
Chemical Engineering at
MIT, Cambridge, MA; he
pioneered the development of
electrospinning of polymers in
the late1900s. http://
www.mit.edu/newsoffice/
2009/electrospun-fibers-
0505.html (accessed 12 June
2010).

7. "History of Polymer and
Plastics for Students"
(on-line). American Chemistry
Council 2010. http://www.
americanchemistry.com/
s_plastics/hands_on_plastics/
intro_to_plastics/students.
html (accessed 12 June 2010).

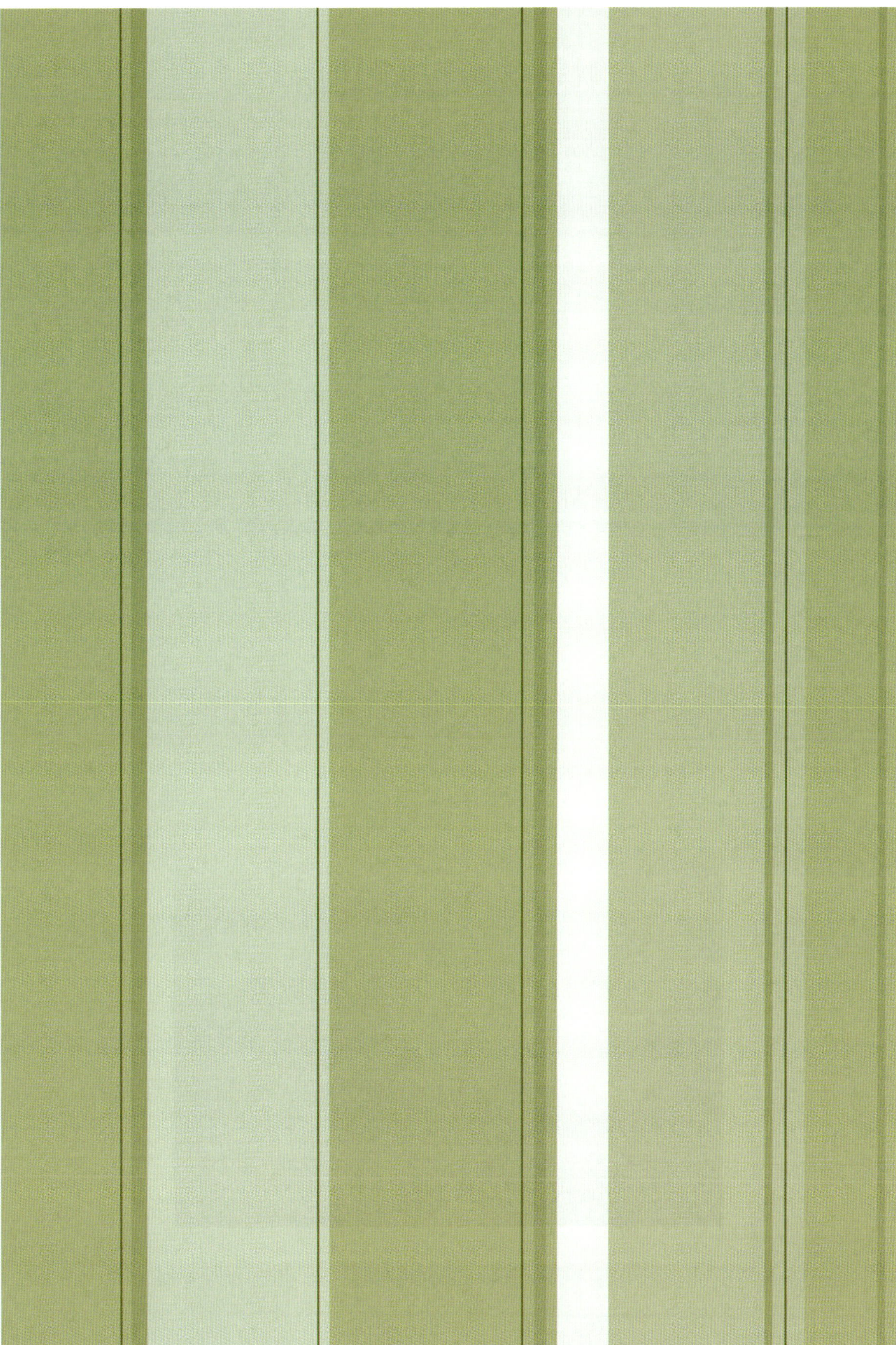

Moundville: Forgotten Textile Fragments Reveal the Past

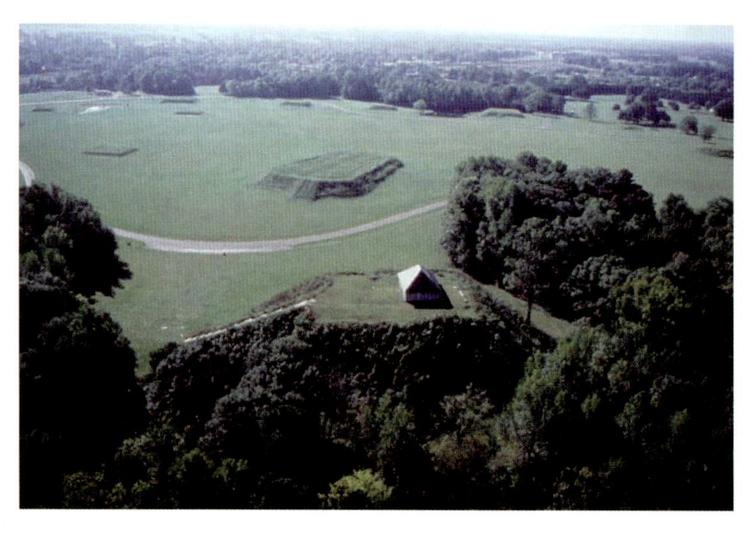

Abstract

The multi-mound site of Moundville in west central Alabama provided the samples, dated to Moundville II (AD 1250–1400) and III (AD 1400–1550) phases. Mound W, Mound R and the Rhodes site within the palisaded area provided textile remains. Textile fragments from Mound W and R are charred and small in size. The Rhodes site provided a copper breastplate with textile pseudomorphs. The fragments provide a wealth of information about technology, their social significance and use, and aspects of ritual and cultural values through dispersal. Methodology included nondestructive physical analysis of samples, light microscopy, and environmental scanning electron microscopy. Chemical analysis spectra were collected using X-ray energy dispersive spectroscopy. It was evident that the fibers from the charred samples were of two types of plant tissue, xylem and sclerenchyma. Fiber type was not determinable for the Rhodes specimen. Even though the yarn and fabric structures were comparable between the specimens collected from domestic areas and the elite burial, the fineness of the yarns that were associated with the breastplate as a prestige good indicate a refining process used for the fibers. As indicated by the specimens available, there were boundaries between residential and apparently moderate elite burials at Moundville.

Keywords: Mississippian, Moundville, pswudomorph, charred, twining, fibers

VIRGINIA WIMBERLEY AND AMANDA THOMPSON

Virginia Wimberley holds a Ph.D. in Archaeological Textiles from Ohio State University, a M.Ed. in Man-Environment Relations from Pennsylvania State University, and a B.S. in Home Economics Education from Juniata College in Huntington, PA. She is currently an assistant professor at the University of Alabama in the Department of Clothing, Textiles, and Interior Design, the College of Human Environmental Sciences. Contact information: Box 870158, 306D Doster Hall, Tuscaloosa, AL 35487-0158, vwimberl@ches.ua.edu

Amanda Thompson holds both M.S. and Ph.D. in Textile Science with a minor in Anthropology from Ohio State University and a B.A. in Anthropology from Brigham Young University. She is currently an associate professor at the University of Alabama in the Department of Clothing, Textiles, and Interior Design, the College of Human Environmental Sciences. Contact information: Box 870158, 306D Doster Hall, Tuscaloosa, AL 35487-0158, amanda.thompson@ua.edu

Textile, Volume 8, Issue 3, pp. 348–367
DOI: 10.2752/175183510X12868938341600
Reprints available directly from the Publishers.
Photocopying permitted by licence only.

Moundville: Forgotten Textile Fragments Reveal the Past

Introduction

Textiles embody information concerning their composition and the technology needed in their formation process. Fibers, dyes, pre- and post- treatments, yarn formation, and fabric construction processes can be determined from physical and chemical examination of the textile product (Emery 1966; Sibley et al. 1991; Drooker 1992; Kuttruff 1993; Sibley et al. 1996; Song et al. 1996; Spanos et al. 2007; Thompson and Simon 2008; Jakes et al. 2009). Information gleaned from textiles has been used to understand cultural concepts such as status (Cassman 2000; Kuttruff 1993; Schreffler 1988), boundaries between cultural groups (Church 1984; Petersen and Wolford 2000), socio-technical change (Hyland and Adovasio 2000) and specific cultural activities, which include labor expenditure, craft specialization, dissemination of textile skills, and burial practices (Sibley 1986; Schreffler 1988; Sibley et al. 1991; Minar 2001; Thompson and Jakes 2005).

The Moundville textile fragments, from early and mid-1970s excavations, have remained unanalyzed until the current study. They were considered insignificant when compared to other cultural remains such as pottery, stone palettes, and metallic artifacts. This article will focus on the physical analysis and some chemical analysis to describe the types of fabric present and the characteristics of the yarns and fibers and whether these fabric characteristics differ by where they were placed in the site. This information can help derive what sociological status can be gleaned from charred and mineralized fabric and their provenience.

The first consideration in analyzing perishable goods such as textiles is an assessment of the state of preservation of the fabric. Archaeological textiles are preserved due to factors that inhibit microbial growth. Usually a textile is preserved by components within the archaeological environment such as the anaerobic setting of water sites, desiccation from desert environments, or extreme temperatures found in frozen locations. The textiles found at Moundville and housed at the Office of Archaeological Research (OAR) survived due to two other preservation processes: association with metallic objects within the burial and as charred remains from exposure to fire. The two different preservation processes have different outcomes for the surviving fragments. When a fabric is exposed to metallic objects such as copper, two developments can occur. First, the metallic ions can inhibit bacterial growth and preserve the textile. This is the basis upon which many of the anti-bacterial fabrics of today are founded (Nakashima et al. 1992;

Nakashima et al. 2002; Gabbay et al. 2006; Foksowicz-Flaczyk and Walentowska 2008). Secondly, the organic components of the fabric can be slowly replaced by metallic ions mineralizing the textile to produce a "fossil" or pseudomorph of the fabric. Both of these processes may occur over time to the specimen. In the case of mineralization and the resulting pseudomorph the fabric's interlaced pattern is still discernable as are often the fiber and yarn details (Jakes and Howard 1986; Good 2001). The resulting mineralized specimen will be discolored and stiffened and, if still attached to the metallic object, not easily removed intact, as exemplified by samples studied by Wimberley (2004).

Charring of fabric often occurs due to cremation burial rituals (Thompson 2003; Thompson and Jakes 2005). Carbonization of textiles may also occur due to domestic mishaps (Thompson and Simon 2008). When a textile fragment survives due to charring, much of its organic matter has been carbonized (Srinivasan and Jakes 1997; Thompson and Jakes 2005). The textile structure and yarn detail is still discernible in most cases; however, the fabric is friable and fragile with most of the visual information such as coloration having been lost (Sibley and Jakes 1994; Jakes et al. 2009).

Textiles in this study from the Moundville site in Alabama are charred or in some cases preserved by their proximity to copper; thus two different processes of preservation are responsible for the fragments that were reviewed.

Moundville Site and the Mississippian Tradition

The samples used in this research came from the archaeological site of Moundville, Alabama (Figure 1). Moundville is a multi-mound cultural ceremonial center along the Black Warrior River and part of the civilizations of the Tombigbee River drainage area (Figure 2). The Tombigbee societies reached their cultural zeniths during the period beginning in 900 CE and ending in the late 1500s. Moundville was part of the Southeastern United States manifestation of a cultural tradition and level of social organization referred to as Mississippian. Its development was dependent upon the concomitant development of the intensification of maize cultivation. Mississippian societies stretched eastward from Illinois to Georgia and northward from Alabama to Ohio and varied considerably in their size and social complexity. They were characterized at the upper end of the continuum by large multiple-mound centers, such as Cohakia and Moundville, and at the lower end by the single-mound local center with its surrounding farmsteads as seen at Lubbub Creek and Hiwasee Island (Blitz 1993; Welch 1990; Jenkins and Krause 1986).

In terms of social complexity Mississippian societies were at the level of developing and maintained chiefdoms and ranked societies. Carneiro (1981) defined the chiefdom as being "an autonomous political unit comprising a number of villages or communities under the permanent control of a paramount chief" (45). The term "ranked societies," as used by Fried (1967), described the situation where the society had "fewer positions of valued status than individuals capable of handling them" (109–10). This stratified society then had power evident in the handling of maize production and storage and the defense of ceremonial centers, as well as the "preferential access to valued craft items" (Blitz 1993: 3). Chiefs maintained residences on the upper surface of the flattened tops of the earthen mounds, created by pooled labor commitments of the local and surrounding farmstead inhabitants. Multi-mound sites have mounds located around open plazas. Also characteristic of these stratified societies was the presence of part-time craftsmen producing items associated with symbolic imagery (Bourne 1973; Griffin 1985; Peebles and Kus 1977; Steponaitis 1986). Frequently the valued craft items were constructed from raw materials available only through extensive exchange networks, resulting in sharks' teeth from the Gulf of Mexico and copper and flint from the Midwestern United States being utilized in northwestern Georgia and west-central Alabama (Welch 1991; Marcoux 2000; King 2007). Trade in items with Southeastern Ceremonial Complex symbolism and finished prestige goods were also part of the exchange network among Mississippian sites (Brown et al. 1990). Drooker (2007) has indicated that some finished textiles, in particular those constructed with the spaced octagonal openwork (as described by Emery 1966), were part of the trade network of items for status differentiation and not made at sites such as Etowah, though they were part of the burial goods with high-status individuals in Mound C.

Figure 1
Overview of Moundville Site (Johnson 2005: 2).

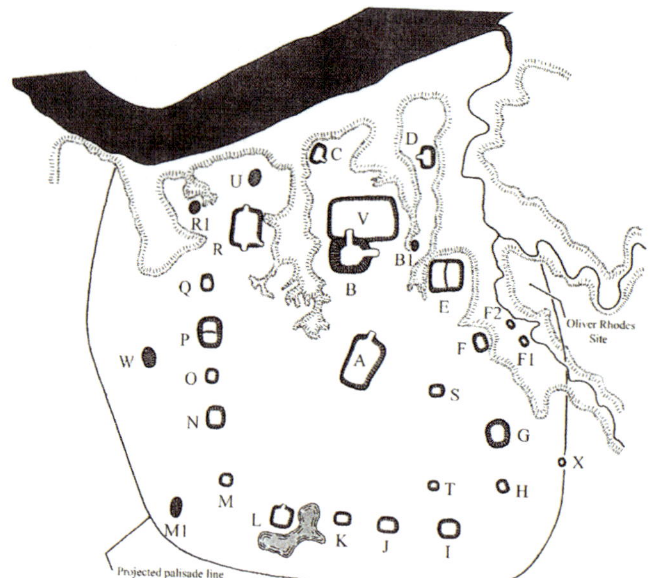

Figure 2
This view of Moundville is on the Eastern side of the site with the Black Warrior River behind and to the right. It is looking across the plaza area. Photograph courtesy of the University of Alabama Museums.

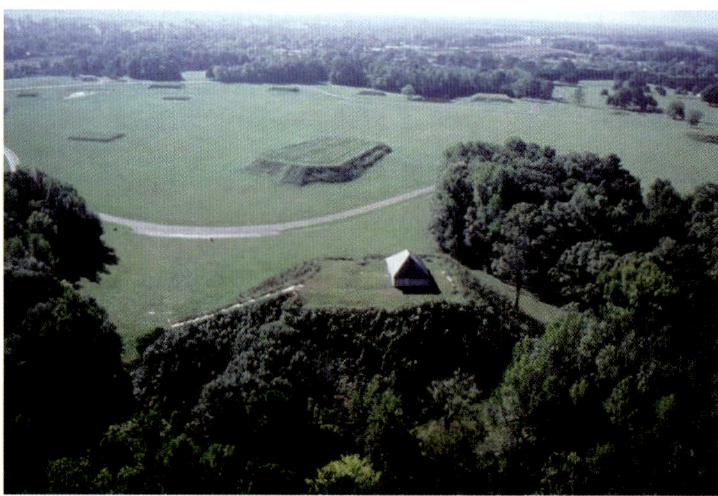

Moundville Chronology

The regional center of Moundville in the Black Warrior River Valley in west-central Alabama, developed at the end of the twelfth century after local inhabitants intensified their cultivation of maize and established several single-mound local centers with associated farmsteads (Blitz 1993). From 1250 to 1400, Moundville grew to include twenty mounds positioned around an extensive plaza and functioned at the top of a three-tiered settlement hierarchy, encompassing several single-mound centers and their farmsteads. This center produced and disseminated prestige goods and ritual objects adorned with the symbolic images of the Southeastern Ceremonial Complex such as bilobed arrows, eagle warrior, hand with eye, weeping eye, and serpents (Steponaitis 1991; Blitz 1993; Brown et al. 1990). Eventually during the fifteenth century, Moundville residents moved away from the site to other residential areas and the center became used as a ritual center and necropolis. The site grew to include twenty-nine mounds around the plaza.

The site has been extensively studied by a variety of archaeologists performing excavations and analysis of the burial populations and accompanying grave goods. The most extensive resulting in an explanation of Moundville social and political organization was accomplished by Christopher Peebles (1979). Through the analysis of 2,000 burials, Peebles demonstrated that the Moundville chiefdom had a high-ranking or superordinate social group based on inherited or ascribed status and a subordinate group based on achieved status. The superordinate group was buried in mounds as adults with copper axes, copper-covered beads, pearl beads and ritualized skeletal parts; or as adults and children in mounds and cemeteries near mounds with accompanying copper earspools, stone disks, bear teeth, and mineral pigments; and a group of adults, children, and infants in mounds and cemeteries near mounds with shell beads, galena cubes, and copper gorgets. The

subordinate group encompassed 95 percent of the burial samples and 63 percent of these individuals had no associated grave goods. Of the remaining subordinate interments, several clusters of individuals possessed bone awls, projectile points, ceramic vessels including effigy vessels and water bottles, stone celts, and shell gorgets. Prentice (1987) and Welch (1991) refined the description of the social and political organization by pointing out the difference between status items which were restricted in use to a specific segment of the population and wealth items which were valued by all in society since they give the possessor prestige.

Based upon the study of burial remains and pottery-style analyses, the chronology of Moundville has been established and refined to the following time periods: West Jefferson Phase, 900–1050; Moundville I from 1050 to 1250; Moundville II from 1250 to 1400; and Moundville III from 1400 to 1550 (Johnson 2005; Knight and Steponaitis 1998). The samples addressed in this article are primarily from Moundville II and III.

Specific Areas of the Moundville
Mound W

Although labeled as a mound, Mound W (Figure 1) was not a mound but described as a "… low natural rise west of the plaza and mound P" (Walthall and Wimberly, 1978: 121). Johnson (2005) argued that there was no evidence to support the "… statement that the area was naturally elevated before the establishment of the recognized occupied surfaces" (28). Instead it appeared to be a mound

built by "… several superimposed episodes of domestic debris and house floors, not a deliberate platform construction of mound fill episodes" (71). Burials were part of several of the later and thicker strata. Walthall and Wimberly (1978) submitted samples for radiocarbon dating: charred cloth (possibly a woven fiber bag), wood and cane fragments, a chenopodium seed, an amaranthus seed, and several eight-row corn-cob fragments all documented at forty inches (100 centimeters) below the surface. The organic components have been proposed to be from either a pit or midden debris and would be from one of the earliest two levels of the mound. A radiocarbon date of 1260±85 (uncorrected) was determined based on these organic remains (Walthall and Wimberly 1978). This would place the organic remains within the Moundville II time period. Since no other cloth has been documented in the Mound W excavation reports it has been assumed that the OAR charred cloth used for this study was used for the radiocarbon dating.

Area North of Mound R

The Michigan Field School Excavations in the 1970s worked on several areas of the Moundville site. A number of charred textile samples came from an area north of Mound R (Figure 2), close to the escarpment for the Black Warrior River. This area had continual occupation for Moundville I as a residential site. It appears to have been discontinued in use except for burials during Moundville II. By Moundville III the area was in use again perhaps as a midden dump and burial site

Figure 3
Breastplate *in situ* on soil block as it is housed in the Office of Archaeological Research, Moundville, Alabama.

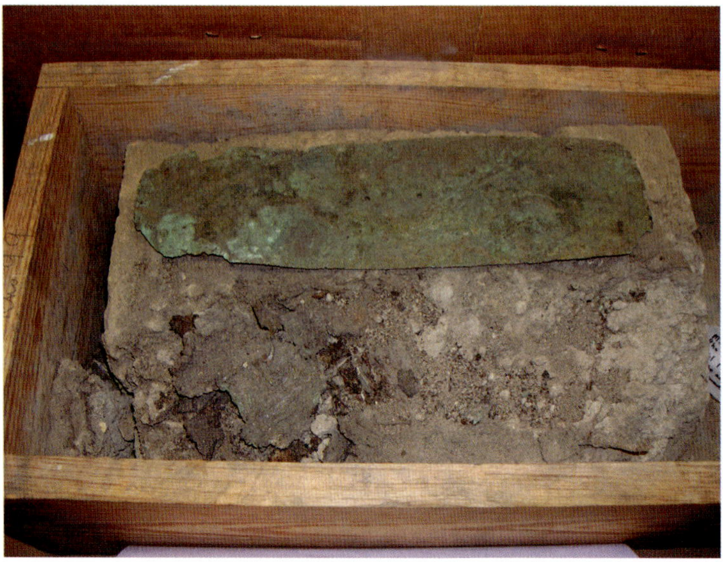

with four to eight burials (Scarry 1981, 1995). The charred textile fragments investigated in this study came from features 61A and 64A at a depth of 44 inches (112 centimeters) and 50 inches (127 centimeters) respectively. Additionally there are textile samples labeled B and C that came from this general area but no further provenience was provided.

Rhodes Site
Thirdly, the Rhodes site (Figure 2) was part of Moundville and was located inside the palisade but across the creek, behind and slightly north of the present-day Archaeology Lab. This area had burials interred during all three (I, II, III) Moundville phases. The copper breastplate with a pseudomorpic textile attached was found in association with Burial 1936. The copper breastplate from the Rhodes site was extracted from its *in situ* location as part of a soil

block (Figure 3) as it was stored in the OAR. Soil under the plate was probed for any textile remains, but only two talons and colored clay nodules resting on cane were found. Additionally the soil block and breastplate were analyzed by X-ray imaging for possible artifacts associated with burials but no additional dense items were found. Prior to our analysis there appears to have been a resin placed on the breastplate and surrounding soil areas to aid in preservation until the soil block could be more closely studied. Since it was not part of the NAGPRA inventory, there was no information as to age and gender of the person interred in the burial or whether other burial goods were associated with it. Peebles (1979) in his study of Moundville skeletal remains determined that males of the superordinate group were most associated with copper artifacts. Peebles (1979) also determined based on ceramic data that Burial 1936 could be temporally assigned

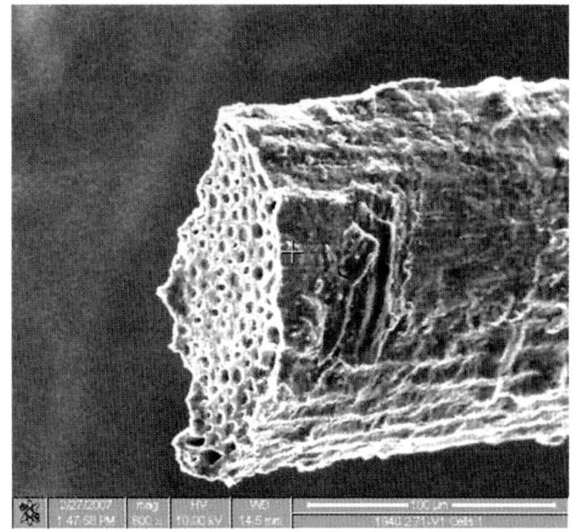

Figure 4
Fiber from Mound W charred specimens ESEM photograph. The high count of voided areas indicates this fiber type to be xylem. Xylem tissues carry nutrients, are vascular bundles, and have numerous small pits.

to the early Moundville III time period. During Moundville III, the Rhodes site portion of Moundville was "... expanded with larger structures and richer burials (Powell 1988: 10)."

Methods

For the textile analysis of the charred and pseudomorphic samples the methodology included nondestructive physical analysis of samples for determination of fragment size, yarn size and type, textile construction, and thread count. For the area north of Mound R nine charred samples were available. For Mound W an additional four charred samples were analyzed. For the Rhodes site one breastplate with an attached pseudomorph was examined.

Light microscopy was done with a Microcolor 2000 system with a Leica macroscope, a Nikon Ds5M camera and CVS 9000 software and NIS Elements Acquisition and Analysis program for specimens from north of Mound R, Mound W, and the Rhodes site. A FEI Quanta 3D environmental scanning electron microscope (ESEM) was used to acquire secondary electron images and qualitative chemical identification of the fibers through X-ray energy dispersive spectroscopy (XEDS). The XEDS detector was equipped with a beryllium window and used Genesis software. The images were collected at settings of 1 torr, 10.00 kiloelectronvolts, and 1.7 nanoamperes for samples. The ESEM was chosen because the samples could be used as they were from the collection and no carbon coating was needed for preparation.

Results

ESEM analysis provided evidence of two fiber types within the charred samples. From the interior cellular structure and exterior surface, it was evident that the fibers were plant. The high count of voided areas indicated this fiber type to be xylem. Xylem tissues carry nutrients, are vascular bundles, and have numerous small pits; an example of this type of fiber from Mound W is in Figure 4.

The second fiber type is sclerenchyma, a supportive fiber tissue of the plant that appears denser with fewer voided areas; an example of this type of fiber from Mound W can be found in Figure 5. This type of plant tissue is typically referred to as bast fiber, examples of which are ramie, hemp, and flax. It is not surprising that these two fiber types are in association because of their location within plants.

XEDS spectra supported the visual identification of the fibers as being from plant sources. Figure 6 is a representative spectrum. Several peaks (iron, magnesium, aluminum, silica, phosphorus, and calcium) are indicative of the samples being associated with soil. Since most of the soil components are bonded with oxygen, that explains the high oxygen peak. Since there was no sulfur peak that would indicate a protein fiber, the plant origin of the fibers was verified. There was a large carbon peak which would be expected since the samples are charred.

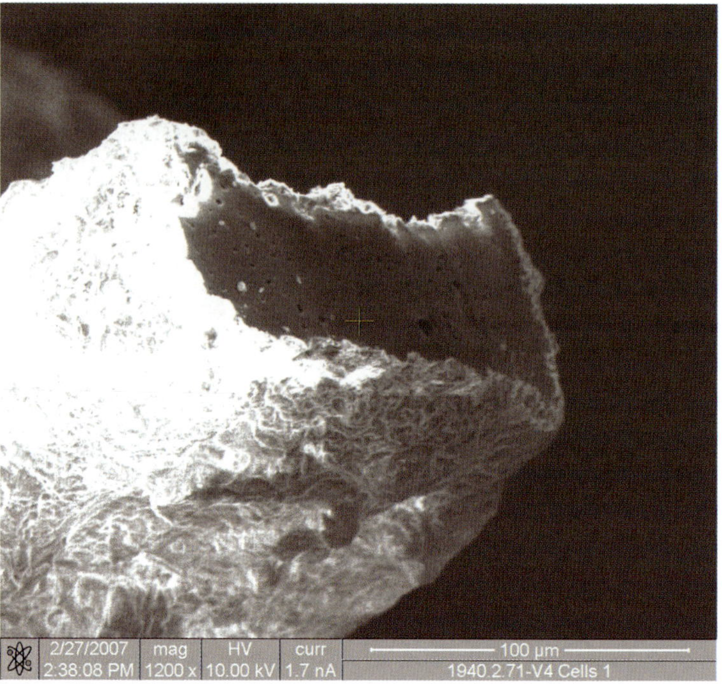

Figure 5
Fiber from Mound W charred specimens ESEM photograph. This is an example of sclerenchyma, typically referred to as bast fibers, a type of supportive fiber tissue of the plant that appears more dense with fewer voided areas.

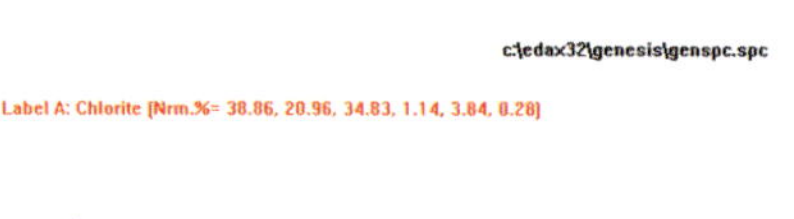

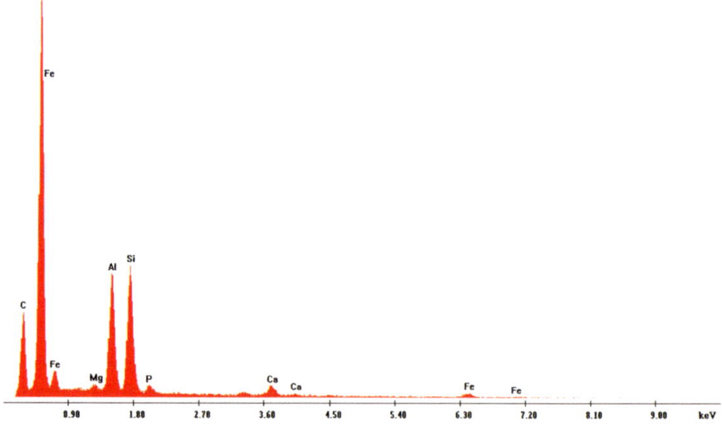

Figure 6
Representative XEDS spectrum from charred textile specimen.

Tables 1 and 2 list the results of Scarry's (1986) analysis of flora remains for the Moundville center during Moundville I, II, and III chronology for potential fiber donors. It is reasonable to consider that efficiency in collection of fibers would be teamed with collection of resources that could also provide

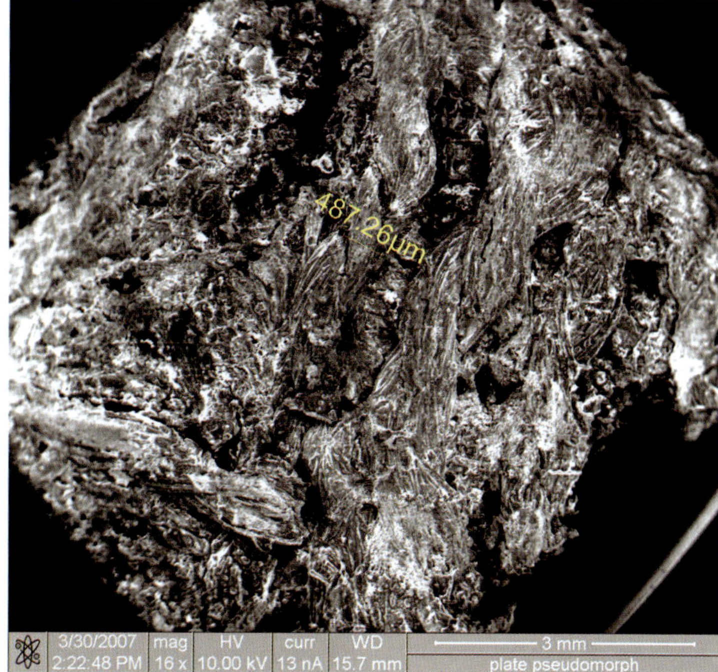

Figure 7
ESEM picture of pseudomorphic textile fragment as seen on the Rhodes breastplate. S plying of the yarns is observed.

food and basketry materials, such as white oak for basketry and mulberry for fiber. The White site (Scarry 1986) was a subservient supplier of materials to Moundville, and Table 3 lists the carbonized seed finds from the late Moundville phase at this site. Some of these food-source plants are another example of dual use of resources. Some of these can provide fiber for textiles and some can provide colorant materials—specifically bedstraw, pokeweed, and sumac. A demand of the chiefdom was that the farmsteads provide resources to those in residence at the ceremonial center at Moundville (Blitz 1993; Brown et al. 1990; Peebles and Kus 1977).

Fiber data for the Rhodes site breastplate pseudomorph could not be collected due to coating of the surface with resin. Key characteristics of the fibers could not be viewed and, therefore, the fiber types could not be identified.

Yarns were only present on the obverse side of the copper breastplate next to the soil. Yarns attached to the breastplate were on average 0.68 millimeters in diameter for the plied yarns; very few measurements were able to be made due to how the pseudomorph was adhered to the breastplate. Both S and Z plying were present. Ply direction was documented by an ESEM micrograph showing S plied yarns as seen in Figure 7 and Z plied yarns as seen in Figure 8.

All yarns in the charred samples had two plies and were S twisted with the singles having negligible or low Z twist. Table 4 lists yarn diameters for all the available charred specimens from the two Mound areas. Diameters of the yarns of the charred samples ranged for active elements from 4.87 to 1.06 millimeters, which included one appreciatively larger textile fragment that had thick and thin singles composing the yarns. Even though this was a larger fragment there still was not enough of this sample to know if this was done for surface effect or was an anomaly. In looking at the diameters of the active elements there is a variation between the area north of Mound R which has a range of 1.06 to 2.15 millimeters in comparison to Mound W with a range of 1.93 to 3.08 millimeters: e.g. Mound W's active yarns are generally thicker. The passive elements for the charred samples varied from 2.25 to 2.17 millimeters, which is a much narrower range, and therefore appear to be more

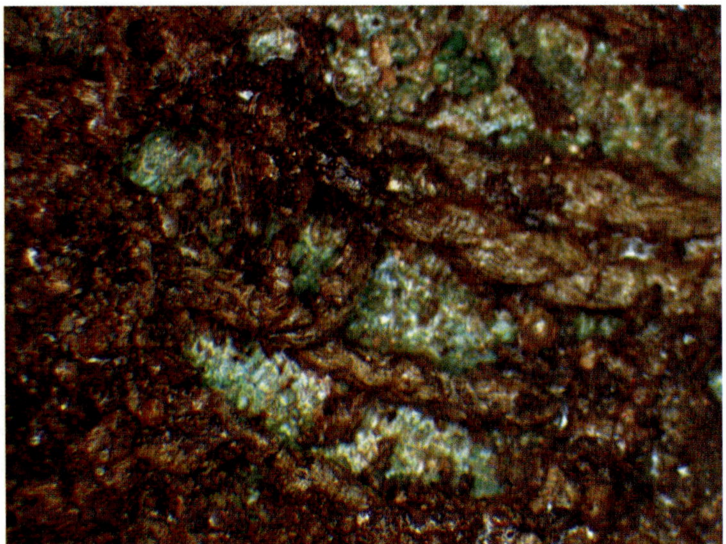

Figure 8
Pseudomorphic textile fragment as seen on the Rhodes breastplate, light micrograph. Z plying of the yarns is observed.

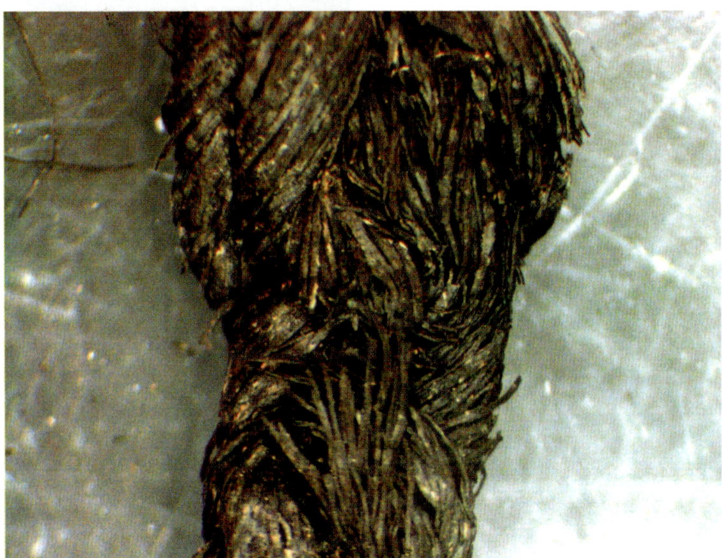

Figure 9
Mound W charred three-strand braid.

consistent. The measurements composing the diameter of the singles may be varying as a function of the fiber size due to processing.

The only fragments that did not have two-ply yarns are the two braid samples from Mound W and Michigan Field School excavations north of Mound R that had comparatively thick singles employed in a three-strand braid as seen in Figures 9 and 10. The diameters in the yarns that make up the three-strand braids are much larger than the active yarn diameters in the two-strand twining. An example of two-strand twining is in Figure 11, a specimen from the Michigan Field School

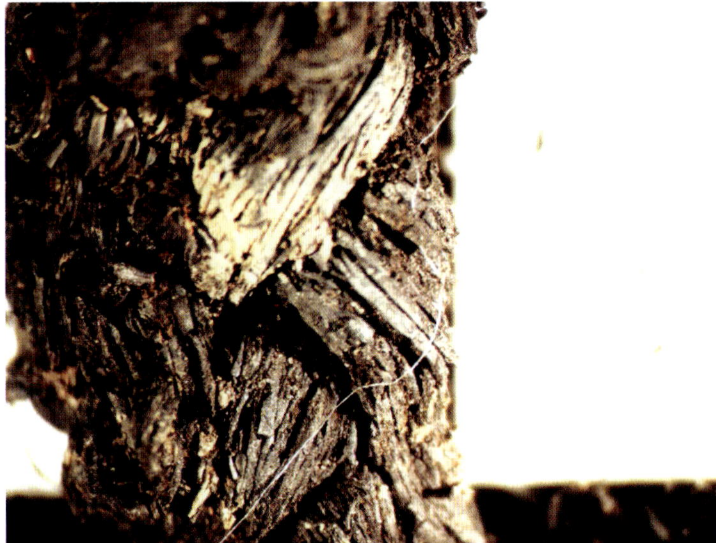

Figure 10
Michigan Field School Excavations North of Mound R labeled C unknown provenience charred three-strand braid.

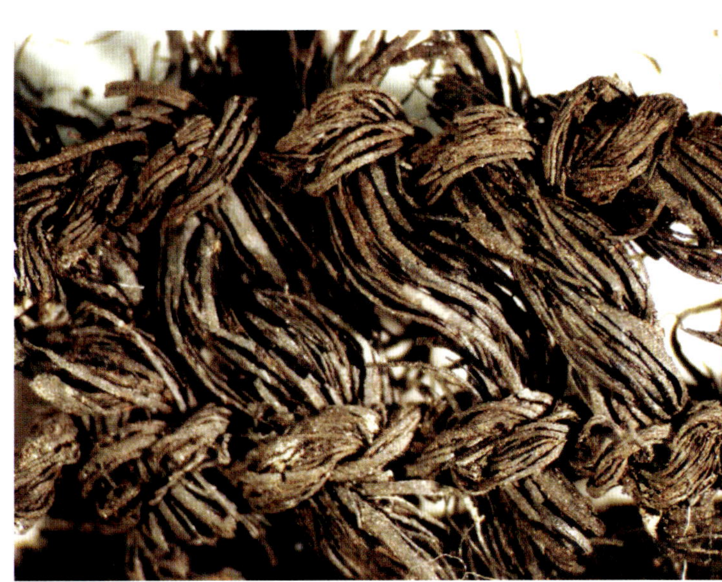

Figure 11
Charred textile fragment from Michigan Field School excavations North of Mound R labeled C unknown provenience. The specimen has two-ply yarns with two identified active yarns and five passive yarns.

excavations north of Mound R labeled "C unknown provenience" had two-ply yarns with two active yarns and five passive yarns. Warp and weft is not designated in twining when there are no selvages/finished edges.

There are two basic structures: three-strand braid, as seen in Figures 9 and 10, and two-strand twining as seen in Figure 12. Measurements have been listed in Table 5 for the charred fabric structures. The two-strand twining structure varied by thread count as illustrated in Figures 12, 13, and 14. The majority of the two-strand twined specimens had 5 millimeters (Figure 12) or more space between the active elements. One specimen had spacing at 1 mm for the active element (Figure 13); it could have been classified as compact two-strand twining. The other characteristic of the textile structures that varied was the spacing between the passives elements. The majority

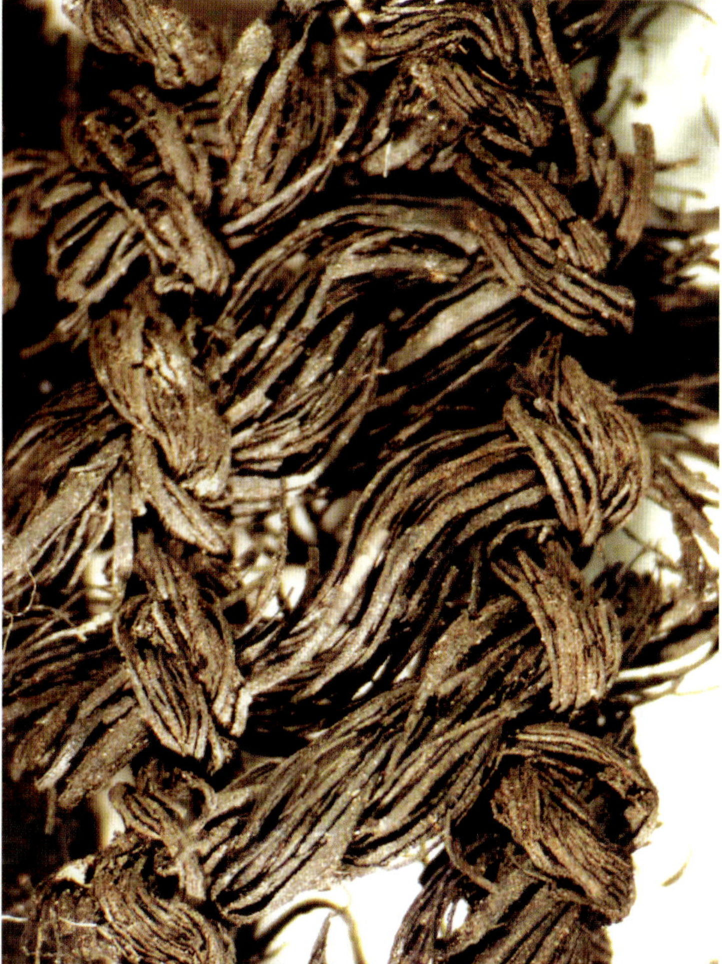

Figure 12
Charred textile fragment from the Michigan Field School Excavations North of Mound R, example of two-strand twining. There is space of 5 millimeters or more between the active elements; the passive elements are abutted.

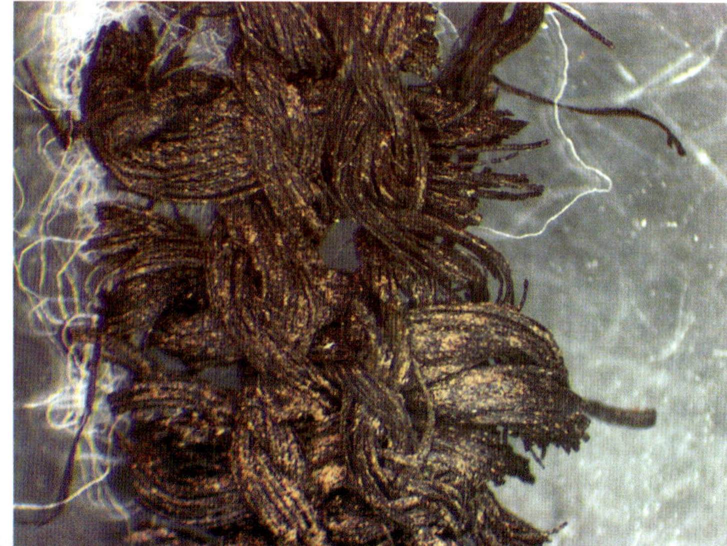

Figure 13
Charred textile fragment from the Michigan Field School Excavations North of Mound R, example of two-strand twining. There is space of 1 millimeter between active elements.

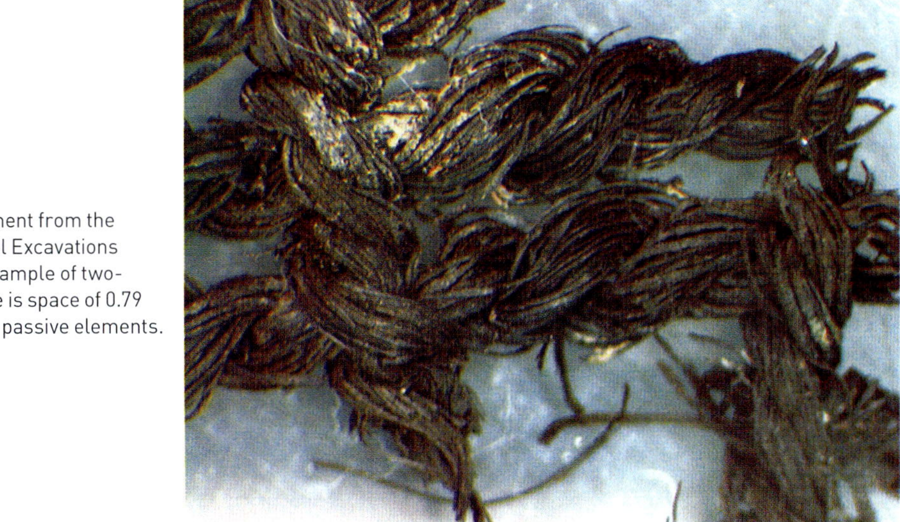

Figure 14
Charred textile fragment from the Michigan Field School Excavations North of Mound R, example of two-strand twining. There is space of 0.79 millimeters between passive elements.

of the passive yarns were adjacent to one another, while there was one example that had a spacing of 0.79 millimeters as seen in Figure 14. Yarn spacing was not calculated for the pseudomorph from the Rhodes site because observed fragments did not have more than one active element available.

Discussion

All three specimen sites are from outside the central plaza and mound area and had multiple uses as residential, midden, and burial locations. Steponaitis (1998), who analyzed the burials and display goods at Moundville, commented that though Moundville was a major Mississippian ceremonial center, few burials could be characterized as lavish, and those exceptions identified as such were found only in three mounds (C, D, H) and the Rhodes site.

What can be said about the surviving interlaced textile fragments from the Moundville site? First, there was no identifiable animal fiber. Any fibers identifiable were of plant origin; specifically sclerenchyma and xylem were found in either a charred or mineralized state. If animal fibers had also been charred they should have had at least an equal chance of survival as the plant fibers that were found. Animal fibers are more difficult to ignite than plant, self-extinguish when ignited, and shrink away from the area where the flame is applied. Individual feathers tend to ignite and burn easily. If the feathers are used in groups there is less area available around the feather material for oxygen and burning is slower. Pseudomorphic formation should not have been influenced by a particular fiber type.

Other Mississippian sites similarly have had a predominance of plant-fiber textiles where some were supplemented with animal fibers and feathers (Schreffler 1988; Drooker 1992; Sibley and Jakes 1994). Feather usage was usually associated with higher-ranking individuals at these sites. Since the majority of these samples are from Moundville areas associated with non-elites, feathers would not be accepted. Soil at Moundville does not seem to be a contributing factor to the paucity of protein fibers. The soil is characterized at Moundville as sandy loam which has a neutral to near-neutral pH. The soil alkalinity/acidity should not have been a factor in fiber survival. There could be a preservation problem with the lack of copper association with the textiles which would affect both animal and plant fiber. The fact that no animal or feather fibers were documented could be a result of excavators not recognizing fibrous material during early excavation at Moundville when nonperishable artifacts were considered more significant. Conclusions as to the lack of any animal fibers or feathers being present and their significance for social stratification cannot be made with the fourteen specimens.

A second area of analysis is the consideration of twist being employed in yarn formation. In order to form a yarn, fibers have to be of such a length that either twist is not needed to create a unit or shorter fibers are held together in a continuous strand by clockwise Z or counterclockwise S twisting. This characteristic of twist direction alternates as more units are joined to form plied yarns; therefore, if a single were spun Z it must be plied S in order to keep the yarn from unraveling. While there are only two choices of twist direction at initial twisting or ply twisting, twist direction has been the subject of much debate and study by archaeologists trying to understand the archaeological record. Twist direction has been studied from the point of view of skill or knowledge acquisition, namely learning frameworks (Minar 2001; Crown 2001; Wallaert-Petre 2001). Twist direction has also been investigated as a possible method of tracking movements of peoples across landscapes by use of final twist percentages in cordage or cordage-marked pottery (Minar 2000; Peterson and Wolford 2000). There seems to be a consistency of twist direction used by individuals within a residency area—namely that people are taught to spin in a particular twist direction for a singles yarn and then ply with the opposite direction to keep the yarn from unraveling that overrides the tendency of a fiber to rotate in a particular direction (Bird 1956; Adovasio and Maslowski 1980; Kent 1983; Minar 2000; Petersen and Wolford 2000). While Minar (2001) illustrates in the Southeastern United States that there maybe separation of groups both temporally and geographically by final twist direction, she cautions that this can only "... potentially define a specific community of practice" (397).

At Moundville, charred textile specimens which are not associated with burials or high-status artifacts were made with Z or negligible twist singles which were then plied with S twist or braided. What is interesting is that the Rhodes-site pseudomorph from a burial with a high-status artifact (breastplate) has both S and Z plied yarns. While the sample is small and we do not know if this paired use of twist is an anomaly or not, it is a separating factor for Rhodes versus specimens from Mound W and the area north of Mound R. In terms of learning frameworks or spatial tracking the Moundville textile sample is too limited. There seems to be nothing else in the archaeological data for Moundville that would lead one to believe that there are two separate production groups between Rhodes, Mound W, and the area north of Mound R.

Braid was documented from Mound W and the area north of Mound R as charred fragments. The braids are the only textiles made from single yarns. Their uses may have been as a decorative element on a textile surface or they may have functioned as a means of closure or as an attachment for decorative copper symbol badges. It is interesting to note that there is a significant difference in the single yarn diameters between Mound W (4.87 millimeters) and the specimen from the area north of Mound R (8.18 millimeters). This area (area north of Mound R) along the riverbank has also been shown to be a manufacturing area for display goods (Marcoux 2000; Steponaitis 1998); therefore, the function of the braid might be for something other than apparel. The larger braid single diameter at 8.18 millimeters would provide a greater strength without using a plied yarn. Using a braid instead of a plied yarn might provide enhanced tensile strength and stability of the component parts upon extensibility. The braids which were composed of 4.87 millimeter singles could have had different usage than those braids composed of 8.18 millimeter single yarns.

The third area of analysis was fabric construction. For the charred samples, there were no alternate pair twining examples, which are typical of other Mississippian sites (Schreffler 1988; Drooker 1992). Textile structures of the specimens from Moundville were categorized as: 1) spaced twined with space between active elements, no spacing between the passive elements was the majority; 2) there was a smaller subset of spaced twined with spacing between the passive elements; 3) compact twining with no spacing between active elements; and 4) three-strand braiding. The breastplate pseudomorph from the Rhodes site has possibly two-strand spaced-weft twining based on the observation of one active element and a group of passive yarns. There appear to be fringes. The use of fringe as decoration is in line with Steponaitis's (1986) findings that display goods functioned as "costumery" and religious iconography. Yarns from the pseudomorph were on average 0.6 millimeters finer than yarns from the charred samples. The charring process causes shrinkage (Srinivasan and Jakes 1997) in fibers and the pseudomorphic process generally causes an expansion in the fibers as the metallic salts are absorbed and replace the organic

portions of the fibers (Jakes and Howard 1986). Even with the shrinkage caused by charring and the slight expansion caused by absorption of copper corrosion, the breastplate yarns remain much finer than the yarns in the charred textiles.

Even though the yarn and fabric structures are comparable between the specimens collected from domestic areas and those associated with an elite burial, the fineness of the yarns that are associated with the breastplate as a prestige good indicate an extraction process that would result in finer plant-fiber bundles. The use of both S and Z plying twist in creating two-ply yarns in association with the breastplate with no occurrence of Z plying in the charred specimens from Mound W and the area north of Mound R may be another significant factor for elites. Another status-differentiation factor associated with the breastplate textiles is their association with two raptor-bird talons which were located under the breastplate on top of matting. Welch (1991) indicates in his study of artifact classes found at the Moundville ceremonial center in comparison with those at single mound sites that bird talons are a status indicator since they appear only at the Moundville center. This indicates from the specimens available that there are boundaries between residential and apparently moderate elite burials.

Implications and Further Research

While archaeologists at Moundville are looking at other types of artifacts for their analysis of status differentiation, it is hoped that

this research utilizing what limited textile evidence is available from Moundville will supplement their findings for the analysis of group dynamics at this site. Even with this small sample we are seeing differences between elites and non-elites in ritually included textiles versus randomly deposited textiles.

Archaeological records indicate there should be additional breastplates that have attached pseudomorphs from the Moundville site that were unavailable for this study. Future work would involve the location of these breastplates and analysis of the fiber, yarn, and fabric structures of these pseudomorphs to increase the data base for generating hypotheses about the groups participating in the Moundville society. The authors would also like to look at the possible remains of cordage associated with copper earspools from these same study areas within the site. Access to these other pseudomorphic textiles attached to breastplates or textiles associated with copper earspools would increase the number of elite textiles in comparison to midden-deposited textiles for drawing sociological conclusions.

Acknowledgments

The authors would like to gratefully thank the Office of Archaeological Research at Moundville and its staff for the loan of the artifacts and the use of their library. Special thanks to Eugene M. Futato.

References

Adovasio, J.M. and Maslowski, R.F. 1980. "Textile Sand Cordage." In T.F. Lynch (ed.) *Guitarrero Cave*, pp. 253–90. New York: Academic Press.

Bird, J. 1956. Appendix 2. "Fabrics, Basketry and Matting as Revealed by Impressions on Pottery." In W.A. Fairservis (ed.) *Excavations in the Quetta Valley, West Pakistan* 45(2): 372–7. New York: Anthropological Papers of the American Museum of National History.

Blitz, J.H. 1993. *Ancient Chiefdoms of the Tombigbee*. Tuscaloosa and London: University of Alabama Press.

Bourne, E.G. (ed.). 1973. *Narratives of the Career of Hernando de Soto in the Conquest of Florida*. Reprinted AMS Press, New York. Originally published 1922, New York: Allerton.

Brown, J.A., Kreber, R.A., and Winter, H.D. 1990. "Trade and the Evolution of Exchange Relations at the Beginning of the Mississippian Period." In B.D. Smith (ed.) *The Mississippian Emergence*, pp. 251–80. Washington, D.C.: Smithsonian Institution Press.

Carneiro, R.L. 1981. "The Chiefdom: Precursor of the State." In G.D. Jones and R.R. Kantz (eds) *The Transition to Statehood in the New World*, pp. 37–79. New York: Cambridge University Press.

Cassman, V. 2000. "Prehistoric Andean Ethnicity and Status: The Textile Evidence." In P.B. Drooker and L.D. Webster (eds) *Beyond Cloth and Cordage: Archaeological Textile Research in the Americas*, pp. 253–66. Salt Lake City: University of Utah Press.

Church, F. 1984. "Textiles as Markers of Ohio Hopewell Social Identities." *Mid-Continential Journal of Archaeology* 9: 1–25.

Crown, P.L. 2001. "Learning to Make Pottery in the Prehispanic American Southwest." *Journal of Anthropological Research* 57(4): 451–70.

Drooker, P.B. 1992. *Mississippian Village Textiles at Wickliffe*. Tuscaloosa, AL: University of Alabama Press.

Drooker, P.B. 2007. "Octagonal Openworks and Mississippian Boundaries." In Proceedings of the 72nd Annual Meeting of the Society for American Archaeology, April 25–9. Austin, TX, pg. 135.

Emery, I. 1966. *The Primary Structures of Fabric*. Washington, D.C.: Textile Museum.

Fried, M.H. 1967. *The Evolution of Political Society: An Essay in Political Anthropology*. New York: Random House.

Foksowicz-Flaczyk, J. and Walentowska, J. 2008. "Eco-friendly Antimicrobial Finishing of Natural Fibres." *Molecular Crystals and Liquid Crystals* 484: 207–12.

Gabbay, J., Borkow, G., Mishal, J., Magen, E., Zatcoff, R., and Shemer-Avni, Y. 2006. "Copper Oxide Impregnated Textiles with Potent Biocidal Activities." *Journal of Industrial Textiles* 35(4): 323–35.

Good, I. 2001. "Archaeological Textiles: A Review of Current Research." *Annual Review of Anthropology* 30: 209–26.

Griffin, J.B. 1985. "Changing Concepts of the Prehistoric Mississippian Cultures of the Eastern United States." In R. Badger and L.A. Clayton (eds) *Alabama and the Borderlands: From Prehistory to*

Statehood, pp. 40–63. Tuscaloosa, AL: University of Alabama Press.

Hyland, D.C. and Adovasio, J.M. 2000. "The Mexican Connection: A Study of Sociotechnical Change in Perishable Manufacture and Food Production in Prehistoric New Mexico." In P. B. Drooker and L.D. Webster (eds) *Beyond Cloth and Cordage: Archaeological Textile Research in the Americas*, pp. 141–60. Salt Lake City: University of Utah Press.

Jakes, K.A. and Howard III, J.H. 1986. "Replacement of Protein and Cellulose Fibers by Copper Minerals and the Formation of Textile Pseudomorphs." In H. Zeronian and H. Needles (eds) *Conservation and Characterization of Historical Paper and Textile Materials*, pp. 277–87. Advances in Chemistry Series No. 212. Washington, D.C.: American Chemical Society.

Jakes, K.A., Thompson, A., and Baldia, C. 2009. "Revealing Clues from Textile Dust through Microscopy, Infrared Spectroscopy, and X-ray Microanalysis." *Textile: The Journal of Cloth and Culture* 8(3).

Jenkins, N.J. and Krause, R.A. 1986. *The Tombigbee Watershed in Southeastern Prehistory*. Tuscaloosa, AL: University of Alabama Press.

Johnson, P.A. 2005. "The Occupational History of Mound 'W' at Moundville, Alabama." Master's thesis. University of Alabama, Tuscaloosa.

Kent, K.P. 1983. *Prehistoric Textiles of the Southwest*. Santa Fe, NM: School of American Research.

King, A. (ed.). 2007. *The Southeastern Ceremonial Complex: Chronology, Content, Context*. Tuscaloosa, AL: University of Alabama Press.

Knight, V.J. and Steponaitis, V.P. (eds). 1998. *Archaeology of Moundville Chiefdom*. Washington, D.C.: Smithsonian Institution Press.

Kuttruff, J.T. 1993. "Mississippian Period Status Differentiation through Textile Analysis: A Caddoan Example." *American Antiquity* 58(1): 125–45.

Marcoux, J.B. 2000. "Display Goods, Production, and Circulation in the Moundville Chiefdom: A Mississippian Dilemma." Masters thesis. University of Alabama, Tuscaloosa.

Minar, C.J. 2000. "Spinning and Plying: Anthropological Directions." In P.B. Drooker and L.D. Webster (eds) *Beyond Cloth and Cordage: Archaeological Textile Research in the Americas*, pp. 85–99. Salt Lake City: University of Utah Press.

Minar, C.J. 2001. "Motor Skills and the Learning Process: The Conservation of Cordage Final Twist Direction in Communities of Practice." *Journal of Anthropological Research* 57(4): 381–406.

Nakashima, T., Yoshioka, M., Fuse, G., and Akio, E. 1992. "Study on Antimicrobial and Deodorant Finish of Textiles, Part 2: The Ability of Wool Fabrics finished with Copper, Zinc, or Tin to Maintain their Bactericidal Efficacy after Laundering and Pre-wash Light Exposure." *Bokin Bobai* 20(2): 69–76.

Nakashima, T., Matsuo, M., Yaida, O., and Sakagami, Y. 2002. "Effects of Laundering and Light-exposure on the Antimicrobial Activity of Cotton Fabrics Finished with Metal Salts." *Biocontrol Science* 7(2): 83–90.

Peebles, C.S. 1979. "Moundville: The Organization of a Prehistoric Community and Culture." Ph.D. dissertation, University of California Santa Barbara.

Peebles, C.S. and Kus, S.M. 1977. "Some Archaeological Correlates of Ranked Societies." *American Antiquity* 42: 421–48.

Petersen, J.B. and Wolford, J.A. 2000. "Spin and Twist as Cultural Markers: A New England Perspective on Native Fiber Industries." In P.B. Drooker and L.D. Webster (eds) *Beyond Cloth and Cordage: Archaeological Textile Research in the Americas*, pp. 101–18. Salt Lake City: University of Utah Press.

Powell, M.L. 1988. *Status and Health in Prehistory: A Case Study of the Moundville Chiefdom*. Washington: Smithsonian Institution Press.

Prentice, G. 1987. "Marine Shells as Wealth Items in Mississippian Societies." *Midcontinental Journal of Archaeology* 12: 193–223.

Scarry, C.M. 1981. "The University of Michigan Moundeville Excavations: 1978–1979." *Southeastern Archaeological Conference Bulletin* 24: 87–90.

Scarry, C.M. 1986. "Change in Plant Procurement and Production during the Emergence of the Moundville

Chiefdom." Ph.D. dissertation, Ann Arbor, MI: University of Michigan, University Microfilms.

Scarry, C.M. 1995. *Excavations on the Northwest Riverbank at Moundville: Investigations of a Moundville I Residential Area.* Tuscaloosa, AL: University of Alabama Museums Office of Archeological Services Report of Investigations 72.

Schreffler, V.L. 1988. "Burial Status Differentiation as Evidenced by Fabrics from Etowah Mound C, Georgia." Unpublished doctoral dissertation, Ohio State University, Columbus.

Sibley, L.R. 1986. "Use of Pseudomorphic Evidence in the Reconstruction of Ancient Fabric Technologies." In J.S. Olin and M.J. Blackman (eds), *24th International Archaeometry Symposium,* Smithsonian Institution Press.

Sibley, L.R. and Jakes, K.A. 1994. "Coloration in Etowah Textile from Burial No. 57." In D.N. Scott and P. Meyers (eds) *Archaeometry of Pre-Columbian Sites and Artifacts,* pp. 395–418. Getty Conservation Institute, J. Paul Getty Trust, Los Angeles, CA.

Sibley, LR., Jakes, K.A., and Larson, L.H. 1996. "Inferring Behavior and Function from an Etowah Fabric Incorporating Feathers." In J.B. Petersen (ed.), *A Most Indispensable Art,* pp. 73–87. Knoxville, TN: University of Tennessee Press.

Sibley, L.R., Swinker, M.E., and Jakes, K.A. 1991. "The Use of Pattern Reproduction in Reconstructing Etowah Textile Remains." *Ars Textrina* 15: 179–202.

Song, C.A., Jakes, K.A., and Yerkes R.W. 1996. "Seip Hopewell Textiles Analysis and Cultural Implications." *Midcontinental Journal of Archaeology* 21(2): 247–65.

Spanos, M., Wimberley, V. and Thompson, A. 2007. "Osceola's Garter: An Analysis of a 19th Century Native American Textile." *Florida Anthropologist* 60(2–3): 139–52.

Srinivasan, R. and Jakes, K.A. 1997. "Optical and Scanning Electron Microscopic Study of the Effects of Charring on Indian Hemp (*Apocynum cannabinum L.*) Fibers." *Journal of Archaeological Science* 24: 517–27.

Steponaitis, V.P. 1986. "Prehistoric Archaeology in the Southeastern United States, 1970–1985." *Annual Review of Anthropology* 15: 363–404.

Steponaitis, V.P. 1991. "Contrasting Patterns of Mississippian Development." In T.K. Earle (ed.) *Chiefdoms: Power, Economy, and Ideology,* pp. 193–228. Cambridge and New York: Cambridge University Press.

Steponaitis, V.P. 1998. "Population Ttrends at Moundville." In V. Knight, and V. Steponaitis (eds) *Archaeology of the Moundville Chiefdom,* pp. 26–43. Washington, D.C.: Smithsonian Institution Press.

Thompson, A.J. 2003. "Textiles as Indicators of Hopwellian Culture Burial Practices." Ph.D. dissertation. Columbus, OH, Ohio State University.

Thompson, A.J. and Jakes, K.A. 2005. "Textile Evidence for Ohio Hopewell Burial Practices."

Southeastern Archaeology 24(2): 137–41.

Thompson, A. and Simon, M. 2008. "An Analysis of Textile Fragments from the Janey B. Goode Site." *Mid-Continental Journal of Archaeology* 33(2): 155–82.

Wallaert-Petre, H. 2001. "Learning How to Make the Right Pots: Apprenticeship Strategies and Material Culture, a Case Study in Handmade Pottery from Cameroon." *Journal of Anthropological Research* 57(4): 471–93.

Walthall, J.A., and Wimberly, S.B. 1978. "Mississippian Chronology in the Black Warrior Valley: Radiocarbon Dates from Bessemer and Moundville." *Journal of Alabama Archaeology* 24(2): 118–24.

Welch, P.D. 1990. "Mississippian Emergence in West-Central Alabama." In B.D. Smith (ed.) *The Mississippian Emergence*, pp. 197–224. Washington, D.C.: Smithsonian Institution Press.

Welch, P.D. 1991. *Moundville's Economy*. Tuscaloosa, AL: University of Alabama Press.

Wimberley, V.S. 2004. "Preserved Textiles on Hopewell Copper." In P.B. Drooker (ed.) *Perishable Material Culture in the Northeast*, pp. 69–85. New York State Museum Bulletin 500. Albany, NY: State University of New York.

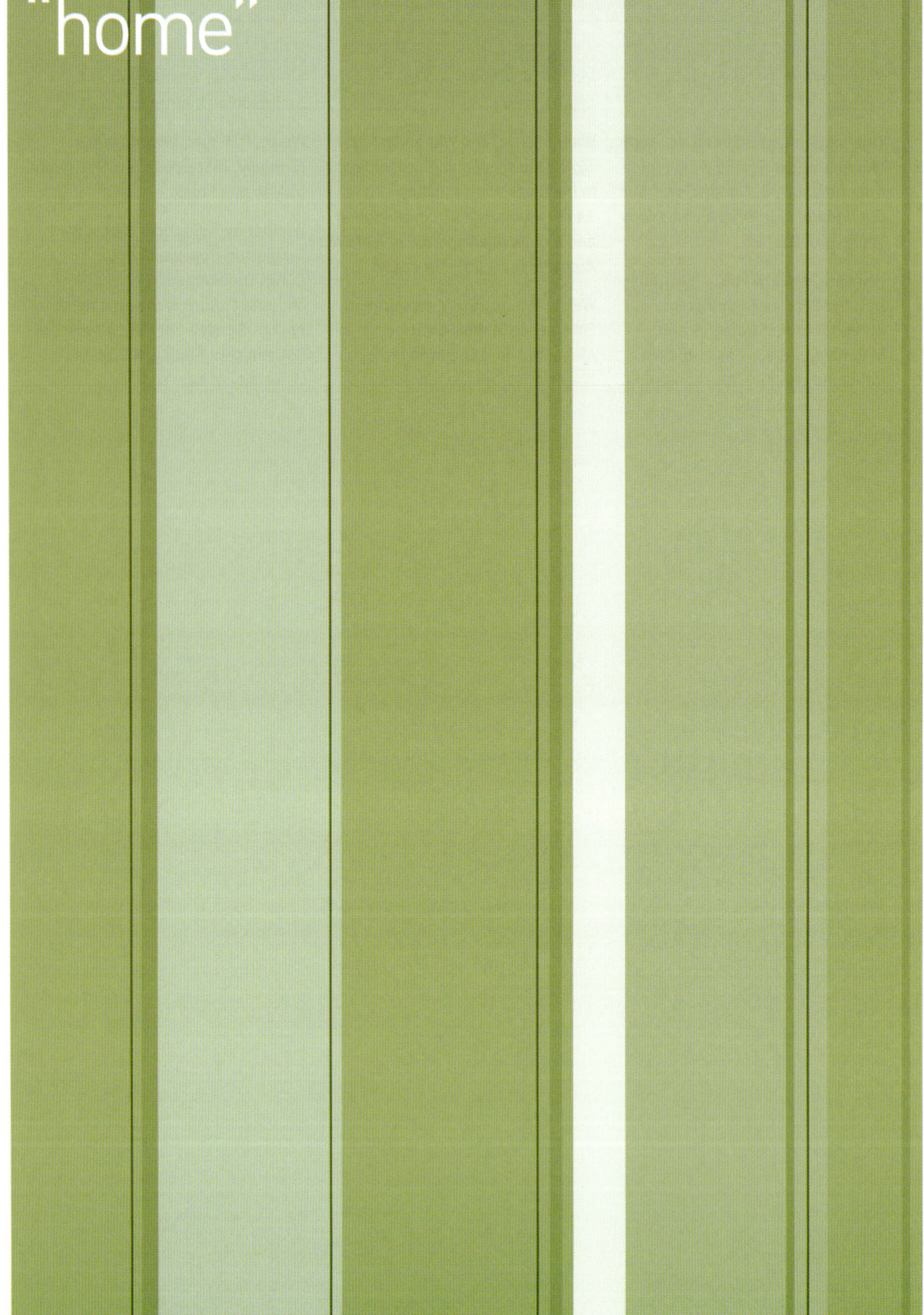
"home"

"home"

> "Saw
> myself dead"—red leaves, wet leaves,
> flat water—he's dead, voice—
> I
>
> little arcs of dust on a couch,
> smoke goes violet, faces crumble,
> the lake the green lake on the
> phone perfect more perfect than
> perfect on the bed—

He's lived a long life. You see. And that doesn't matter to me. That doesn't help. Is he dying? She thinks he's moving in the right direction. Getting his strength back. Is he dying? He's lived a good life. That doesn't matter. I don't know what I'm saying. I thought I could come here and—what— just walk in and be with them. Trying to follow my breath, to have compassion, remember everything. Breathe and pray. Help him. He's coughing. He's lived a good life. Is that what you say?

Easy to say they've had a great love story. They have a great love. A great love story. She said it's a wonderful world. And she said when we die we become dark matter. She kept saying it has to be that. She kept saying there's no escape. There's no getting out of the universe. When we die— what we are has to become something. It has to be dark matter. That's what she said. The news was on. He was half-awake. He couldn't hear.

JOSEPH LEASE

Joseph Lease chairs the MFA Program in Writing at California College of the Arts.

Textile, Volume 8, Issue 3, pp. 368–371
DOI: 10.2752/175183510x12868938341646
Reprints available directly from the Publishers.
Photocopying permitted by licence only.
© 2010 Berg. Printed in the United Kingdom.

                         dust, leaves and
               straws and plastic bags, forks
               and dirt, gum: the world did
               only paint and lie, Miss USA
               gone wild, high school football,
               in the shadow of
                                   the silo,

               what
               if bodies,
               nature means dust,
               hello, sweet—hello,
               dust goes violet,
               faces turn to
                            dust,

       Our bodies
       changing
       somewhere
       becoming
       rain

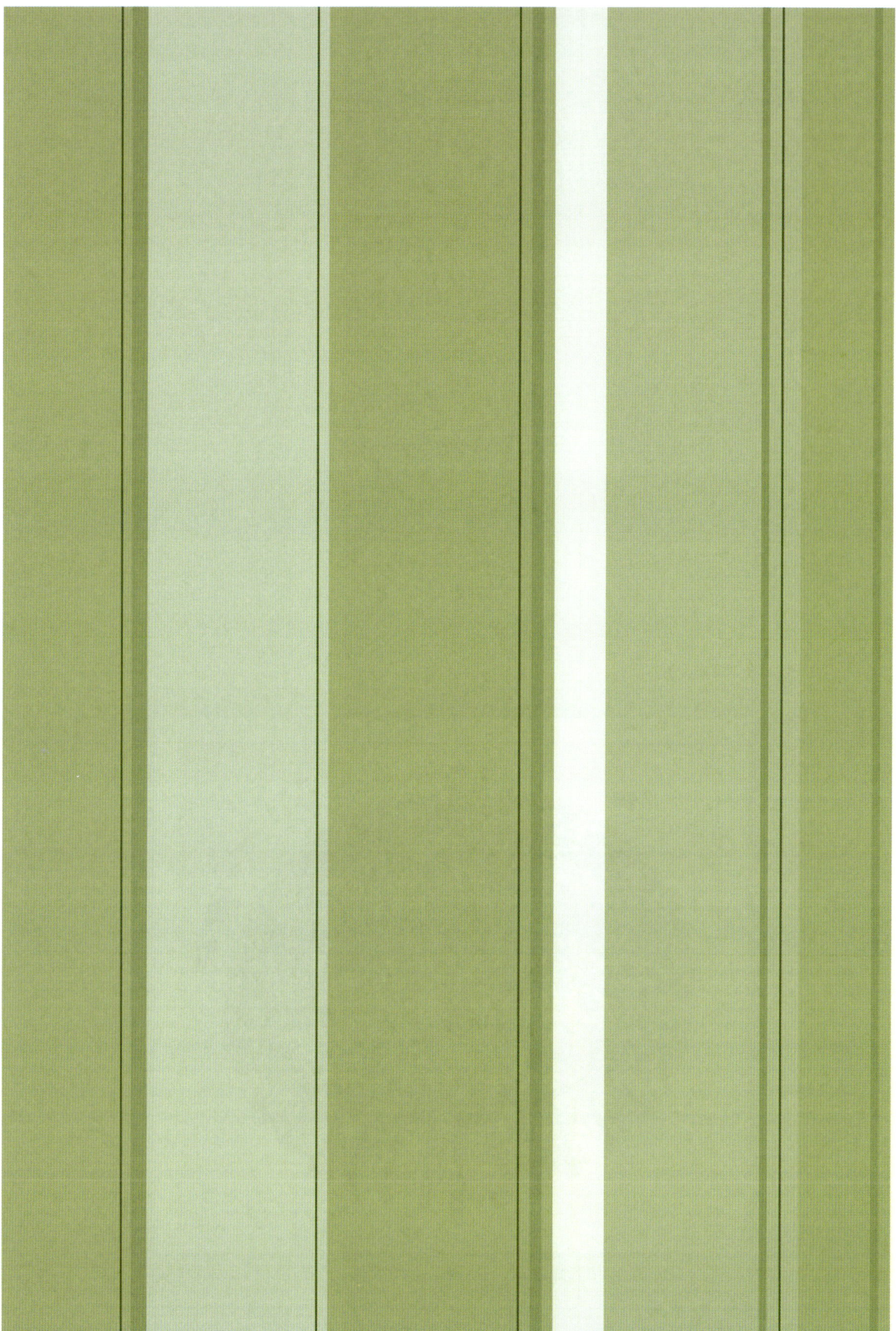

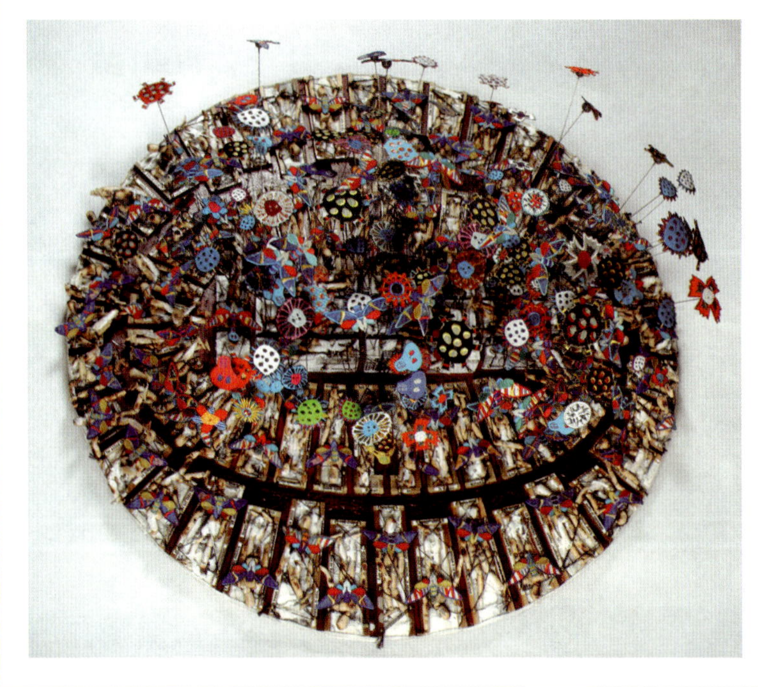

Exhibition Review
Pretty Deadly: New Work by Michael Brennand-Wood

The Naughton Gallery, Queen's University, Belfast, October 16–November 8, 2009

Pretty Deadly was Michael Brennand-Wood's first solo show in Northern Ireland and this exhibition brought together pieces made during the last five years as part of a celebration of his eight years as a Research Fellow in Textile Art at the School of Art and Design at the University of Ulster in Belfast. Curated by Dr Joseph McBrinn of the University of Ulster, the theme of the exhibition drew upon images referencing fairy tales, folklore, and literature and, as with all good fairy tales, the twenty-nine compositions on display in the Gallery explored the dichotomy of good versus evil through oppositions including: chaos and order; attractive and repellent; real and sublime; beauty and pain; universal and personal.

As the title of the exhibition suggests, seen together these works function as a visual *Fleur du mal*. The use of flowers as subject matter has formed an integral part of Brennand-Wood's work since *Stars Underfoot* 2002, although by 2004 the fresh flowers were replaced by computerized embroidered flowerheads and joined by butterflies and skulls made in the same manner. This choice of subject offered plenty of scope in terms of decorative elements of color and texture and at first glance the exhibits brought a carnival atmosphere to the gallery space. The wall-mounted pieces (see Figure 2) worked particularly well in the relatively narrow space of the gallery; they invaded the spectator's space with their spiky protuberances drawing attention to themselves, yet this aggression was ameliorated by the bright, playful colors of the flower- and seed-heads, military badges and insignia that sit atop wires. However, lingering beneath this gaudy surface lie the Baudelairean association of flowers with decadence and decay. Brennand-Wood comments in the catalogue

REVIEWED BY
JULIETTE MACDONALD
Juliette MacDonald is based at Edinburgh College of Art. Juliette@eca.ac.uk

Textile, Volume 8, Issue 3, pp. 372–377
DOI: 10.2752/175183510x12868938341682
Reprints available directly from the Publishers.
Photocopying permitted by licence only.

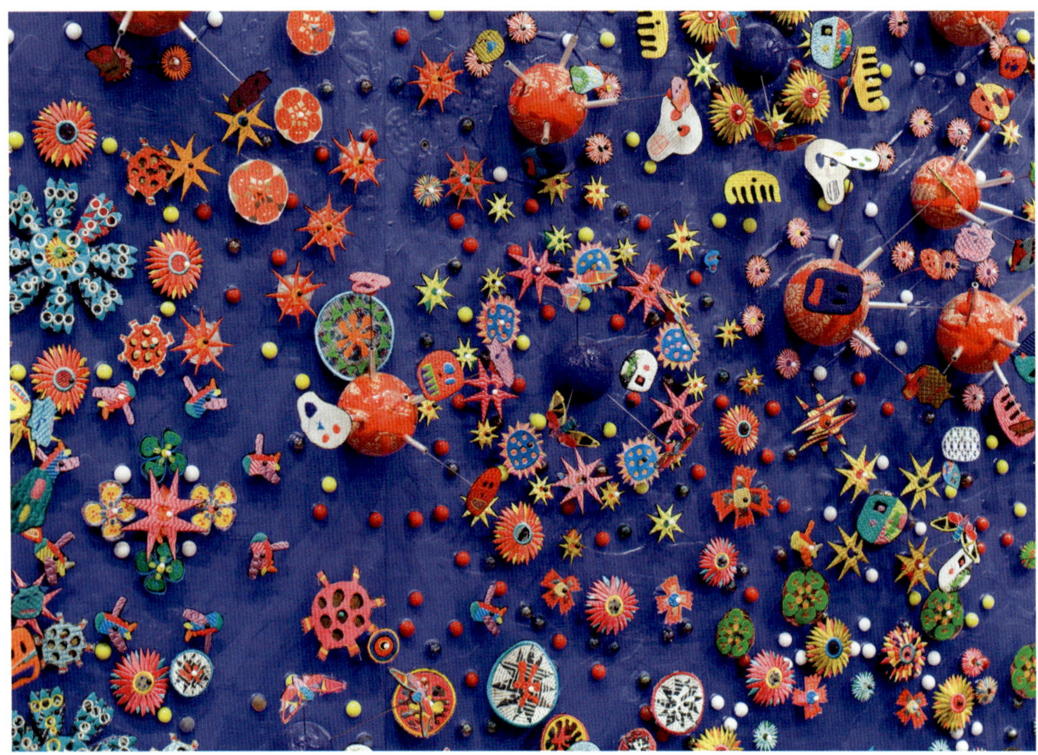

Figure 1
Stars Underfoot—the Slow Reveal, detail.

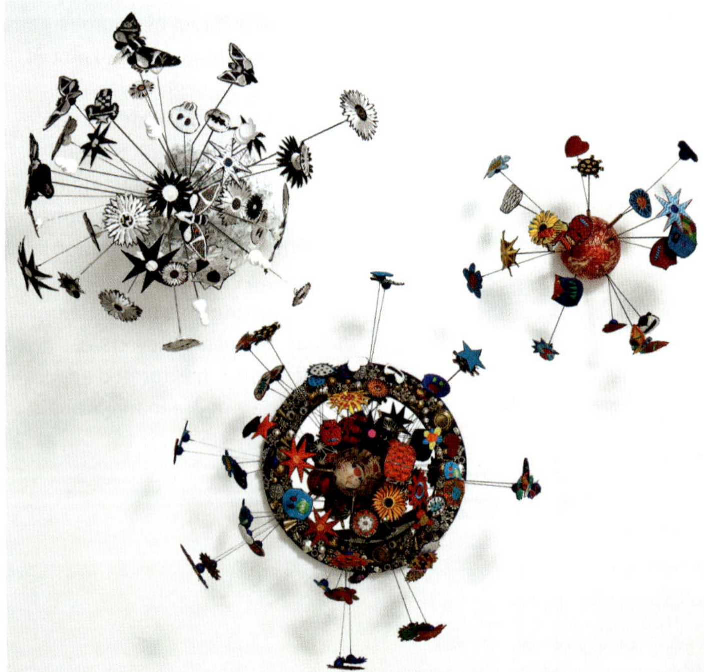

Figure 2
Vase Attacks.

that: "the direct use of pretty elements to seduce the viewer is quite deliberate and in my mind analogous to the use of beautiful flowers to render death, palatable and less offensive."[1]

Holding Pattern (Figure 3), created in 2007, was one of the larger circle form pieces in the exhibition (90 cm in diameter and 55 cm deep). Based on an arena-style seating plan, hundreds of small wooden figures were burnt and buried into the frame. Resting either directly on top of the bodies or hovering just above them are bright red and blue butterflies interspersed with equally colorful flowers, skulls, and seed-heads trapping the bodies onto their gruesome globe. These visual juxtapositions, and the allusion to the arena and the gathering of large crowds, comment on the continuing fascination Western society has with commodifying leisure. However, as McBrinn notes in the catalogue, in Northern Ireland the arena format offers an extra layer of meaning as former prisons are now being converted into cultural and sporting stadia.[2]

The 7-meter-long, panoramic *Stars Underfoot—the Slow Reveal* (2007–8) (Figure 4) dominated the central section of the gallery.

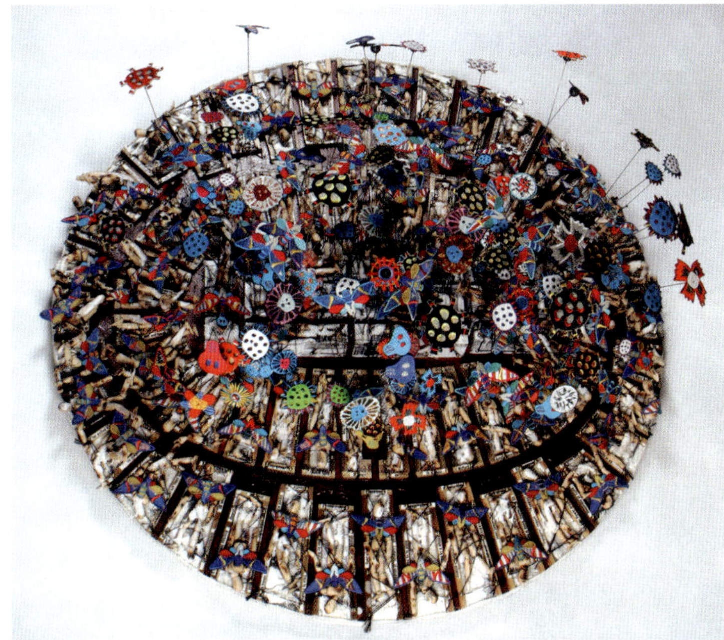

Figure 3
Holding Pattern.

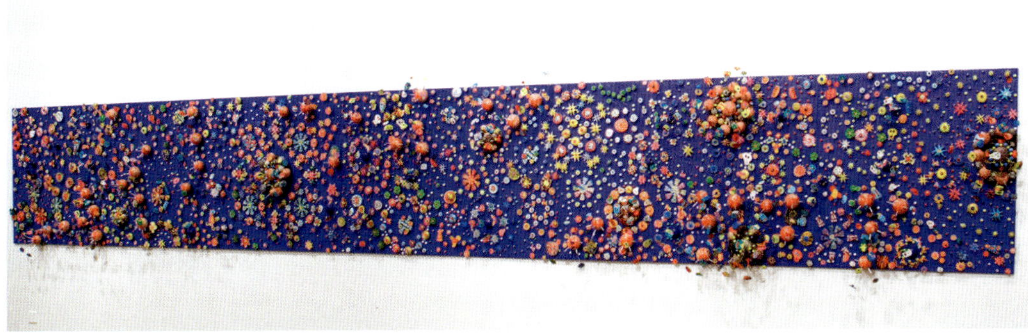

Figure 4
Stars Underfoot—the Slow Reveal.

Its dense blue background is decorated with a constellation of flowers reminiscent of a Turkish carpet or runner, and as such provides visual relief to some of the visually and symbolically weightier pieces surrounding it. There is without doubt a joyful exuberance provided by the sheer size of the composition and its blast of color and texture. However, it too functions as a critical commentator; in the catalogue Brennand-Wood points out that while some in the West might demonize Islamic politics and religion there are clearly no qualms evident in terms of appropriating elements of its material culture and associated aesthetics.[3]

While much understanding could be gained purely by examining the exhibits, the illustrated catalogue provides a thoughtful and informed response to the work. The images are plentiful and clear and the essay functions especially well in that it gives an insight into the primary and secondary research resources that were the inspiration for Brennand-Wood's work. It is an ideal companion for negotiating the diversity of meanings to be found in the pieces and the profound intentions of the maker.

The many layers of association and reference in his work ensured that the exhibition achieved a good balance between the sensual and the thought-provoking. With his evident interest in the human ability to create cruelty and beauty, chaos and order, one feels compelled to agree with McBrinn's suggestion that Brennand-Wood would make an original, intriguing, and challenging Official War Artist.[4]

Notes

1. Brennand-Wood quoted in McBrinn 2009.
2. McBrinn. 2009.
3. Brennand-Wood quoted in McBrinn 2009.
4. McBrinn 2009, n. 18.

Reference

McBrinn, J. 2009. Catalogue Essay. *Pretty Deadly Catalogue.* The Naughton Gallery at Queen's University, Belfast.

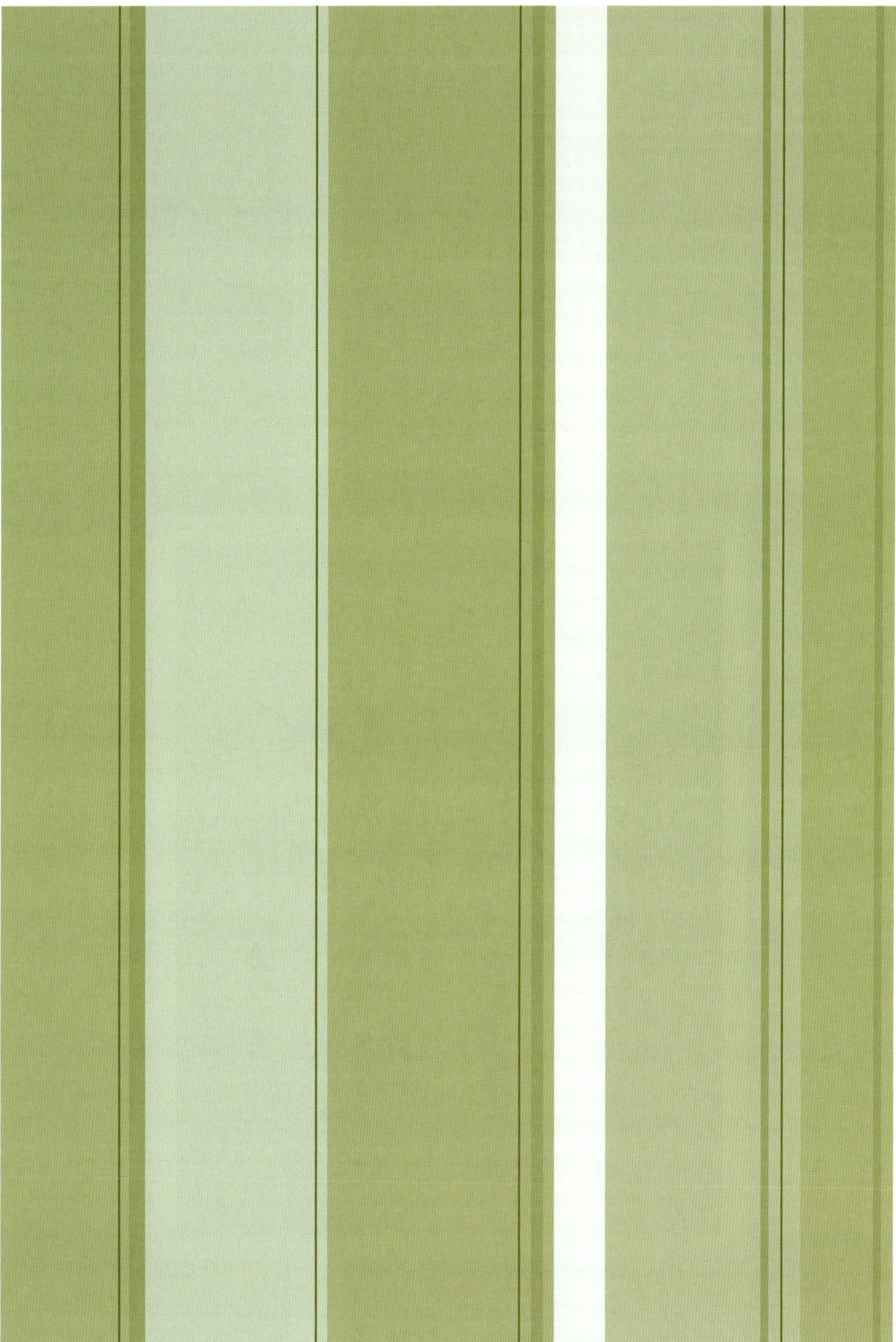

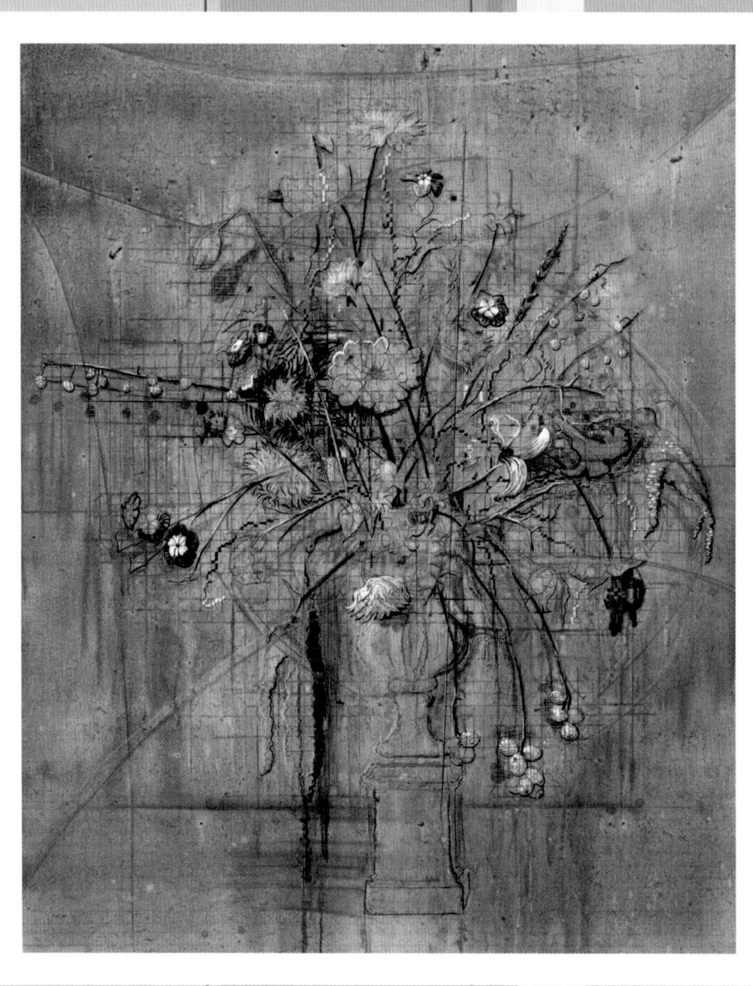

Exhibition Review
Michael Raedecker

Camden Arts Centre, May 1–June 28, 2009

During what promised to be the beginnings of a longed-for "barbeque summer" the cool, sparsely populated interior of Camden Arts Centre made a welcome respite from the baked pavements and roaring traffic of North London.

Upstairs from a well-served cafeteria, gardens, and a fashionably minimal entrance area, Raedecker's exhibition of paintings began in the corridor, which serves as a long gallery and also as a conduit to other, more conventionally proportioned gallery rooms. This corridor is possibly an architecturally pertinent factor to the success of Raedecker's show; his work is haunting, eerie, and has a postapocalyptic atmosphere. The painted concrete/brick walls of the corridor contribute to a sensation of being unsettled; of mentally rolodexing through the popularly imagined "*unheimlich*" interiors of prisons, asylums, bunkers, slaughterhouses, and other worrying places.

Raedecker's work and in this case, the curation of it, leaves space for imagination; the work is unarguably well executed and aside from his irritating and probably unnecessarily self-conscious titles, allows the viewer to engage with suggested yet unimposed narratives.

Not a single person inhabits these images: there is evidence of presence but no one is there. In *Superficial*, a solitary place setting sits unsullied upon a tablecloth that has a patterned surface craftily stitched with embroidery onto a canvas washed with grey scale glazes.

There is no chair to anchor the scene to that of prosaic domesticity; instead this apparition hovers uncannily, resonating with absence and bringing to mind tales of the mysteriously abandoned *Marie-Celeste*.

Other paintings depict beautifully rendered plants; *Penetration* (an example of why Raedecker really should stick

REVIEWED BY
NICOLA DONOVAN

Nicola Donovan is a mid-career artist and part-time lecturer based at Spike Island, Bristol. She has a BA and MA in Fine Art and is currently studying for a PhD at Nottingham Trent University, in a practice-based exploration of what artists and museums can do together to excite interest in museum collections. nsdonovan@hotmail.com

Textile, Volume 8, Issue 3, pp. 378–383
DOI: 10.2752/175183510x12868938341727
Reprints available directly from the Publishers.
Photocopying permitted by licence only.

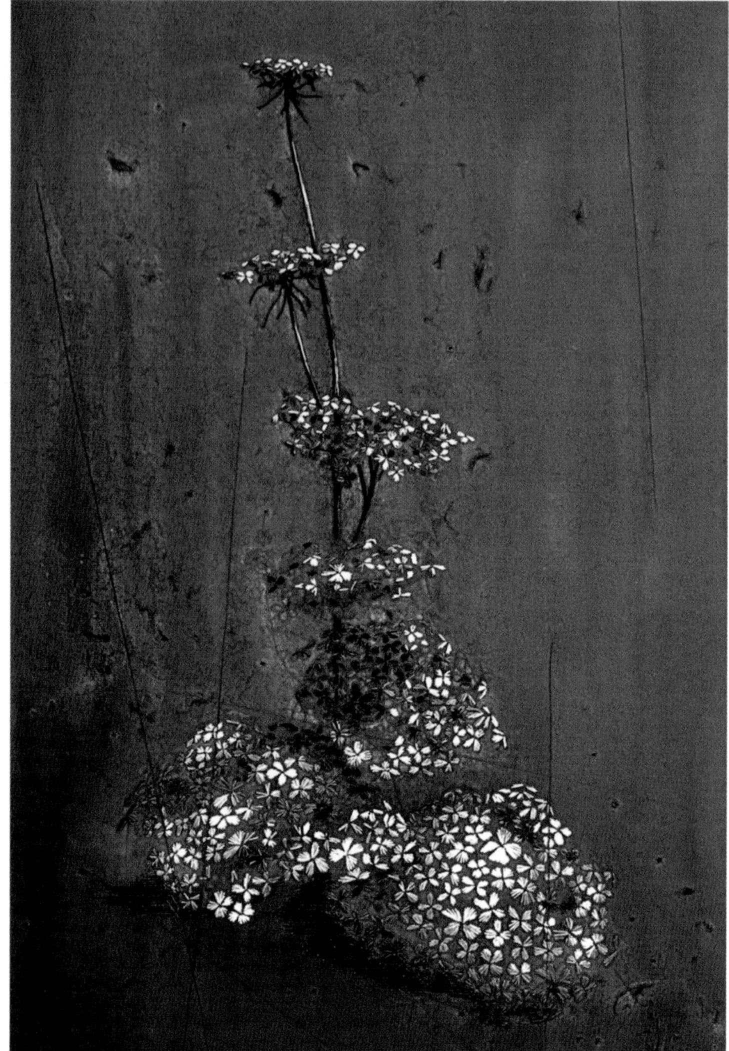

Figure 1
Penetration. 2005. Acrylic and thread on canvas. 98 × 62 cm. © Hauser & Wirth, Zürich and London. Collection Ann and Steven Ames, New York. Courtesy the artist and Hauser & Wirth, Zürich and London.

to images and leave words well alone) is a quiet but powerful image of a tall, common weed in flower, its petals carefully observed with satin stitch to correspond haptically with the unmistakable silky feel of a live petal, or perhaps ultra-thin and sensitive skin. Dessicated, discolored and spent blossoms are formed using knots of thicker, fibrous thread, each mark controlled, accounted for, and earning its right to a place in the frame.

However, the skill and accomplishment of this image is undermined by the inept word-smithing of its title, which renders it nothing but a botanical phallus, complete with climbing veins and a generous, be-flowered testicular bulge. Raedecker has a habit of throwing out such in-articulacy, which is perhaps the

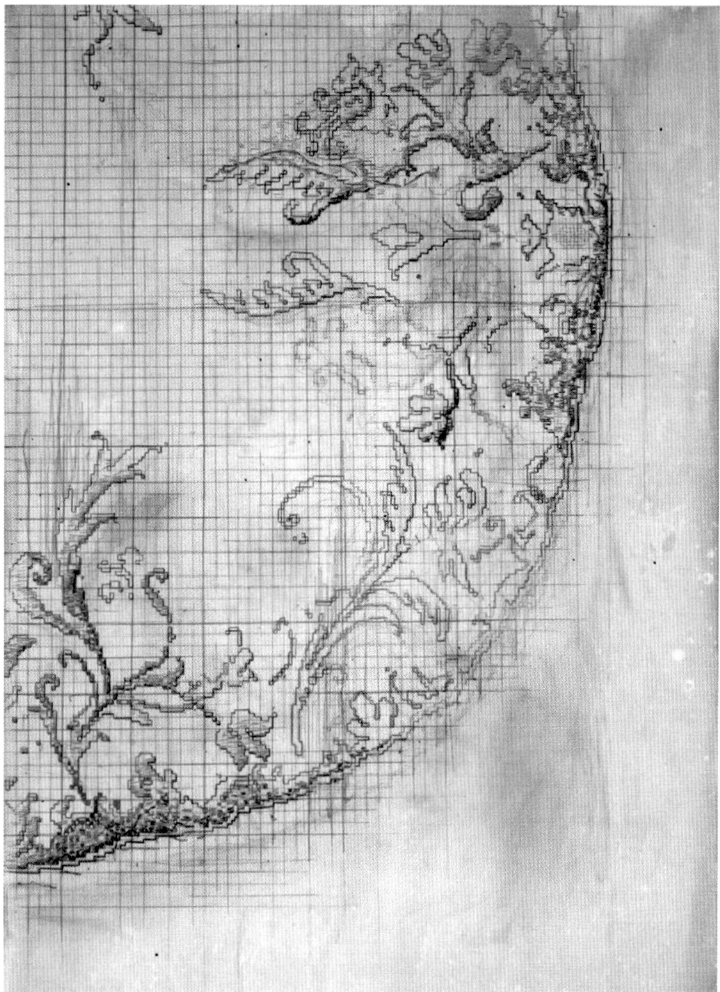

Figure 2
Servile. 2009. Acrylic and thread on
canvas. 180 × 124 cm. © Andrea Rosen,
New York. Courtesy the artist and
Andrea Rosen, New York.

result of feeling pressurized into explicitly engaging with on-going discussions regarding Gender and Stitch.

The title *Penetration* robs the viewer of the opportunity to develop a "conversation" with the image; its direct textual hammer-blow fixes meaning into tight confinement, leaving little space for speculation and thus reads as more petulant than playful. The image and title suggest that the wild, forceful weed depicted is ennobled by its masculinization, that it somehow is improved beyond any feminine connotations by being imbued with Byronic virility. This clumsily arranged marriage of text and image saps the strength of Raedecker's work, as does the introduction to the exhibition pamphlet which cites his current practice as being deeply concerned "with what might be called the 'feminine.'"[1]

It could perhaps be argued that Raedecker merely follows the great Romantic tradition of assuming the emotional, intuitive "feminine" in order to feed his intellectual and creative "masculine" genius, or maybe it is just quite simply a defence of his stereotypically "unmasculine" interests. However, while acknowledging the value of discourse regarding gender and stitch, it could be argued that Raedecker's use of stitch and his depiction of domestic subjects such as washing lines, cakes, and tablecloths has nothing to

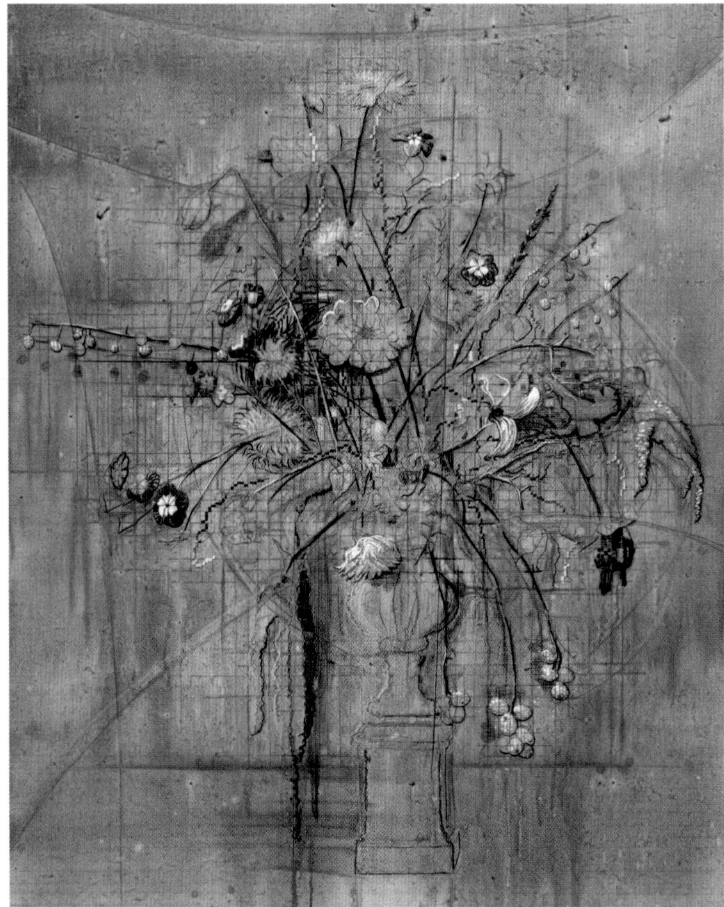

Figure 3
Corrupt. 2008. Acrylic and thread on canvas. 162 × 130 cm. © Andrea Rosen, New York. Collection De Heus-Zomer. Courtesy the artist and Andrea Rosen, New York.

do specifically with femininity, or masculinity.

Drawing on his art historical heritage as a native of Amsterdam, Raedecker plunders the traditions of landscape and still life, easing them into the modern world with depictions of contemporary mundanity. He makes use of traditional methods—i.e. drawing, painting, embroidery, and perhaps even tapestry, a process historically connected to "masters" such as Da Vinci and Goya.

Raedecker makes pictures about the emptiness of life; they express a melancholy that reflects the de-saturated experience of day-to-day existence for a society that is confused about its priorities and purpose. As such perhaps he is indeed a direct descendant of his vocational and geographical forebears. The dominant palette of rain-sodden, leaden cloud greys contributes to the gloomy pessimism of these embroidered paintings, relieved only by an occasional bipolar breakout into technicolor flora-scapes.

A lighter mood is detected in Raedecker's delight with tricking and deceiving the unwary audience; a first glance at one of his large canvasses will report sketchy graphite/pencil marks, a few brushstrokes and paint spatters with a wash ground. Closer inspection reveals that almost every mark, bar the background wash, is made using thread and needle punctures.

The meticulous control and application required to successfully render these paintings calls for an obsessive's touch, and the advantage of being an obsessive attending to one's obsessive activity is that it keeps existential anxiety at bay. So, as Raedecker works the speckles, dots, and strikes that pretend to be splatters of paint or pencil marks, he may actually be deeply engaged in avoiding the void that his images reflect.

On a more optimistic note, this work is truly accessible by a wide audience; the clearly visible labor-intensive nature of Raedecker's working methods alone is a cause for wonder and admiration. Easily identifiable significant drawing and embroidery skills along with recognizable subjects help to engage audiences on many levels. These images really are very cleverly worked, an image of street lamps in Raedecker's interminable damp mizzle are so convincingly diffused that it is difficult to resist a compulsion to rub focus back into un-misted eyes.

Raedecker's people-free landscapes utter the transient nature of our existence: our buildings, objects, possessions, and creations remain regardless of whether we live or die; we are at once material and immaterial. His careful, meticulous embroidered paintings reveal a tenderness toward our "pitifulness" and are perhaps his way of leaving the world with a document of our times. We can hope that future generations will see these domestic and contemporarily familiar spaces that Raedecker traced with studied observation and ancient methods, but will they detect the attendant anxious ennui which he seems to identify so well?

Note

1. J. Hutchinson. *Michael Raedecker Catalogue.* Camden Arts Centre (ISBN 1 90047092 6).

Book Reviews

Book Review

The Bayeux Tapestry: New Interpretations,
Martin K. Foys, Karen Eileen Overbey, and Dan Terkla (eds),
Woodbridge and Rochester, NY: Boydell Press, 2009

This volume of essays about the Bayeux Tapestry is testimony to the apparently inexhaustible fascination of this most famous of medieval embroideries. Shirley Ann Brown's chapter begins "Great works of art both give pleasure and teach," and we are encouraged to infer that the Tapestry (as some of the contributors still call it) is indeed one of the most skillfully contrived pieces of visual rhetoric in the history of art. This perception is a relatively recent one. Only two or three decades ago the majority view was still that this was a relatively straightforward depiction of the events leading up to the Norman Invasion of England in 1066. It was the pictorial realization of the written histories, particularly that of William of Poitiers, occasionally offering worthwhile additional information and sometimes puzzling contradictions. That has now changed; its interpretation is a growth industry revealing just how rich, complex, and rewarding an object it is. That the volume under review here introduces both new data and some fruitful approaches to the subject is further indication that this particular piece of needlework is in a class of its own.

The approaches of Gale Owen Crocker and Michael Lewis focus on facture, on the information provided by the techniques and processes, and on "errors" of manufacture. Here the "embroideriness" of the Tapestry is critical. Both authors are concerned with the sequence of production and what it might imply about the design process itself and changes of mind that occurred while the work was in hand. Owen Crocker's chapter considers the evidence from the reverse of the embroidery insofar as there is a photographic record. She amply demonstrates the potential of the reverse for answering a number of critical questions while justifiably lamenting the lack of textual or pictorial information from the quite recent restoration. In the fullness of time, one may hope for a detailed survey and analysis of the data, though in the nature of things they are likely to raise as many questions as they answer.

Two other chapters, by Karen Overbey and Dan Terkla, deal in different ways with what eleventh-century audiences might have known or thought. Terkla is concerned with Norman

Textile, Volume 8, Issue 3, pp. 384–386
DOI: 10.2752/175183510x12868938341763
Reprints available directly from the Publishers.
Photocopying permitted by licence only.
© 2010 Berg. Printed in the United Kingdom.

REVIEWED BY
T. A. HESLOP
University of East Anglia, T.Heslop@uea.ac.uk

mythmaking, on the Normans' sense of their identity, and how the Tapestry plays into it. Overbey's focus is the relics of Bayeux on which Harold swore his oath (*sacramentum fecit*) to William. She argues very plausibly that one of the reliquaries is that commissioned by Bishop Odo for the relics of Saints Rasyphus and Ravennus, but realistically that an English audience would have been unlikely to know. Implicitly it would have been the patron, Odo himself, who cared.

This raises the issue addressed by Elizabeth Pastan and Stephen White: "Problematizing Patronage." The laudable aim here is to point out some of the tacit assumptions made by writers on the Tapestry about the degree of involvement of Odo in the commissioning and designing process. Less helpful to my way of thinking is the ensuing suggestion that Odo was the "benefactor," and that the perspective on the events depicted is that of St Augustine's Abbey at Canterbury. This is posited on the supposed even-handedness of the treatment of Normans and Saxons. But how even-handed is it? If Madeline Caviness's view, argued at length, that the English are shown as emasculated, as a third sex," is valid, then the vanquished are being derided as inadequate and inferior by the standards of virile militarism.

Those persuaded by the postmodern position that there is no such thing as "correct" interpretation will have no difficulty with these contrasting arguments. They indeed say as much about the writers' situation as about the Tapestry itself. It is, however, striking that, however sophisticated the "problematizing," it is difficult for authors to resist the temptation to offer a new, better (implicitly more "correct") interpretation. A possible exception is Martin Foys's unpicking of the issues around the representation of Harold's death, which suggests that our own uncertainties about what is shown mirror medieval uncertainty about what actually happened, possibly fed by contemporary chroniclers themselves using interpretation of the Tapestry as if it were information.

This question of what and how we experience through seeing is the subject of the chapters by Richard Brilliant, "Making Sounds Visible," and Valerie Allen on "the Nature of Things." Here it is possible to conclude only that, for me, the Tapestry is neither as noisy nor as haptic as it is for these writers. Would an eleventh-century viewer have heard the "clip clop" of horses' hooves or felt the texture of a coat of mail when they viewed the embroidery? Surely that too is a matter for each individual to decide.

Book Review

Tartan, Jonathan Faiers, Oxford: Berg, 2008

This is a fascinating and thought-provoking book that is guaranteed to make the reader consider tartan from new perspectives. At the outset it is clear that the author, Jonathan Faiers, is intent on moving tartan away from the somewhat wearied discussion of the myths and speculations that surround its relationship with "ben and glen" sentimentality and concerns with tracing its "traditional" origins that have so often been associated with texts on tartan. These themes are not entirely abandoned but rather are considered from fresh points of view. Similarly, _Tartan_ does not offer a chronological evaluation of the development of tartan but seeks to "position tartan within broad philosophical, political and cultural contexts" in order to assess its impact domestically and globally. Faiers states that his intention is to attempt to redress the gap left by most considerations of tartan which ignore the diversity and richness of its history, commenting that:

> In order to achieve this, an a-historical and heterogeneous approach will be adopted which, whilst utilizing previous studies of the subject, will provide an alternative, more inclusive and

> interdisciplinary assessment of tartan as a highly complex and persistent cultural phenomenon.

This is perhaps an ambitious undertaking but one that Faiers accomplishes with erudition and enthusiasm.

Michel Foucault's _heterotopia_ and Mikhail Bakhtin's _chronotope_ provide the main theoretical framework. These approaches are blended and used in order to understand how tartan operates across a number of sociocultural spaces. This methodology enables Faiers to evaluate tartan in both real and fictional spaces such as the interior of Balmoral Castle, Hampden Park football stadium, fashion runways, and Hollywood film sets. With this breadth of research and depth of knowledge the author brings a ludic quality to his cultural examination of tartan. He argues that following its prohibition in 1746 tartan has transformed "rhizomatically" (referencing Deleuze and Guatarri). Opposite this discussion is an image of a bi-colored variety of dahlia, itself a rhizome, named "Tartan." The inclusion of the decorative flower head simultaneously underlines the theoretical stance as well as demonstrating the ubiquity of tartan.

Textile, Volume 8, Issue 3, pp. 387–388
DOI: 10.2752/175183510x12868938341808
Reprints available directly from the Publishers.
Photocopying permitted by licence only.

REVIEWED BY
JULIETTE MACDONALD
Edinburgh College of Art, j.macdonald@eca.ac.uk

The book is divided into three parts: Tartan and History; Tartan and Dress; and Tartan's Embrace. In the first part the technical aspects of tartan are considered; the sett, weaving, and use of color, and its ancient roots are considered. Here Faiers is careful not to fall into the trap of trying to establish first recorded appearances or usage of the term. This first section attempts to create the cultural contexts for the cloth and examines subsequent historical "fabrications." Again the images used to support his ideas are informative and varied: Rod Stewart on stage in 1983, a child's tartan sock from *c*.1851, a couple at the 2005 Inverness Highland Games dressed in belted plaid and short tailored kilt standing in front of an Aberdeen Angus Steak bar. The second part begins by mapping tartan's relationship "to fashionable dress, [and the] many socio-cultural territories [that] need to be surveyed ... Tartan as masquerade, as protest, as conqueror, as disruption, as erotic." It is in this section that the complexity of ideas is fully explored, and the dialogue between tartan and fashion and the romanticized and eroticized is fluently articulated. The images in this section are equally eloquent, the juxtaposition of a portrait of Charles Edward Stuart as a Harlequin with Noddy Holder, lead singer from Slade, demonstrating the textile's potential to be both fashionable and representative of opposition and revolt. Part three considers the abstraction and fetishization of tartan. Here tartan and the tourist industry is critiqued followed by a deconstruction of the material's associations with modernity, escapism, fantasy, colonization. Finally Faiers examines tartan's "translation" by designers such as Junya Watanabe and Jun Takahashi. It is with part three that Faiers implicitly makes the strongest case for the integration of textile studies with other modes of cultural critical enquiry.

The simultaneous consideration of pattern, cloth, and garment is both the main strength and the weakness of the book. The ideas are germane and provocative and create a wealth of connections. However, as is perhaps inevitable with an undertaking of this size, many of the ideas would benefit from further examination and analysis. In the section on erogenous zones, Piet Mondrian's use of horizontal and vertical lines representing universalities is discussed and the idea is briefly paralleled with the rise of interest in tartan as both a textile and a pattern. Given that this is such an engaging idea it seems a pity that so few lines are devoted to it. That said, it can only be considered a positive that despite the detail and expanse of information the reader is still left wanting more.

Having read the book one becomes aware of tartan's extraordinary versatility, its possibilities as both a radical and traditional material, and the local and global contexts within which it operates.

Book Reviews

Roze Hentschel, *The Culture of Cloth in Early Modern England: Textual Constructions of a National Identity*. (Farnham, UK: Ashgate, 2008).

Maria Hayward, *Rich Apparel: Clothing and the Law in Henry VIII's England*. (Farnham, UK: Ashgate, 2009).

In her imaginative and persuasive book, Rose Hentschel explores early modern English literary texts defending wool and woolen fabrics as an English industry in need of protection and appreciation. Her analysis of literary texts includes romance, here shown, surprisingly, to be a vehicle of social protest on the part of distinctly non-fictional shepherds, a chapter on Thomas Deloney's ballad and city comedy *Jack of Newbury*, pamphlets encouraging New World settlements as places to raise and sell English wool, and fiery satire of dishonest cloth merchants and luxurious imported fabrics that competed with English wool and styles of dress. One of the strengths of Hentschel's book is that she relates these literary texts to a detailed material and political history of wool, as typified in her first chapter about the importance of sheep not only as the conventional trimmings of literary pastoral but as a point of conflict between shepherds deprived of their livelihood by agricultural takeovers and the noblemen who hoped for greater profit from the lands their farmers cultivated. That is, Hentschel situates the literary texts in the social realities of the period, so she is able to base her very perceptive readings on a context that frequently allows her to say something new about well- and lesser-known writing of the period.

A study focused on the sartorial realities underlying the satirical debates analyzed by Hentschel is Maria Hayward's subject in *Rich Apparel: Clothing and the Law in Henry VIII's England*. Basing her conclusions on three state sumptuary edicts made in 1510, 1514, and 1553 and a high number of inventories in wills (over 1,300, including most regions of England and 95 by London testators) recorded in parish records and the prerogative court in London (where property of people with holding in more than one parish were put through probate), she concludes that higher-ranking Englanders, including ecclesiastics, were more likely to infringe these laws than people of lower social standing

REVIEWED BY
ANN R. JONES
Smith College, Massachusetts;
arjones@smith.edu

Textile, Volume 8, Issue 3, pp. 389–390
DOI: 10.2752/175183510x12868938341844
Reprints available directly from the Publishers.
Photocopying permitted by licence only.

and that the dress of city dwellers, including cloth merchants and men who wore livery, became more elaborate and was better tolerated as the sixteenth century went on. The details of her study are fascinating: the fabrics, dyes, cuts, and accessories belonging to the wealthy especially are of dazzling complexity, and in both her text and her glossary she is generous with definitions and explanations of what items in the inventories meant—although one wonders whether it is really necessary to include "Fox: a red furred quadruped with a bushy tail"! As visual evidence she includes portraits, tomb rubbings, paintings of court scenes, and even an analysis of Holbein's drawings of nobility and gentry. This is a book that will be studied for years by costume historians and by social historians interested in the gradual transformations of rank and wealth throughout the sixteenth century.

One could not do better than to read these books in tandem: Hayward's for the empirical facts of who wore what, and Hentschel's for the period's emotional and imaginative responses to these realities. Together, they offer a richly informative and often entertaining interdisciplinary pair.